The Victory Ode: An Introduction

FOR ALAN

THE VICTORY ODE
An Introduction

by
Mary R. Lefkowitz
Wellesley College

NOYES CLASSICAL STUDIES

NOYES PRESS
PARK RIDGE, NEW JERSEY

Copyright © 1976 by Mary R. Lefkowitz
Library of Congress Catalog Card Number 76-11650
ISBN: 0-8155-5045-6

Published in the United States by
NOYES PRESS
Noyes Building
Park Ridge, New Jersey 07656

Library of Congress Cataloging in Publication Data

Main entry under title:

The Victory ode.

    Translation of selections from Pindar and Bacchylides.
    Includes bibliographical references
    1. Odes—History and criticism. 2. Pindarus.
Pythia. 3. Bacchylides. I. Lefkowitz, Mary R.,
1935-   II. Pindarus. Pythia. Selections. English.
III. Bacchylides. Works. Selections. English.
PA3118.03V5   884'.01   76-11650
ISBN 0-8155-5045-6

TABLE OF CONTENTS

Introduction 1
    Notes 5
Chapter I 8
    Pythian 2: Preliminary Responses 8
    Pythian 2: A First Reading 13
    Notes 34
Chapter II 42
    Bacchylides' *Ode* 5 43
    Pindar's *Olympian* 1 76
    Notes 98
Chapter III 104
    Pindar's *Pythian* 1 105
    Bacchylides' *Ode* 3 125
    Pindar's *Pythian* 3 142
    Notes 157
Chapter IV 164
    Pythian 2: A Second Reading 164
    Conclusions 170
    Notes 174

PREFACE

Anyone who tries to read the odes of Pindar and Bacchylides in the original Greek experiences at first a pervasive despair. Memorable words and phrases strike the ear; the narration of a myth intrigues; but the satisfaction of being able to understand another language and another's process of thought that draws us to the study of antiquity remains tantalizingly unattainable.

Much of the trouble derives from the way we go about reading this difficult literature, armed with dictionaries, surrounded by commentaries and translations. This book instead asks only an open mind and patience. It seeks to bring the reader directly into contact with the poetry itself, through close line-by-line discussion of six poems, using non-technical language, assuming no previous knowledge of either poet's work. A special working translation helps both to explain difficulties in grammar and to call attention to distinctive word choice in the Greek.

Concentration on style made possible by this approach leads to the surprising and satisfying discovery that virtually every word in a victory ode has significance, no matter how digressive or irrelevant it might at first seem. Extraordinary language sets particular events into a larger generic framework, and endows words with meaning that could not ordinarily be perceived. The book invites the reader to share in appreciation both of the amazing potential of a complex art form and in the innovative linguistic talents of two great poets.

Completion and publication of this study were made possible by grants from the American Council of Learned Societies, The Radcliffe Institute, and Wellesley College. Friends and colleagues have generously provided advice and criticism; in particular I would like to acknowledge here my gratitude to Ernst Badian, Deborah Dickman Boedeker, Anne Burnett, Douglas Frame, Bernard Knox, Martin Ostwald, Emily Vermeule, Jennifer Wheat, and James Zetzel. Martha Gillies, Robert Noyes and Paul Stecher of Noyes Press have responded with insight and tolerance to a demanding manuscript.

Special thanks are due to BSB B. G. Teubner Verlagsgesellschaft, Leipzig, for permission to reproduce from *Pindari Carmina,* edd. Snell-Maehler (Ed. 6, 1971) and from *Bacchylidis Carmina,* edd. Snell-Maehler (Ed. 10, 1971).

Introduction

In the first half of the fifth century B.C., winners in the Olympic games received acclamation and awards that set them apart from other men: free maintenance for life by their city, commemorative inscriptions, and elaborate celebration on their return home. Odes were written to celebrate some of the victories at Olympia and other games, composed by famous poets, and performed by choruses. Some forty-five odes by the Theban poet Pindar, and fifteen written by Bacchylides of Ceos have survived antiquity, a literature large enough to provide a sense of the form and purpose of the victory ode, of each poet's style, and of their historical environment. The distinctive qualities of fifth century art and literature are reflected in the odes: the conflict between fixity and movement, the striving of the individual for supremacy, the importance of family and race.

How the odes describe success is as interesting as what they say about it. Through them we can see more clearly how in the Greek drama myth can be used as commentary on present action. The juxtaposition in the odes of individual achievement, general observations of human behavior, ancient legend and fable, prefigures the structure of Platonic proof, where historical example is used to verify hypothesis, and abstraction is reinforced by myth. Even later lyric poems, both Hellenistic and Roman, follow structural connections set in the odes. Centuries later poets like Ben Jonson and Thomas Gray turned to the format of the victory ode to express the relation of present to past. Disuse of the ode's formal structure in poetry reveals by contrast our own tastes and predilections: our impatience with inherited structures of expression and of thought, our sense that the past is foreign and generally irrelevant.

But the victory odes, for all their importance, have remained virtually inaccessible. As Thoreau observed, "Pindar is an empty name to all but Greek scholars," and even among classicists, Pindar is more admired than understood.[1] It is possible to appreciate his innovative language and his ability to revitalize convention, in the same way that we respond enthusiastically to the difficult poetry of Gerard Manley Hopkins and of T.S. Eliot. Yet for the most part scholars tend to read Pindar's work in excerpts, since it is hard to assimilate into modern written idiom the structuring techniques of a poetry that was meant to be heard rather than looked at, where references to the poet mark transitions, and repetition of word and theme binds different subjects together. The works of Bacchylides, particularly, seem to have elicited little enthusiasm, since his poetry draws its strength from recollection of traditional epic contexts and language, and accordingly appears flat and unimaginative. The remoteness of archaic culture, with its unfamiliar names and places, discourages even the most patient modern readers. It is hard to reconstruct the ambience of athletic contests, or to derive excitement from the elaborate recollection of an obscure myth. Scholarly criticism has tended to reflect and to accommodate contemporary reaction. The poems are read as biography rather than as fiction; striking images are withdrawn from context; conventionalities (rather than innovations) of thought and language are categorized.[2]

Yet at no time since the fifth century B.C. have scholars been better prepared to understand the techniques and expressions that have long seemed incomprehensible. The discovery in recent years of the principles of oral composition has made possible new understanding of the structure of the longer poems. The development of linguistic science enables us to analyze once baffling metaphors, and to see where associative patterns in our own language block understanding. Our sensitivity to psychology helps us account objectively for differences in religious practices and cultural values. Recent criticism, especially the work of Bundy, Young, Köhnken, Lloyd-Jones, Greengard and Skulsky, has helped solve many of the problems anachronism and ignorance have created for us.[3] But their studies, since they are addressed to scholars who have assimilated much misinformation in the process of their training, are necessarily as much destructive of misinterpretation as they are indicative of new approaches. The student new to Pindar, who knows some Greek and simply wants to try to understand an ode, finds himself entering in the middle of a contest, whose rules he must learn by assimilation, and whose participants will be described to him only by their opponents.

This book, which assumes no previous knowledge of Pindar or Bacchylides, is meant to be an introduction to the virtually lost literature of the victory odes. I try to anticipate at least some of the modern reader's negative reaction to this difficult poetry, and to demonstrate a basic method of reading that he can then apply to the many odes that are not discussed in the book. My intention is to let the reader discover for himself how scholars have evolved such categories as "first" and "second praise" and to see for himself how themes are developed, without stating categorically in advance what he ought to expect. Detailed interpretative discussions of controversial passages have been put into the notes, not in

Introduction

order to deceive the reader into thinking that scholars can or should agree on every point, but to keep attention on the ode as a whole rather than as the fractional sum of its more celebrated parts.

The book is also intended as an introduction for the scholar, not to the significance of a literature which he already knows and appreciates, but to the aspect of Pindar's and Bacchylides' poetry that has received relatively little consideration in recent criticism, their language. Following a suggestion of David Young's, I have emphasized the function of thematic repetition as a unifying element in the odes, a process whose effectiveness has now again been confirmed by Skulsky.[4] Some observations in Carola Greengard's recent dissertation encouraged me to try to account explicitly for the consistent differences in diction within each ode. I will try to show how the complex metaphorical statements at the beginning of odes are developed and elaborated in successive expressions of praise (or blame), in the narration of the myth, and in the relatively straightforward recapitulation of praise in the ode's conclusion. I will argue that the connotations of words and metaphors in different odes vary because they derive their meaning from the ode's central myth rather than from some external set of symbolic patterns. I will also try to show why the odes, both of Pindar and Bacchylides, speak their praise so predominantly in descriptions of failure and of envy. I hope that others will test and refine what I say on these topics in interpreting the many odes that I have not considered in this book.

Since not even experienced classicists can comfortably read Pindar and Bacchylides at "sight," I have included in the discussion of each Greek passage a line for line translation, which differs from other available translations in several respects. I try to follow the word order of the original closely, to give some impression of the suspense possible in an inflected language like Greek, where words can be arranged in the order that best suits meaning and poetic form. Ambiguities in the original are represented ambiguously in English, with neutral words which do not readily convey a single connotation. Each time the same Greek word occurs within the ode, I try to represent it by the same word in English, so that the reader can get some sense in his own language also of the repetition that helps connect the different sections of the ode. The results occasionally sound strange, in comparison to accepted literary translations. As the poet Cowley said, "if a man should undertake to translate *Pindar* word for word, it would be thought that one *Madman* had translated another."[5] But the attempt to replicate in an artificially elemental English the repetition and ambiguity of the Greek at least avoids the discontinuity imposed on the Greek text by more idiomatic translation, and additional explanatory sentences can provide the line's basic sense in more ordinary terms. To illustrate the problem briefly: in *Olympian* 1, βάλλειν ("throw") denotes three related actions, the crowning of poets' plans (ἀμφιβάλλεται,

8), Tantalus' trying to push away (βαλεῖν, 58) the stone that Zeus has hung above his head, and Oenomaus putting off (ἀναβάλλεται, 80) the marriage of his daughter. All standard translations render these three related words with three different English terms, e.g., Conway's "play round, strike, holds back." I translate instead, "throw around, throw, throws off."[6]

In the book I discuss only six odes in detail, all written for the same victor, Hieron of Syracuse: *Pythian* 2, the most difficult of all Pindar's odes; *Olympian* 1, the most famous; Bacchylides' *Ode* 5, written for the same occasion as *Olympian* 1; Pindar's *Pythian* 1, Bacchylides' *Ode* 3, and Pindar's *Pythian* 3, as illustrations of the flexibility of both format and emphasis in the odes; then *Pythian* 2 again to try to answer questions unresolved in the first reading. I chose to consider odes for Hieron because it seemed simpler in an introductory book not continually to involve readers in the intricacies of new information about unfamiliar places, dates, and names. Hieron was the logical candidate, because Pindar and Bacchylides wrote more odes for him than for any other victor. His relative importance means that odes for him are somewhat atypical, but especially deserving our attention, because of the extraordinary admiration for Hieron that both poets express.

Professional Pindarists may judge my beginning with *Pythian* 2 somewhat capricious.[7] My intention is to confront directly the interpretative problems that keep us from understanding Pindar and the function of a victory ode: uncertainty of place and date, swift changes of expression, and a concentration on wrong action that seems particularly out of place in a celebration of victory. One other advantage of beginning with this problematic ode, in a book about the victory ode as a genre, is that lack of information about its historical setting compels us to concentrate on general questions of form and style. My hope is that the complex *Pythian* 2 will serve as introduction not only to the agonies of interpretation but to the positive reasons for reading Pindar and Bacchylides, even in translation. In this latter sense the discussion of *Pythian* 2 will work like a proem of a victory ode, as an initial statement, not immediately clear in all particulars, that is developed and elaborated in the lines that follow.

This book is an attempt only to describe the general scope and poetics of the victory ode. It is, like the translations in it, designed as a means to better understanding, not as a series of definitive statements about individual passages. No such final statements are in fact possible. Changing patterns of culture will always interfere with our ability to evaluate or interpret perfectly all of any ancient poem, even if we were somehow miraculously to recover the factual information that now seems irretrievably lost. When I first went to Olympia, I remember arguing with a senior scholar about the meaning of the opening phrase of Pindar's *Olympian* 1, ἄριστον μὲν ὕδωρ, "the best is water." I thought Pindar meant that water reflected the brilliance of light, but also quenched thirst and sustained life. My older colleague said, "that is not the point at all; Pindar was referring to the four elements."[8] In attempting now, after years of study, to come up with a more comprehensive answer, I claim only to have made progress toward the kind of complete understanding one ideally would like to have.[9] But the definitive "meaning" of a poem sometimes eludes even its authors, as T.S. Eliot warns—perhaps Pindar himself would not have wanted to tell us the reasons why he chose to begin with water, and not with sunlight or with gold.[10]

NOTES

Since comprehensive bibliographies of both Pindar and Bacchylides are available, I have only mentioned in the notes works that have been directly helpful to me in writing this book or that are not listed in the bibliographies. For further information, the reader should consult Douglas L. Gerber, *A Bibliography to Pindar, 1513–1966* (*Amer. Philol. Assoc. Monograph* 28, 1969) and his "A Survey of Publications on Greek Lyric Poetry Since 1952," *Classical World* 61 (1968): 373-385, and *Bacchylidis Carmina cum Fragmentis*[10], ed. Bruno Snell and Herwig Maehler (Leipzig, 1971) pp. lv-lxi.

1. Henry David Thoreau, "Pindar," *Dial* IV (1844): 379.

2. See, e.g., C.M. Bowra, *Pindar* (Oxford, 1964), who does not analyze any ode in detail but instead discusses Pindar's thought under a variety of rubrics, and is in general more concerned with establishing the historical context of a poem than with how it functions as a work of art; see Anne P. Burnett's review in *Class. Philology* 63 (1968): 234-237. Concentration on formal elements and use of traditional material in the odes similarly leaves little impression of the poet's style or aesthetics; see, e.g., Erich Thummer, *Pindar: die Isthmischen Gedichte* (Heidelberg, 1968) I, pp. 19-158, and David Young, *Pindar Isthmian 7, Myth and Exempla* (*Mnemosyne Suppl.* 15; Leiden, 1971); Richard Hamilton, *Epinikion: General Form in the Odes of Pindar* (The Hague, 1974); and the discussion of the limitations of such studies in my "Pindar's Lives," *Classica et Iberica* (*Festschrift Joseph M.-F. Marique;* Worcester, Mass., 1975) pp. 71-93, in my review of Hamilton in *Classical World* 69 (1976): 340-41, and in Peter W. Rose, "The Myth of Pindar's First Nemean," *Harvard Studies in Class. Philol.* 79 (1975): 145-49.

3. Elroy L. Bundy, *Studia Pindarica, Univ. Calif. Publ. in Class. Philol.* 18. 1-2 (Berkeley, 1962) pp. 1-92; David C. Young, *Three Odes of Pindar (Mnemosyne Suppl.* 9; Leiden, 1968); Adolph Köhnken, *Die Funktion des Mythos bei Pindar* (Berlin, 1971); Carola Greengard, *Studies in the Structure of Pindar's Epinician Odes* (diss. Columbia Univ., U.M. Microfilm #74-12722); Hugh Lloyd-Jones, "Modern Interpretation of Pindar: The Second Pythian and Seventh Nemean Odes," *Journal of Hellenic Studies* 93 (1973): 109-137; Susan D. Skulsky, "πολλῶν πείρατα συντανύσαις: Language and Meaning in *Pythian* 1," *Classical Philology* 70 (1975): 8-31.

4. On the importance of repetition in Pindar's odes, and the difficulties involved in describing its usage, see Skulsky (n.3) p. 31 and David Young, "Pindaric Criticism," in *Pindaros und Bakchylides,* ed. W.M. Calder, III, and J. Stern, *Wege der Forschung* vol. 134 (Darmstadt, 1970) pp. 27-28, 30-31, 35. Young's observations about Pindar (p. 27) could equally well be applied to Bacchylides: "He saw myriad relationships between a number of events, ideas, and problems, and he could express them artistically. The principal means of so doing are repetition and cross-reference." As Young observes (p. 28), even if we cannot determine the degree to which repetition was used (and heard) consciously, at the very least looking for recurrent words requires us to read the text closely, "which is, after all, obviously the best method of understanding it."

5. Abraham Cowley, "Pindarique Odes" (1668) in *Poems,* ed. A.R. Waller (Cambridge, Eng. 1905) p. 155, conveniently reproduced in Roy Arthur Swanson, *Pindar's Odes* (Indianapolis, 1974) pp. 223-224. The dramatist Lessing, citing Cowley, also observed: "it is immeasurably easier to write a learned commentary on all of Pindar than to translate a single ode well"; see Letter 31 (1759) in *Sämmtliche Schriften,* ed. K. Lachmann (Berlin, 1838–40) VIII, p. 65.

6. Geoffrey S. Conway (London, 1972). In John Sandys' translation (Cambridge, Mass., 1946) the three cognate words are rendered, respectively, as "enfoldeth, thrust, deferring." Richmond Lattimore (Chicago, 1947) has "winds, at the stroke, puts aside"; Carl Ruck and William Matheson (Ann Arbor, 1968), "enweaves, free, postpone"; C.M. Bowra (Baltimore, 1969), "clothed, cast, put back"; Roy Arthur Swanson (n. 5), "wrapped, released, refuses." William J. Slater, in his Lexicon to Pindar (Berlin, 1969) translates more precisely, "put around/crown with, throw/cast away, postpone."

7. But see Burnett, review of *Pindar* by C.M. Bowra, (above, n. 2): "one inevitably asks of a new book on Pindar, 'what advance has been made with *Pythia* 2?'"

8. See, e.g., Henry Miller, *The Colossus of Maroussi* (New York, 1941) p. 11 (which I had not read at the time), describing his first impressions of Greece: "*The glass of water* . . . everywhere I saw the glass of water. It became obsessional. I began to think of water as a new thing, a new vital element of life. Earth, air, fire, water. Right now water had become the cardinal element."

9. My dissertation, "Τῶ καὶ ἐγώ: The First Person in Pindar," *Harvard Studies in Class. Philol.* 67 (1963): 177-253, attempted to use stylistic criteria to determine whether certain passages in the odes were spoken in the persona of the chorus;

"The Influential Fictions in the Scholia to Pindar's *Pythian* 8," *Classical Philology* 70 (1975): 173-185, approaches the same problem by questioning the historicity of the evidence for a choral speaker. "Bacchylides' *Ode* 5: Imitation and Originality," *Harvard Studies in Classical Philology* 73 (1969): 45-96 considers the effects of nuances of diction and the use of thematic repetition.

10. See Eliot's preface to his Notes on *The Waste Land*: "Not only the title, but the plan and a good deal of the incidental symbolism of the poem were suggested by Miss Jessie L. Weston's book on the Grail legend: *From Ritual to Romance* (Cambridge). Indeed, so deeply am I indebted, Miss Weston's book will elucidate the difficulties of the poem much better than my notes will do; and I recommend it . . . to any who think such elucidation of the poem worth the trouble."

Chapter I

Pythian 2: Preliminary Responses

One's first reaction to any poem by Pindar is to feel that one is confronting a series of unrelated fragments. *Pythian* 2 especially is a kind of Stonehenge: we can gather from a first impression that words and sentences have been in *an* order. But the erosion of many centuries keeps us from seeing immediately what the order is, or, in fact, for what purpose the arrangement as a whole was intended. The poet seems to say that he is celebrating a victory in the chariot race by Hieron of Syracuse, but at which festival, and when?

Having once read the ode through, we can, like a tourist, leave the site with the consolation of having seen something significant, even if we don't know exactly what it is. This was Thoreau's approach; he translated from all of *Pythian* 2 a single line: "a plain-spoken man brings advantage to every government" (86).[1] Or we can remain, like an archaeologist, on the site and try to reconstruct the purpose of what we see, on the assumption that there is a describable meaning to the poem, even if we can't recognize it without considerable study: certainly Greek words, like the stones on Salisbury plain, do not ordinarily find themselves in such configurations.[2]

We can begin by reviewing the available methodology. The least expensive, and in many ways most appealing technique, is hypothesis. With luck, we may never need to leave our armchair. This was the method chosen by the first explicators of Pindar, the Hellenistic scholars whose works form the basis of the "scholia" or marginal commentaries in the surviving manuscripts of Pindar. It is not surprising that these critics, like ourselves, needed to find explanations for what they read. The Greek language had undergone some radical changes in two hundred years; they lived in urban Alexandria, in a society as remote from the Greek villages of Pindar's day as nineteenth century London from the town of Shakespeare's time. Professional athletes were now hired to compete in the games; poetry had become an ornamental, rather than central means of communication.[3] Poets composed in writing, their audiences read, where in Pindar's day poets recited and audiences listened. Confronted with the complex language of Pindar's text, its historical obscurity, and the insistent concentration in the ode of statements about failure and envy, the Alexandrian scholars resorted to "probability" (εἰκός) to determine meaning, and came up with biographical constructions to explain what had appeared to them to be the most anomalous features of the poem.[4] The scholia preserve these interrelated guesses: (1) *re* the ode's occasion, for either the Nemean, Olympian, or Pythian games, or perhaps it is not a victory ode at all; (2) in response to references to travel, Pindar was not in Syracuse for the ode's performance but sent it by messenger; (3) in response to references to envy and slander, other poets, especially Bacchylides, were slandering Pindar behind his back, so that Pindar had fallen out of favor, a hypothesis which seems to be confirmed by a reference to the poet's wearing a yoke in the ode's last stanza (93–94):[5]

φέρειν δ' ἐλαφ'ρῶς ἐπαυχένιον λαβόντα ζυγόν
ἀρήγει·

This interpretation is attractive, because it casts the poet in a role of heroic isolation, as long as one does not look back at the poem and see that Pindar is not speaking of "dragging" (ἕλκειν) a yoke, but of taking a yoke and bearing it lightly on his neck (**φέρειν λαβόντα**) i.e., wearing it willingly. The Alexandrian commentators appear to have done what some archaeologists also have been tempted to practice: distorting evidence in order to fit the pattern of the theoretical reconstruction.

We will learn more if we adopt the kind of methodology modern archaeologists would use: a survey of the site to determine its use, now and in the past; a careful description of all evidence in its exact provenience, layer by layer; comparison of what we find to similar structures elsewhere. The excavation of *Pythian* 2 will require us to ask what odes, in the fifth century and in later European literature, were meant to do, and to account for the position and function of every word in the poem, and to discuss similar phenomena in other odes. The results of such an undertaking will bear as little resemblance to the fictions of the Alexandrian scholars as the blue monkeys on the Thera frescoes to the famous "blue boy" erroneously reconstructed from fragments by the first excavators at Cnossos. And, like the blue monkeys, what we find will not necessarily be what we would have created ourselves or what we would like to read into what we see before us. Perhaps the most difficult task we have in understanding *Pythian* 2 is to disengage ourselves from the present, to read Zeus when he says θεός, not God; to remember that when he talks about Centaurs he means literal horse-men, not literary metaphors of bestiality.[6]

An ode, as we might define it from what became of it after Pindar, is a long discursive poem celebrating a particular topic or occasion, of which it generally approves; inevitably there is some consideration of the role of the appraiser, the poet or the persona through which the poem is spoken, so that the ode seems at once forensic and autobiographical—one thinks of Keats' *Ode to a Nightingale*, which describes both what the nightingale does and the poet's reflections on it, "thy plaintive anthem fades/Past the near meadows, over the still stream..../Was it a vision, or a waking dream?/Fled is that music:—do I wake or sleep?"[7] Thus we might expect an ode like *Pythian* 2 would praise the victor or victory in a reflective fashion, without the urgency imposed by the close definition of the sonnet form, and we might not be surprised if the poet's role figured rather more largely than it would in a more strictly narrational genre, such as a Homeric hymn.

With these general considerations in mind, we can begin to examine the components which make up our "site," words in their particular situations. Contemporary practice and tradition can help us anticipate more clearly why what is where, and how the parts we see can in combination form a comprehensible whole. Homeric epic can provide some clues to principles of organization. We know that in the case of Homeric books unity is achieved not by overt designation of subject, but by covert repetition and elaboration of theme. For example, *Iliad* 6 begins with Adrastus begging Menelaus to free him so his father can ransom him; later Diomedes and Glaucus tell their genealogies; the book ends with Hector holding his son Astyanax in his arms. We also know that in epic, transitions to new themes are made by reference to the poet, his audience, or his poetry. We know that myth and fable are used in epic as illustrations of appropriate conduct. In *Iliad* 6, Diomedes uses the story of his ancestor Lycurgus to show that men should not fight with gods. In Hesiod's *Works and Days*, the fable of the hawk and nightingale illustrates how the strong treat the weak, and especially how kings treat poets.

In some Homeric speeches, metaphor and myth are used in combination to reinforce advice: in *Iliad* 6 Glaucus illustrates a general statement by first comparing the generation of men to the generation of leaves, and then by describing the achievement and failures of his own ancestor Bellerophontes. The comparison of human life to the life of nature is made both explicity ("so of men one generation grows, another ceases," 149) and implicitly, in the account of Bellerophontes' life, with its triumphs and sudden isolation and madness. The techniques of thematic repetition, bardic transition, and narrative illustration would have been instinctive by Pindar's day.[8] We see them used by Pindar's contemporary Aeschylus in the *Oresteia*, where the story of the hare killed by the eagles presages later action, either recounted, like Iphigenia's death, or realized in the drama, like Cassandra's death, and later Clytemnestra's and Aegisthus'. The full meaning of the story of the hare and the eagles is not immediately clear, but slowly developed and elaborated.[9] Similarly, in *Pythian* 2, Pindar might expect his audience to grasp his meaning only gradually, not in the condensed action of the poem, but later in the myth and the description of victor and poet that follow. Stating, revising, reconsidering, the ode as it progresses reflects on the celebration of victory, channelling our reactions to the event so we may grasp its meaning through the formalization of recurrence. How deliberate the process is at any point on the poet's part is less important for us to know than the fact of its existence.[10]

We also know that victory odes were intended for public performance, like the choral odes of drama. As such we should not expect from *Pythian* 2 the intimacy of solo songs composed for private parties. But at the same time, because the "I" who speaks in victory odes is the poet rather than the chorus, the dramatic situation of the ode will necessarily involve the poet, and describe his relationship to audience and victor. Combining modes of public and private expression in this way will inevitably produce arresting variation in style, setting formal utterance of moral truth ("god bends any mortal who thinks high," 51) against direct exclamation ("I must keep escaping the close bite of evil talk," 52–53) in collocations that celebrate at once the achievements of community and of individuals.

This blurring of lines that we would draw distinctly is a hallmark of archaic style. What we would call the past can be considered a present reality; so, for Pindar's audience, we find the ancient story of Ixion's lust for Hera introduced, "they tell (φαντί) that Ixion says (λέγειν) this" (21).[11] νόμος, which later particularly connotes "law," in *Pythian* 2 seems in part to retain the spatial connotation it had in early Greek. Pindar will speak of παλάμαι ("hands"), where we might think "contrivance" (40, 75). General advice will be phrased as a personal command or specific reflection: "one should always according to oneself see the measure of everything" (34); "I must keep escaping the close bite of evil talk" (52–53); "learn and become who you are" (72). Generalities will be expressed by accretions of specifics, sometimes analogous, sometimes counterpoised to one another, much in the way that Pindar's contemporary Heraclitus describes god: "god is day night, winter summer, war peace, plenty hunger . . . he becomes another, like fire, when it is mixed with incenses, it is called by the name of each" (67 D–K).[12] Sentences accordingly seem like short trees with many elaborate twigs. In the opening lines of *Pythian* 2, adjectives accompany each noun, and both subject and object have apposites, "great-citied Syracuse, precinct of Ares deep-in-war, god-like nurse of men and horses that-rejoice-in-iron, to you I come, bringing from shining Thebes this song, announcement of earth-shaking four-horse-rig" (1–4). Narrative likewise proceeds by agglutination. Time moves forward and backward or in circles; Pindar tells the story of Ixion in a triple loop: from his punishment to his lust, from his delusion to his punishment, from his lust to his delusion to his punishment (again).[13] Even more remarkable from our point of view is the way hortatory statements are often balanced immediately by illustrations of the opposite type of behavior, e.g., "one should always according to oneself see the measure of everything" (34) is followed by a description of Ixion's lusting for Hera; "learn and become who you are" (72) by the proverb about the child who foolishly thinks an ape is beautiful, as if a complete definition required opposition, right in terms of wrong, beast in terms of man. These negative balancing statements have disturbed readers since the Hellenistic age, because they impart a sense of danger and defeat that seems out of place in a celebration of victory.

These theoretical considerations may help us understand the general intention and structure of *Pythian* 2, but the process of discussion itself will present new problems, not least because we must read what the ancients heard, and must remind ourselves frequently of what they would have remembered. Our own language, with its inflexible word order and special connotations, will often distort meanings that we must then attempt to paraphrase and retranslate. Coping with these difficulties will divert us from the poem; strenuous resummary may call us back; a single line of Greek will thus generate a paragraph of English. It will be tempting to impose on the discussion organizational categories of our own devising: *Pythian* 2 seems at first reading to divide into an introductory section concerning victor and poet, a narration of a myth, and a final long section concerning once again victor and poet. But these delineations, easily charted on paper, are not marked in the ode's metrical structure. Accordingly it may be safest to read the ode as the ancients heard it, stanza by stanza, in triadic units (strophe, with a metrically duplicate antistrophe, and epode) that singers, musicians, and dancers followed. The metrical divisions are not unrelated to meaning: each triad constitutes a complete syntactic unit; sentences are carried over, often with deliberate suspense, from strophe to antistrophe, antistrophe to epode, but stop at the epode's end. The mechanics of the ode's metrical system thus impose certain syntactic expectations, which are lost on us as long as we think in our own language, but that we will ignore at our peril. Comparison with other odes can confirm the validity of these observations, and reveal as well predictable patternings in the ways in which praise can be expressed.[14] Fortunately *Pythian* 2 is not, like Stonehenge, without analogue in genre or in time. What we can learn from it can help us analyze other odes more easily, and what we can find in other odes can in the end help us come back to it with even greater appreciation. Our first reactions as we read the ode—bewilderment at its swift changes of subject, frustration at the vagueness and banality of its general statements, amazement at its stunning metaphors, and perhaps if we have read it in Greek, exhaustion—can, with patience, be replaced by the continuing pleasure of new insight and understanding.

Pythian 2: A First Reading

Μεγαλοπόλιες ὦ Συράκοσαι, βαθυπολέμου
τέμενος Ἄρεος, ἀνδρῶν ἵππων τε σιδαροχαρ-
  μᾶν δαιμόνιαι τροφοί,
ὔμμιν τόδε τᾶν λιπαρᾶν ἀπὸ Θηβᾶν φέρων
μέλος ἔρχομαι ἀγγελίαν τετραορίας ἐλελίχθονος,
5 εὐάρματος Ἱέρων ἐν ᾇ κρατέων
τηλαυγέσιν ἀνέδησεν Ὀρτυγίαν στεφάνοις,
ποταμίας ἕδος Ἀρτέμιδος, ἇς οὐκ ἄτερ
κείνας ἀγαναῖσιν ἐν χερσὶ ποικιλα-
  νίους ἐδάμασσε πώλους.

(1–8, strophe 1)

The first strophe of *Pythian* 2 tells us some of the information we might expect to read in program notes. In the context of a victory celebration, the subject of the song, the occasion, and the author could readily be identified in the first sentence: "I, the poet, come from Thebes (i.e., am Pindar) and bring you, Syracuse, a song which is a message about Hieron's victory in the chariot race."[15] The way this essentially straightforward statement is phrased should be examined closely, if our assumptions about development, based on Aeschylus' methodology, are correct. What is present but inexplicit here will in fact become important later.[16]

The ode begins with praise of Hieron's city, Syracuse, specifically for her military prowess: "O Syracuse with your great city, precinct of Ares deep-in-war." The word order emphasizes the relationship between her greatness and her wars, framing Syracuse between two new adjectives, **μεγαλοπόλιες** and **βαθυπολέμου**, both of which describe general extent (**μεγαλο-, βαθυ-**) and echo each other in sound (-πολιες, -πολέμου).[17] Another appositional phrase provides further elaboration of this first statement: "godlike nurse of men and horses who rejoice in iron," which is in turn expanded in the lines that follow. Reference to divinity (τέμενος and δαιμόνιαι) prepares us for the poet's description of himself as votary "to you (Syracuse) I come, I bear this song from shining Thebes." Syracuse was described as "nurse of men and horses," and now the poet's song is "an announcement of four-horse rig earth-shaking, in which Hieron with his chariot won." The new ἐλελίχθων which is reminiscent of Poseidon's Homeric epithet ἐνοσίχθων, together with **κρατέων,** suggests victory on a battlefield, but "and bound Ortygia high with far-beaming crowns," as opposed to trophies of armor, indicates that the poet is talking of games rather than war. **τηλαυγέσιν** endows Hieron's victory with significance beyond Ortygia and Syracuse: the song itself comes from **λιπαρᾶν** Thebes. Each statement in the stanza successively reflects on every other. The poet paid tribute to Syracuse with a song; Hieron binds Ortygia, "shrine of Artemis of the river," high with crowns. Syracuse is "godlike nurse of men and horses." So in the concluding lines, Artemis is responsible for Hieron's victory, "not without whom (Artemis) did he tame in his gentle hands those mares with intricate reins." Hieron "bound Ortygia high with crowns;" in the last line, the new **ποικιλανίους** also trains our attention on the action of his hands.

The antistrophe begins with continued description of Artemis' support:

ἐπὶ γὰρ ἰοχέαιρα παρθένος χερὶ διδύμᾳ
10 ὅ τ' ἐναγώνιος Ἑρμᾶς αἰγλάεντα τίθησι κόσ-
μόν, ξεστὸν ὅταν δίφρον
ἔν θ' ἅρματα πεισιχάλινα καταζευγνύῃ
σθένος ἵππιον, ὀρσοτρίαιναν εὐρυβίαν καλέων θεόν.
ἄλλοις δέ τις ἐτέλεσσεν ἄλλος ἀνὴρ
εὐαχέα βασιλεῦσιν ὕμνον ἄποιν' ἀρετᾶς.
15 κελαδέοντι μὲν ἀμφὶ Κινύραν πολλάκις
φᾶμαι Κυπρίων, τὸν ὁ χ'ρυσοχαίτα προ-
φ'ρόνως ἐφίλησ' Ἀπόλλων,

(9–16, antistrophe 1)

The opening statement, "the archer maiden (Artemis) with both hands and Hermes god of contests place (on him) bright adornment," responds directly to Hieron's binding Ortygia, Artemis' shrine, high with "far-beaming crowns," in gratitude to the goddess, "not without whom" his victory was won (6–7). The next line again describes Hieron's conduct in victory, but now without reference to any particular place or time, "whenever he yokes down the might of horses to the polished car and to the chariot that persuades the bit." The new adjective **πεισιχάλινος** conveys renewed emphasis on Hieron's kindness; in the strophe, "he tamed in gentle hands those mares with intricate reins" (8).[18] "He calls upon the trident-mover god wide-in-force" provides further illustration of Hieron's piety; in the strophe his winning chariot was described with an epithet that suggested Poseidon's presence, **ἐλελίχθονος** (4).

Reference to the poet's role marks the conclusion of this extended praise of the victor: "for other kings some other man has paid a sounding hymn of praise, requital for achievement." In the strophe the poet spoke of himself "bearing his song as announcement" of Hieron's victory (3-4); now the act of praising acquires the character of formal obligation, ἄποινα. A familiar myth provides ready illustration of the general truth that the achievement of other kings has won praise from other men. "The Cyprians' stories often sing of Cinyras, whom golden-haired Apollo kindly befriended."[19] Artemis, Hermes, and Poseidon have aided Hieron; Apollo's epithet **χρυσοχαῖτα** reminds us of the contribution of divinity to Hieron's victory, the "far-beaming crowns" on Artemis' shrine (6), his "bright adornment" (10). But the exact significance of what the Cyprians say and think, and of Apollo's friendship for their king Cinyras, is not explained until the following stanza.

> ἱερέα κτίλον Ἀφ¹ροδίτας· ἄγει δὲ χάρις
>   φίλων ποί τινος ἀντὶ ἔργων ὀπιζομένα·
> σὲ δ', ὦ Δεινομένειε παῖ, Ζεφυρία πρὸ δόμων
> Λοκρὶς παρθένος ἀπύει,
>   πολεμίων καμάτων ἐξ ἀμαχάνων
> 20 διὰ τεὰν δύναμιν δρακεῖσ' ἀσφαλές·
> θεῶν δ' ἐφετ¹μαῖς Ἰξίονα φαντὶ ταῦτα β¹ροτοῖς
> λέγειν ἐν πτερόεντι τ¹ροχῷ
> παντᾷ κυλινδόμενον·
> τὸν εὐεργέταν ἀγαναῖς
>   ἀμοιβαῖς ἐποιχομένους τίνεσθαι.
>
>   (17-24, epode 1)

The dramatic first words of the epode, **ἱερέα κτίλον**, "priest ram of Aphrodite" would be incomprehensible were it not for the emphasis on taming and control in the lines preceding.[20] Like the ram, Cinyras is leader of his flock, but still under the control of someone else, in this case Cyprian Aphrodite. In his relationship to his people and the goddess, Cinyras illustrates a general truth: "joyful thanks (**χάρις**) for one of their friends leads and in some way shows admiration in return for his deeds." Again the emphasis falls on giving and receiving, but with explicit association with the "joy" (**χάρις**) we first heard of in "men and horses that rejoice in iron" (**σιδαροχαρμᾶν**, 2). The repayment here involves "showing admiration" (**ὀπιζομένα,** "looking to"). The story of Cinyras brings to mind the previous actions of both Pindar and Hieron. Cinyras is a priest, the poet came as votary to the shrine of Ares (3-4), Hieron binds the shrine of Artemis with garlands (6).

As in the case of "some other man for other kings" in the antistrophe (13), the inexplicit generalization "joyful thanks for one of their friends leads and in some way shows admiration" is explained more fully in the following lines: "of you, son of Deinomenes (Hieron), the Zephyrian Locrian maiden sings before her home, from helpless weariness of war through your power she looks forth in safety." The Cyprians' stories sing of Cinyras (15-16); now the Locrian maiden sings of Hieron. The maiden (also παρθένος) Artemis placed bright adornment on Hieron (9), and Hieron himself calls on Poseidon (12). The occasion of the maiden's song, praise of the power that has saved her from πολεμίων καμάτων, was the subject also of the opening lines, μεγαλοπόλιες ὦ Συράκοσαι βαθυπολέμου/ τέμενος Ἄρεος, with their two new epithets.[21] The detail "she looks forth in safety," makes her action an illustration of "joyful thanks for one of their friends leads and in some way shows admiration" (ὀπιζομένα) in return for his deeds.[22] The crowns of Hieron's victory are "far-beaming" (6). This emphasis on seeing prepares us for the sudden change of subject in the following lines. "At the gods' command they tell that Ixion says this to mortals as he is spun round everywhere on his winged wheel: a benefactor repays those who come up to him with gentle exchange." At first these lines seem to break abruptly with the preceding context but a key for our ears comes with "they tell" (φαντί): the Cyprians' φᾶμαι sing of Cinyras (15-16).[23] But θεῶν ἐφετμαῖς λέγειν emphasizes that Ixion's "speaking" is different from the songs that so far have expressed only praise; it is involuntary, as he is whirled on a winged wheel, rather than in willing response to kindness from a god. But his message restates what we learned from the story of Cinyras: τὸν εὐεργέταν ἀγαναῖς ἀμοιβαῖς ἐποιχομένους τίνεσθαι, "a benefactor repays those who come up to him with gentle exchange." The idea is commonplace, "do good to those who honor you," but it is phrased in language that reminds us of the constructive reciprocity between man and god that we have heard about in the lines preceding: ἀγαναῖσιν also described Hieron's hands as he tamed the colts in the first strophe (8). ἀμοιβαῖς and τίνεσθαι are financial terms, like ἐτέλεσσεν and ἄποινα in 13-14. As in the case of the antistrophe (why Cinyras?), we are left at the end of the stanza with yet another riddle to solve: why Ixion on a winged wheel?

Before going on to read the second triad, it might help to stop and reconsider what we have learned so far about the way Pindar works. His method of presentation might roughly be compared to the musical scheme of theme and variation, except that in Pindar, each variation in turn becomes the theme, and the effect is cumulative. Each statement of theme is not completely clear in itself, but depends upon what follows and precedes it. Links are made by verbal repetition (βαθυπολέμου/πολεμίων, σιδαροχαρμᾶν/χάρις, ἵππων/ἵππιον, εὐάρματος/ἄρματα, ἀγαναῖσιν/ ἀγαναῖς, χερσί/χερί, παρθένος/παρθένος, φᾶμαι/φαντί); by sound (-πόλιες/-πολέμου/πολεμίων,-χαρμᾶν/χερσί/χερί), by natural association (ἵππων/πώλους/ἵππιον, τηλαυγέσιν/αἰγλάεντα/χρυσοχαῖτα, στεφάνοις/κοσμον, μέλος/ἀγγελίαν/καλέων/ὕμνον/κελαδέοντι/ἀπυέι, τετραορίας/ εὐάρματος/δίφρον/ἅρματα, ἐτέλεσσεν/ἄποινα/ἀμοιβαῖς/τίνεσθαι, ὁπιζο- μένα/δρακεῖσα). These associative clusters are combined into a new pattern peculiar to this poem, of gifts/light/taming, that deals with the relationship between unequal partners, god and man, man and beast. As we should by now expect, the myth of Ixion will deal directly with this new, not yet fully articulated theme.

> ἔμαθε δὲ σαφές. εὐμενέσσι γὰρ παρὰ Κρονίδαις
> γλυκὺν ἑλὼν βίοτον, μακ¹ρὸν οὐχ ὑπέμεινεν ὄλ-
>   βον, μαινομέναις φρασίν
> Ἥρας ὅτ' ἐράσσατο, τὰν Διὸς εὐναὶ λάχον
> πολυγαθέες· ἀλλά νιν ὕβ¹ρις εἰς ἀνάταν ὑπεράφανον
> ὦρσεν· τάχα δὲ παθὼν ἐοικότ' ἀνήρ
> 30 ἐξαίρετον ἕλε μόχθον. αἱ δύο δ' ἀμπλακίαι
> φερέπονοι τελέθοντι· τὸ μὲν ἥρως ὅτι
> ἐμφύλιον αἷμα πρώτιστος οὐκ ἄτερ
> τέχνας ἐπέμειξε θνατοῖς,
>
>   (25–32, strophe 2)

The story starts with conclusion first: " he learned plainly," i.e., the message he says as he is spun on his wheel, "a benefactor repays those who come up to him with gentle enchange." (24).[24] A narrative explains: "for beside the kind children of Cronus he seized a sweet existence, but he did not wait long for prosperity, when with maddened mind he lusted for Hera, whom Zeus' bed of much pleasure had won." The gods, as in Hieron's case, are "well-intentioned" (εὐμενέσσι); Ixion's life is "sweet." But Ixion acts with violence, seizing where Hieron responds by crowning shrines (6), taming "with gentle hands" (8), and calling on Poseidon for aid (12). The sense of patience and continuity implied in the repeated action of "whenever he (Hieron) yokes the might of horses" (ὅταν... καταζευγνύῃ, 10-11) is denied in Ixion's μακρὸν οὐχ ὑπέμεινεν ὄλβον. Ixion acts alone, μαινομέναις φρασίν, rather than with the support of Artemis and Hermes, or of Apollo and Aphrodite; he lusts for what rightfully belongs (λάχον) to Zeus. The new πολυγαθέες endows Zeus' marriage with the joy that characterized the citizens' gratitude for Cinyras' deeds (17). Poseidon ὀρσοτριαίνας came to Hieron's aid (12) but ὦρσεν describes Ixion's last step εἰς ἀνάταν ὑπεράφανον, a height that indicates that he has moved from his rightful place, "waiting under" (ὑπέμεινεν) for prosperity from his friendship with the gods. The result of his action is predictable in terms of conventional morality: "soon suffering the expected the man seized chosen pain." ἀνήρ explains the nature of Ixion's madness: man is not the equal of a god; his lust for Hera is a crime beyond adultery. ἀνήρ is the last word in the fifth verse of this stanza, as it is also in the first antistrophe ἄλλοις δέ τις ἐτέλεσσεν ἄλλος ἀνήρ (13). The repetition invites comparison of the reciprocity of poet and patron to Ixion's solitary, joyless lust. Instead of seizing (ἑλών) a sweet life, he seizes (ἕλε) "choice" or "seized-out" (ἐξαίρετον) pain and suffering. The emphatic repetition ἑλών/ἕλε indicates to Pindar's audience that this first summary statement of Ixion's story is complete.

"His two wrongs are bearers of labors." The story is told again, in an amplified version. Ixion's first crime is that "he mixed for mortals kindred blood, not without skill." The lines allude to Ixion's use of a trap to kill his father-in-law: to avoid paying the bride-price, he lured him into a pit of coals. The language Pindar uses to describe the crime invites comparison with the right action described earlier in the ode. Ixion's crimes are φερέπονοι; the poet "bears" (φέρων, 3) a song. Hieron associates with immortals; Ixion's actions link him to death, "mixed for mortals (θνατοῖς, "men-who-die") kindred blood." Ixion kills οὐκ ἄτερ τέχνας; Hieron wins "not without Artemis" (ἇς οὐκ ἄτερ, 7). But the phrase "mixed kindred blood" (ἐμφύλιον αἷμα ἐπέμειξε) is new and puzzling; why *mixed*? μείγνυναι in Homer denotes close physical combination, of water and wine, hands in combat, men and women in bed, but never of shedding blood. As in the case of the financial terminology of "for other kings some other man has paid (ἐτέλεσσεν) a song of praise, requital (ἄποινα) for achievement," (13-14), we must wait for a second reference before we can fully grasp the reasons why Pindar chooses to use "mixing" to describe an act of familial violence. The stanza ends in mid-sentence, impelling us toward the antistrophe, to hear his other crime.

> ὅτι τε μεγαλοκευθέεσσιν ἕν ποτε θαλάμοις
> Διὸς ἄκοιτιν ἐπειρᾶτο. χρὴ δὲ κατ' αὐτὸν αἰ-
> εὶ παντὸς ὁρᾶν μέτρον.
> 35 εὐναὶ δὲ παράτ'ροποι ἐς κακότατ' ἀθ'ρόαν
> ἔβαλον· ποτὶ καὶ τὸν Ἰκοντ'· ἐπεὶ
> νεφέλᾳ παρελέξατο
> ψεῦδος γλυκὺ μεθέπων ἄϊδ'ρις ἀνήρ
> εἶδος γὰρ ὑπεροχωτάτᾳ πρέπεν Οὐρανιᾶν
> θυγατέρι Κ'ρόνου· ἅντε δόλον αὐτῷ θέσαν
> 40 Ζηνὸς παλάμαι, καλὸν πῆμα. τὸν δὲ τε-
> τ'ράκναμον ἔπραξε δεσμόν
> (33–40, antistrophe 2)

Ixion's lust is now described in more detail: the Greek word order builds suspense, "when— great— hidden— in— once— bedroom— of Zeus— wife— he tried," saving the worst for last. A general statement follows once again, concerning judgment: "one must always according to oneself see the measure of everything." Essentially this is a version of the traditional advice, γνῶθι σαυτόν: if one knows what is beyond one's reach, one can avoid the insolence that causes one to rise to the high delusion that destroys.[25] We recall the Locrian maiden looking forth in safety through Hieron's power, in the first epode (20), and the fact that Ixion tells his story first of all because his wheel is whirled round where all can see it. But the exact meaning of "one must not always according to oneself see the measure of everything" is not yet completely clear.

Since the first sentences of the antistrophe elaborate on the summary statement of Ixion's lust and insolence, the next sentences expand upon the nature of his punishment: "his bed turned-aside threw him into crowded evil, and also toward him it came, for he slept with a cloud, grasping sweet falsehood, the man in his ignorance." Zeus' "bed of much pleasure" had won Hera (εὐναί, the plural signifies the repeated act, 27), but Ixion's εὐναί throw him into evil. παράτροποι "turned-aside," suggests that the reversal is achieved in Ixion's own terms, i.e., by deceit (παρατροπεῖν means "mislead" in Od.4. 465); the evil into which he is thrown is "crowded;" we have heard how his two wrongs multiply his suffering (φερέπονοι, 31). ποτὶ καὶ τὸν ἴκοντ' begins to suggest how Zeus deceives him: the beds (i.e. the sexual acts) come toward or against Ixion (ποτί can mean either or both).[26]

The ambiguity of ποτί is resolved as the story continues; the encounter is hostile ("against") though it appears to Ixion to be otherwise: "for he slept with a cloud, the man in his ignorance." Before, Ixion had "seized a sweet (γλυκύν) existence" with the gods (26), now "he grasps sweet (γλυκύ) falsehood." He is ἄϊδρις; vision has so far connoted right action "one must always according to oneself see the measure of everything." Again the sentence about Ixion concludes with ἀνήρ in the same metrical position as in the preceding strophe παθὼν ἐοικότ' ἀνήρ (29), and in the first antistrophe ἐτέλεσσεν ἄλλος ἀνήρ (13).

This unusual triple repetition is most emphatic.[27] Ixion is not Ixion, but "man" in the story. He is the negative extreme to which we all can go, the opposite of the man who "one for another" (ἄλλος ἄλλοις) has paid a song, "requital for achievement" (13-14).

The final lines of the stanza describe the man's delusion and his punishment. Again what one *sees* is significant: "for her looks seemed like the highest of Heaven's children, Cronus' daughter, whom Zeus' hands had set as a trap for him, beautiful pain. He made a four-spoked chain--." Cloud, Heaven, highest, all suggest the unattainable, the ἀνάταν ὑπεράφανον into which insolence made him rise (28-29). Dramatically, what Ixion sees is a trap made by Zeus' hands; Ixion had earlier used skill (τέχνα) to murder a kinsman (32).

In the first stanzas of the ode, by contrast, hands are involved in constructive action: Hieron tamed the mares "in gentle hands" (8), Artemis "with two hands places bright adornment" (χερὶ διδύμᾳ ... τίθησι, 9-10).

The recollection emphasizes the differences between right and wrong relationships. *Giving* makes other flourish; *taking* turns back against oneself. Lust becomes its own punishment. τὸν δὲ τετράκναμον ἔπραξε δεσμόν follows as if in expansion of ἄντε δόλον αὐτῷ θέσαν/Ζηνὸς παλάμαι. The means by which attainment becomes defeat is left unexplained, again held in suspense until the next stanza.

> ἑὸν ὄλεθ'ρον ὅγ' · ἐν δ' ἀφύκτοισι γυιοπέδαις
> πεσὼν τὰν πολύκοινον ἀνδέξατ' ἀγγελίαν.
> ἄνευ οἱ Χαρίτων τέκεν γόνον ὑπερφίαλον
> μόνα καὶ μόνον οὔτ' ἐν ἀν-
>   δράσι γερασφόρον οὔτ' ἐν θεῶν νόμοις·
> τὸν ὀνύμαζε τράφοισα Κένταυρον, ὅς
> 45 ἵπποισι Μαγ'νητίδεσσιν ἐμείγνυτ' ἐν Παλίου
> σφυροῖς, ἐκ δ' ἐγένοντο στρατός
> θαυμαστός, ἀμφοτέροις
> ὁμοῖοι τοκεῦσι, τὰ μα-
>   τρόθεν μὲν κάτω, τὰ δ' ὕπερθε πατ'ρός.
>
> (41–49, epode 2)

We learn immediately that the four-spoked chain is Ixion's "own ruin." Now we know how Ixion "spun round everywhere on his winged wheel" can tell the whole story. The wheel is a love charm, and the man, outstretched as on a bed, has his arms and legs chained to its four spokes, turning the act of lust into imprisonment and torture. "And falling in limb-bonds inescapable, he received the announcement shared by many" restates the message of the myth. Violence is repaid with violence, good with good. It is no coincidence that what Ixion receives is an "announcement" (ἀγγελίαν) that the poet brings from Thebes to Syracuse (3). A new compound, πολύκοινον, stresses once again the general applicability of the story. Ixion is called "man" in the narrative; we all share his capacity to be ungrateful to our benefactors.

The remainder of the epode describes more fully how Ixion's two wrongs become "bearers of labor" (31), not just for the wrongdoer himself, but for still others not even present at the scene of the crimes. "Without the Charites she (the Cloud) bore to him offspring high-in-pride, alone a son alone, bearing-no-honor among men or in the right ways of the gods."[28] ἄνευ Χαρίτων immediately suggests that this is a different world from Hieron's, whose Syracusan men and horses "rejoice in iron (σιδαροχαρμᾶν, 2), and for whom, as for Cinyras, "joyful thanks (χάρις) leads and shows admiration" (17).

μόνα καὶ μόνον puts a surprising emphasis on isolation, as if to make the son resemble his father spun on his solitary wheel. Like Ixion with his "high-proud" (ὑπεράφανον) delusion (28), the son is ὑπερφίαλος; Ixion's wrongs are **φερέπονοι** (31); his son is **οὐ γερασφόρος**. The language of the concluding lines makes the son's behavior replicate the father's: "Him she raised and named Centaurus, who mixed himself with the Magnesian mares in the spurs of Pelion, and from this was born an army wondrous, like both parents, the mother below, the father above." Centaurus' name suggests the circumstances of his begetting, **κεντεῖν** ("stab") and **αὔρα** ("breeze"), reminding us of his father's crime.[29] Ixion "mixed (**ἐπέμειξε**) for mortals kindred blood" (32); his son **ἐμείγνυτο** with the Magnesian mares.

The scene of the second "mixing" is the "ankles" (**σφυροῖς**, "foothills") of Pelion; Zeus makes a **τετράκναμον** ("four-legged") chain for Ixion (40), who is held on his wheel in "limb-bonds inescapable" (41). The dual nature of the offspring is explicitly specified: **τὰ μέν...τὰ δέ, κάτω... ὕπερθε**. So Ixion's wrongs are detailed, **τό μέν...ὅτι τε** (31-33).

The setting of this union of man and horses forms a direct antithesis to the opening description of Syracuse, **ἀνδρῶν ἵππων τε δαιμόνιαι τροφοί** (2), where Hieron's gentle taming of horses, with divine support, brings victory in games and war. The force and violence of the second triad are a negative foil for the civilization and cooperation of the first. Through Hieron's power the Locrian maiden looks forth in safety from the weariness of war (19-20). Does the emphasis on a crime of lust in Ixion's story suggest why Pindar talks about a Locrian maiden, and not all Locrians, or Locrian men?

We can expect the implications of the story of Ixion to be developed more fully in the next triad: the interrelationship between sight and judgment, man and god, poet and the ungrateful "man" who acts for himself. The first word of the new triad deals directly with one of these underlying themes, "god."

> θεὸς ἅπαν ἐπὶ ἐλπίδεσσι τέκ'μαρ ἀνύεται,
> 50 θεός, ὃ καὶ πτερόεντ' αἰετὸν κίχε, καὶ θαλασ-
>   σαῖον παραμείβεται
>   δελφῖνα, καὶ ὑψιφρόνων τιν' ἔκαμψε β'ροτῶν,
>   ἑτέροισι δὲ κῦδος ἀγήραον παρέδωκ'· ἐμὲ δὲ χ'ρεών
>   φεύγειν δάκος ἀδινὸν κακαγοριᾶν.
>   εἶδον γὰρ ἑκὰς ἐὼν τὰ πόλλ' ἐν ἀμαχανίᾳ
> 55 ψογερὸν Ἀρχίλοχον βαρυλόγοις ἔχθεσιν
>   πιαινόμενον· τὸ πλουτεῖν δὲ σὺν τύχᾳ
>   πότ'μου σοφίας ἄριστον.
>
> (49–56, strophe 3)

"A god comes up to every mark on his hopes, a god, who catches up with the winged eagle, and passes by the dolphin in the sea, and bends any mortal who thinks high, and gives to others unaging glory." **θεός** is repeated emphatically at the beginnings of the first two lines of the strophe; ἀνήρ ended the fifth line in each of three earlier stanzas (13, 29, 37).

The setting appears to be a race. Ixion's story showed that "one must according to oneself see the measure of everything" (34), but unlike man, god can gauge his achievements by his aspirations ἅπαν ἐπὶ ἐλπίδεσσι τέκμαρ ἀνύεται; he wins contests in sea and air, where men can not compete. His races with dolphin and eagle are described in language briefly reminiscent of the beginning of Ixion's story, παραμείβεται ("exchange places with")/ἀμοιβαῖς ("exchange," 24); πτερόεντα/πτερόεντι (21), as if to suggest that the narrative is reaching a conclusion. In general terms ὑψιφρόνων τιν' ἔκαμψε βροτῶν describes the "man" with his ὑπεράφανον delusion (28), bound to his wheel. κῦδος ἀγήραον is the reward of Cinyras, about whom the Cyprians often sing (15-16), and, by implication, also of Hieron.

We heard in the ode's introduction that kings win "requital" for their achievements through song (13-14). Now again reference to "unaging glory" leads to description of the singer's role "I must keep escaping the close bite of evil talk." The language in which this statement is expressed reflects the message of Ixion's myth. The structure of the sentence, ἐμὲ χρεών, parallels the advice "one must (χρή) according to oneself see the measure of everything" (34). The ungrateful Ixion is caught in ἀφύκτοισι γυιοπέδαις (41), and fell into κακότατ' ἀθρόαν (35); the poet must φεύγειν δάκος ἀδινὸν κακαγοριᾶν. δάκος connotes bestiality, but in Syracuse Hieron's chariot is described by the emphatic new epithet πεισιχάλινος ("that persuades the bit," 11).

Further illustration of wrong conduct follows: "for I saw, being far away, that many times in helplessness blaming Archilochus fattens himself on heavy-spoken hatreds." ψογερόν and βαρυλόγοις ἔχθεσιν distinguish Archilochus' behavior from the poets like Pindar who write for kings "sounding hymns of praise" (14). Archilochus "fattens himself"; Ixion takes for himself when he should give. Reference to vision marks the contrast between Archilochus' actions and Pindar's: earlier in the ode, χάρις for a friend's deeds "shows admiration" (17), and "one must see according to oneself the measure of everything" (34). The Cyprians sing "many times" (πολλάκις) of Cinyras (15); the Locrian maiden looks from the "helpless weariness" of war (καμάτων ἀμαχάνων, 19), but Archilochus τὰ πόλλα is in ἀμαχανία.

The concluding lines of the stanza indicate, in balance, the right course of action: "to have wealth with luck is the best of a fate of skill." In context this generalization acquires specific application. The language of financial transaction in this ode already denotes a constructive relation: "for other kings some other man has paid a sounding hymn of praise, requital for achievement" (14); "a benefactor repays those who come up to him with gentle exchange" (24); "to others (i.e., men unlike

Ixion) god gives unaging glory" (52). σοφία emphasizes the contrast between the good conduct here described and the actions of the "ignorant" (ἄϊδρις) Ixion (37). The poet Archilochus "fattens himself on hatred," i.e. makes his living by slander and invective, but "the best of a fate of skill" (σοφία is a word Pindar chooses elsewhere to describe his craft) is "to have wealth with luck."[30]

> τὺ δὲ σάφα νιν ἔχεις ἐλευθέρᾳ φρενὶ πεπαρεῖν,
> πρύτανι κύριε πολλᾶν μὲν εὐστεφάνων ἀγυι-
>   ᾶν καὶ στρατοῦ. εἰ δέ τις
>   ἤδη κτεάτεσσί τε καὶ περὶ τιμᾷ λέγει
> 60 ἕτερόν τιν' ἀν' Ἑλλάδα τῶν πάροιθε γενέσθαι ὑπέρτερον,
>   χαύνᾳ πραπίδι παλαιμονεῖ κενεά.
>   εὐανθέα δ' ἀναβάσομαι στόλον ἀμφ' ἀρετᾷ
>   κελαδέων. νεότατι μὲν ἀρήγει θράσος
>   δεινῶν πολέμων· ὅθεν φαμὶ καὶ σὲ τὰν
>   ἀπείρονα δόξαν εὑρεῖν,

(57-64, antistrophe 3)

The opening lines of the next stanza now apply the generalization about "having wealth with luck is the best of a fate of skill" also to Hieron, winner in the chariot race, who tamed in his gentle hands those mares with intricate reins" (5-8): "and you plainly have it (i.e. wealth, τὸ πλουτεῖν, 56) to display with a free mind." σάφα and πεπαρεῖν point up the contrast with Ixion, who learned σαφές (25) and whose wheel is "an announcement shared by many" (41). Hieron displays his wealth ἐλευθέρᾳ φρενί, while Ixion who lusted μαινομέναις φρασίν (26) is imprisoned in "limb-bonds inescapable" (41).

Details of Hieron's "having wealth" follow: "ruler lord of many well-crowned streets and an army." The reference to crowns, city streets, and soldiers brings us back to the opening description of Syracuse "with your great city, precinct of Ares deep-in-war, of men and horses that rejoice in iron god-like nurse" (1-2), and of Ortygia bound with "far beaming" στεφάνοις (6). Hieron's στρατός, in the civilized context of "many well-crowned streets," bears little resemblance to the wondrous στρατός of horse-men sired by Centaurs in the hills of Pelion (46).

The next lines return to the poet's role, with a general "if someone now says" that corresponds to "for other kings some (τις) other man has paid" in the ode's introduction (13). But suddenly the speaker's theme becomes negative "says (λέγει) that in possessions or honor any of the men of old up through Hellas was higher." The line describes not a Pindar, who "must escape the close bite of evil talk" (53), but rather an Archilochus, fattening himself on βαρυλόγοις hatreds (55). The connection between this "someone" who says evil, Archilochus, and Ixion becomes clearer in the next line: "he (the someone) wrestles in his gaping mind empty thoughts." Ixion, "with maddened mind" lusted after Hera (26), "grasping a sweet falsehood" (37), caught by the παλάμαι of Zeus (40). Unlike a god, the someone does not judge by established marks, or outstrip competitors (49-51), but instead struggles with himself, as Archilochus fattens himself on hatred (55). As in the line about Archilochus ψογερὸν Ἀρχίλοχον βαρυλόγοις ἔχθεσιν, sound links together selfish futile actions χαύνᾳ πραπίδι παλαιμονεῖ κενεά.[31]

After this restatement of the futility of envy, the opening praise is reiterated in new detail, with some of the same words, but with special concentration on Hieron: "I shall embark on a well-flowered journey, singing about your achievement; in youth boldness lends strength in fearful wars, whence I say that you find boundless glory."[32]

In the first strophe, the poet came to Syracuse from Thebes (3-4), and Hieron bound Ortygia with far-beaming crowns (6); the first antistrophe described song's function as "requital for achievement" (ἀρετᾶς, 14), and told how the Cyprians' stories "sing" (κελαδέοντι) of Cinyras (15). Syracuse was the precinct of βαθυπολέμου Ares (1-2); Hieron freed the Locrian maiden from πολεμίων καμάτων (19). The Cyprian's φᾶμαι sing of Cinyras (15-16); now Pindar himself tells (φαμί) of his patron. The general statement of the preceding strophe, "to others (unlike Ixion) god gives unaging glory" (52) is now applied specifically to Hieron. As usual, the explanation of how Hieron won his glory is not completed within the stanza, but carried over into the first lines of the epode following.

65   τὰ μὲν ἐν ἱπποσόαισιν ἄνδρεσσι μαρνάμενον,
   τὰ δ' ἐν πεζομάχαισι· βουλαὶ δὲ πρεσβύτεραι
   ἀκίνδυνον ἐμοὶ ἔπος ⟨σὲ⟩ ποτὶ πάντα λόγον
   ἐπαινεῖν παρέχοντι. χαῖ-
      ρε· τόδε μὲν κατὰ Φοίνισσαν ἐμπολάν
   μέλος ὑπὲρ πολιᾶς ἁλὸς πέμπεται·
   τὸ Καστόρειον δ' ἐν Αἰολίδεσσι χορδαῖς θέλων
70   ἄθρησον .χάριν ἑπτακτύπου
   φόρμιγγος ἀντόμενος.
   γένοι', οἷος ἐσσὶ μαθών.
   καλός τοι πίθων παρὰ παισίν, αἰεί
                              (65-72, epode 3)

Hieron's "boundless glory" derives in part from "fighting among men driving horses," as we might expect from the opening "Syracuse of men and horses godlike nurse" (2). "And among men battling on foot" recalls with its deliberate balance (τὰ μέν . . . τὰ δέ) the paired specification of Ixion's two crimes (τὸ μέν . . . ὅτι τε, 31, 33) and the description of the army of horse-men (τὰ μέν . . . τὰ δέ, 48). The one-two correspondence connotes completeness, of wrong in the case of Ixion and his monstrous grandchildren, of right "achievement" in the case of Hieron.

The balance is further extended in the next lines, "your older plans hold out to me a word without danger to praise you toward every speech," where reference to age corresponds to "in youth boldness lends strength" in the stanza preceding (63). Again, as in the case of the Locrian maiden who "looks forth in safety through your power" (20), Hieron's military accomplishments provide "a word without danger." But here the adversaries are not soldiers but λόγοι, the speeches made by the people who would vainly assert that there had been in the past someone greater than Hieron (59-60), or by Archilochus in "heavy-spoken hatred" (βαρυλόγοις ἔχθεσιν, 55)—ποτί, as in the case of the bed's turning on Ixion, denotes hostile confrontation (ποτὶ καὶ τὸν ἵκοντ', 36).

The simple greeting that follows "I wish you joy," the conventional "farewell," suggests that the poem might end here, at the conclusion of this third epode, with a closing recollection of the χάρις that shows admiration for a friend's deeds (17). The next lines also take us back to the poem's beginning, "this is sent on the Phoenician trade, a song across the grey salt sea," with its repetition of "I bring this song (τόδε μέλος) from shining Thebes" (3-4).

κατὰ ἐμπολάν denotes yet another of the financial transactions that previously have connoted successful friendship between poets and patrons, men and gods, "requital for achievement" (14), repayment "with gentle exchange" (24). But at the same time these lines begin to elaborate on a theme first articulated in the preceding strophe and antistrophe, the presence of danger in praise. The poet in singing sets out on a sea voyage (62); "the song is sent on the Phoenician trade"—the Phoenicians in Western Sicily and Greece (i.e., the Carthaginians) were perpetual enemies of the Sicilian Greeks.

These reminiscences of war lead up to a surprising statement: "(this song is sent), a Castoreion on Aeolian strings; observe it gladly and meet the joy of the seven-toned lyre." Pindar calls his victory ode, composed in the Aeolian mode and sung to the lyre, a Castoreion war song, since it praises Hieron for his success in war as well as at the games.[33] ἀντόμενος, which can connote confrontation in battle, is juxtaposed dramatically with χάρις of song. Reference to vision, ἄθρησον, again accompanies expression of gratitude: earlier χάρις shows admiration in return for a friend's deeds (17), and the Locrian maiden looks forth in safety as she sings of Hieron (20).

"Learn and become who you are" reinforces the command to "observe (the song) gladly." The advice is traditional, a version of the maxim γνῶθι σαυτόν. But it is stated here in the language that described Ixion's realization of his limitations: **ἔμαθε σαφές** (25).[34] What must Hieron learn? Pindar has already said that "no one of the men of old in Greece was higher in possessions or in honor" than Hieron (60), and that he won "boundless glory" for his successes in war (65).

But learning fully who he is must involve something more than understanding the extent of his material wealth or military accomplishments, or the song would not go on to a strange new theme: "beautiful is an ape among children always." The ape of the fables is a fraud, a counterfeit man, who seems to have human intelligence because he has a humanoid form. Comparison to a real man reveals his inadequacy; as Heraclitus said, "the most beautiful ape is ugly compared to the human race," and "the wisest of men seems an ape compared to god, in wisdom and in beauty and in everything else" (B 82, 83 DK).

What Pindar means by the line about the children and the ape becomes clearer when we remember that Archilochus told the fable of the ape and the fox to his enemy Lycambes: the ape was named king of the beasts, but the fox was jealous, and told the ape of a treasure he had found for him, and led him to meat set in the trap. The ape ate the meat without thinking and was caught in the trap. "With such intelligence how did you expect to be king?" asks the fox. Lycambes is the deluded ape and Archilochus, the fox.[35] The story in essence describes Ixion's predicament. The ape deludes himself in his greed and accepts a gift from a seeming friend, that turns out to be a trap.

In the ode **καλός** describes both the ape and Ixion's "beautiful pain," i.e., the cloud that Zeus made as a trap for him (39-40). If Ixion is the ape who then are the children, and where is the fox? What meaning does the story have for Hieron and the poet? Only the emphatic **αἰεί** at the end of the stanza hints that the story has something to do with measuring: Ixion's story showed that "one must always (**αἰεί**) according to oneself see the measure of everything" (34).

καλός. ὁ δὲ ῾Ραδάμανθυς εὖ πέπραγεν, ὅτι φρενῶν
ἔλαχε καρπὸν ἀμώμητον, οὐδ' ἀπάταισι θυ-
μὸν τέρπεται ἔνδοθεν,
75 οἷα ψιθύρων παλάμαις ἕπετ' αἰεὶ βροτῷ.
ἄμαχον κακὸν ἀμφοτέροις διαβολιᾶν ὑποφάτιες,
ὀργαῖς ἀτενὲς ἀλωπέκων ἴκελοι.
κέρδει δὲ τί μάλα τοῦτο κερδαλέον τελέθει;
ἅτε γὰρ ἐννάλιον πόνον ἐχοίσας βαθύν
80 σκευᾶς ἑτέρας, ἀβάπτιστος εἰμι φελ-
λὸς ὣς ὑπὲρ ἕρκος ἅλμας.

(73-80, strophe 4)

The third triad made explicit the connection between the myth and Hieron and the poet, by converting themes from the introduction into more specific praise, and by making the action of detractors seem to resemble the conduct of Ixion, introducing new references to danger in the process. The fourth triad provides answers to the unsolved riddles of the third epode, continuing the story of the ape, repeating his epithet "beautiful." The reduplicated καλός is emphatic, like the double θεός (49, 50) and the triple ἀνήρ (13, 29, 37).

That "beautiful" is meant to illustrate misjudgment is illustrated by reference to another story: "Rhadamanthys did well when he won from his mind worthy harvest, and did not delight his heart with delusions, such things as always follow a mortal through the hands of whisperers." The Greek audience would remember what king Rhadamanthys said "if a man should sow evil, he would reap evil gain. If he should get as he gives, the marker (δίκη) would be straight" (Hesiod, fr. 286 M-W).

In Pindar's account, οὐδ' ἀπάταισι θυμὸν τέρπεται ἔνδοθεν emphasises that Rhadamanthys is not like Ixion, whom "insolence moved into high-proud delusion"(αὐάταν, 28) and who "embraces a sweet falsehood (ψεῦδος γλυκύ) in his ignorance" (37). Zeus' παλάμαι (40) made a trap for the "ignorant man;" the children mistakenly judge the ape "beautiful" (72), but Rhadamanthys is not deceived by delusions, "such things as always (αἰεί) follow a mortal through the hands (παλάμαις) of whisperers." The story of Rhadamanthys directs the lesson of Ixion and of the ape from the general pattern of right giving and receiving to the specific problem of giving and receiving (i.e., hearing) speech.

The next lines reveal that Pindar has converted Rhadamanthys' saying into a new moral to Archilochus' fable. The fox suffers too, since the one who does evil gets it in return: "low speeches of slanders are an evil unconquerable for both; they are completely like the tempers of foxes."[36] The language connotes powerlessness and confinement. Evil is ἄμαχον; Ixion was trapped in "limb-bonds inescapable" (41); Archilochus blamed in "helplessness" (54); before Hieron's power saved her, the Locrian maiden was caught in "helpless weariness of war" (19). ἄμαχον κακὸν ἀμφοτέροις διαβολιᾶν ὑποφάτιες makes explicit what Pindar implied earlier in his statement about δάκος κακαγοριᾶν (53). Slander harms both slandered and slanderer: Archilochus fattens himself not with food but with "heavy-spoken hatred" (55-56). ἀτενὲς ἴκελοι establishes the analogy with Archilochus' fable of the fox and the ape.

But Pindar does not let the fox enjoy the victory she wins in the traditional tale: "for gain how is this so gainful?" The repeated κέρδει ... κερδαλέον is false, like the καλός ... καλός ape. The "beautiful" in Ixion's eyes turned out to be "pain" (40); his two wrongs were "bearers of labors" (31). Rhadamanthys said "if a man should sow evil (κακά), he would reap evil gain (κακὰ κέρδεα, Hesiod, fr. 286 M-W). We cannot help but suspect that for the foxes the "gainful" will likewise prove not gainful at all.

The concluding lines of the strophe move from foxes to fishing nets: "for as when another set of ropes holds deep labor in the sea, I come undipped, like a cork above the fence of the salt water." References in the third triad to singing this ode as beginning a sea voyage prepare us in part for this sudden shift in language: "I shall embark on a well-flowering journey, singing about your achievement" (62-63); "this is sent on the Phoenician trade, a song across the grey salt sea" (**πολιᾶς ἁλός**, 67-68). But now the poet is a cork whose role is contrasted that of "other equipment" (**σκευᾶς ἑτέρας**) that holds **ἐννάλιον πόνον βαθύν**.

πόνος earlier in the ode connoted the results of Ixion's two wrongs, mixing kindred blood and lusting for Hera (**φερέπονοι**, 31). The poet's aloofness from the ropes, **ἀβάπτιστος εἰμι**, matches his remoteness (**ἑκὰς ἐών**, 54), from blaming Archilochus. Again the stanza seems to end in a puzzling new complex of associations, that will be worked out only in subsequent lines. But the exposition of Archilochus' fable in this strophe has at least made clear the dominant focus of the poem's concluding triad: the role of the poet. In the first and third triads Pindar had spoken of his positive gift to Hieron, and only hinted at the damage he might possibly do by failing to praise him sufficiently, or by "evil talk." The poet's good actions in the first triad were balanced in the second by a description of the man who did not repay kindness. Accordingly we might expect the fourth triad likewise to be the inverse of the third, dealing, like the second triad, with the results of ingratitude.

> ἀδύνατα δ' ἔπος ἐκβαλεῖν κραταιὸν ἐν ἀγαθοῖς
> δόλιον ἀστόν· ὅμως μὰν σαίνων ποτὶ πάντας ἄ-
> ταν πάγχυ διαπ'λέκει.
> οὔ οἱ μετέχω θράσεος. φίλον εἴη φιλεῖν·
> ποτὶ δ' ἐχθρὸν ἅτ' ἐχθρὸς ἐὼν λύκοιο
> δίκαν ὑποθεύσομαι,
> 85 ἀλλ' ἄλλοτε πατέων ὁδοῖς σκολιαῖς.
> ἐν πάντα δὲ νόμον εὐθύγλωσσος ἀνὴρ προφέρει,
> παρὰ τυραννίδι, χὠπόταν ὁ λάβ'ρος στρατός,
> χὤταν πόλιν οἱ σοφοὶ τηρέωντι. χρὴ
> δὲ πρὸς θεὸν οὐκ ἐρίζειν,
>
> (81-88, antistrophe 4)

The antistrophe continues to deal with the subject developed in the strophe: the destruction caused by the man who speaks evil. The scene now changes from wilderness back to civilization: "it is impossible for a deceitful citizen to throw out a word that wins among good men"—**ἐν ἀγαθοῖς**, as opposed to children or animals; the deceitful citizen has no negative effect.

The relevance of this new statement is conveyed by recollection. The poet earlier had an ἀκίνδυνον ἔπος (66) to speak about Hieron's achievement, but the deceitful citizen cannot "throw out" (ἐκβαλεῖν in Homer connotes wasted effort) an ἔπος κραταιόν. Hieron "won (κρατέων) in his chariot (5); his δύναμις saves the Locrian maiden (20), but the deceitful citizen's attempt is ἀδύνατα. δόλιον marks his action as inimical: Zeus set a δόλον for Ixion (39), responding in kind to Ixion's own deceit and lust, where before he had given Ixion a "sweet existence" (26).

The next line fixes the association between beasts, evil speakers, and enemies firmly in our minds: "all the same he fawns toward everyone and weaves his delusion complete."[37] As in the case of the bed's coming toward Ixion (36) and the word without danger that the poet can speak toward every speech (ποτὶ πάντα λόγον, 66), ποτὶ πάντας denotes a potentially hostile confrontation. ἄταν πάγχυ διαπλέκει marks his resemblance to Ixion and his ἀυάταν (28) and to the whisperers' ἀπάταισι (74). διαπλέκει suggests the preparation of a snare, like the traps laid by Ixion for his father-in-law, by Zeus for Ixion, and the fox for the ape.

Pindar in the next lines explicitly disassociates himself from the "deceitful citizen": "I do not share his boldness." He will use his boldness instead for positive ends, as Hieron's θράσος once lent strength to Syracuse (63-64). He will help his friends and hurt his enemies (not his friends!), as traditional morality decrees. As Solon said, "so may I be sweet to my friends, bitter to my enemies, respected by friends, to enemies fearful to see" (13. 5-6). "May it be mine to love a friend. Toward an enemy since I am an enemy like a wolf I shall run below, trading one way then another on crooked paths."[38]

φίλον εἴη φιλεῖν states the familiar ethic with repetition to emphasize the reciprocity characteristic of right action in this poem (17, 24); a balancing statement about enmity follows, where ποτί, which before denoted potentially hostile encounters, now describes open conflict, ποτὶ ἐχθρὸν ἅτ' ἐχθρός. λύκοιο δίκαν ὑποθεύσομαι again casts hostile action in the familiar terminology of bestiality. The world of enemies is an uninhabitable wilderness in which wolves tread the narrow paths of the forests. Speakers of evil also have a "close bite" (53). As the wolf "runs under" (ὑποθεύσομαι), διαβολιᾶν ὑποφάτιες ("under-speakings") follow a man through the hands of whisperers (75-76). πατέων ὁδοῖς σκολιαῖς suggests that he stalks his prey, with the premeditation Ixion used to trap his father-in-law, and which Zeus used to trap Ixion.

Greek ethics do not demand mercy for an enemy, even from a god: παλάμαι designates the hostile action both of Zeus' hands (40) and the whisperers' (75). As in the story of Ixion, the world of wild beasts is contrasted with civilization, and the expression λύκοιο δίκαν denotes the marking off essential to law and order.[39] Where men stay within the defined area (νόμος) and abide by the markers (δίκαι), no wrong will be done, and good, as Rhadamanthys suggests, will be repaid by good: "if he should get as he gives, the marker (δίκη) will be straight" (Hesiod, fr. 286 M-W).

The concluding lines of the stanza further describe the difference between civilized and bestial behavior: "into everything the straight-tongued man bears his right way forth, in a tyranny, and when a hungry army, and when the skilled watch a city." Once again the subject is a speaker. In the ode's opening line the poet "bears" song to Sicily (φέρων, 3-4). Now the straight-tongued man bears his "right way" into everything he does, where Centaurus, by contrast, was described as "bearing-no-honor among men or in the right ways of the gods"(οὔτ' ἐν ἀνδράσι γερασφόρον οὔτ' ἐν θεῶν νόμοις, 43), and Ixion's wrongs were "bearers of labors" (φερέπονοι, 31).[40] ἀνήρ is repeated for the fourth time (13, 29, 37), reminding us of mortal potentials and limitations.

The language that describes the areas in which the straight-tongued man succeeds continues to evoke the setting of the myth: παρὰ τυραννίδι (Ixion, before he violated the reciprocity of friendship, lived εὐμενέσσι παρὰ Κρονίδαις, (25-26); ὁ λάβρος στρατός is set emphatically in a separate clause, like Centaurus' horse-men offspring, the στρατὸς θαυμαστός (46-47), while Hieron is "ruler lord of many well-crowned streets and an army" (στρατοῦ, 58). The last of the three areas, χὦταν πόλιν οἱ σοφοὶ τηρέωντι seems to describe Syracuse, μεγαλοπόλιες in the ode's opening; "skill" (σοφία) referred to Hieron as well as to Pindar (56); vision in the ode connotes knowledge and understanding (34, 37, 54). The sudden shifting of terminology in this passage would be incomprehensible without Ixion's story in the background, and the characterization of evil speaking as the conduct of beasts and of enemies in the example of Archilochus (52-56).

The last line of the stanza returns to an earlier theme: "one must not fight against a god." We have already heard that "a god comes up to every mark on his hopes; a god, who catches up with the winged eagle and passes by the dolphin in the sea" (49-51). χρὴ δέ reiterates the format of the advice about judgment: "one must (χρὴ δέ) see according to oneself the measure of everything" (34). The advice, which could be applied easily to Ixion, now seems intended for the "straight-tongued man." How and why are more fully articulated in the ode's final stanza, where all these statements about evil talk are made to refer directly to the context of the victory ode.

> ὃς ἀνέχει τοτὲ μὲν τὰ κείνων, τότ' αὖθ' ἑτέροις
> ἔδωκεν μέγα κῦδος. ἀλλ' οὐδὲ ταῦτα νόον
> 90 ἰαίνει φθονερῶν· στάθμας δέ τινες ἑλκόμενοι
> περισσᾶς ἐνέπαξαν ἕλ-
> κος ὀδυναρὸν ἑᾷ πρόσθε καρδίᾳ,

πρὶν ὅσα φροντίδι μητίονται τυχεῖν.
φέρειν δ' ἐλαφ⌐ρῶς ἐπαυχένιον λαβόντα ζυγόν
ἀρήγει· ποτὶ κέντρον δέ τοι
95 λακτιζέμεν τελέθει
ὀλισθηρὸς οἶμος· ἀδόν-
τα δ' εἴη με τοῖς ἀγαθοῖς ὁμιλεῖν.

(89-96, epode 4)

The reiteration of the earlier description of god's powers continues, but now the stress falls more heavily on the reasons for human envy than on the workings of divine justice. Instead of "who bends any mortal who thinks high, and gives to others unaging glory" (51-52), we hear "who holds up the deeds of some and gives others great glory." Again reference to success is followed immediately by comments about envy. After "god . . . gives to others unaging glory," the poet said, "I must keep on escaping the close bite of evil speaking" (52-53).

Now the scene has become an athletic contest: "but this does not soothe the intentions of the envious. Some drag a standard that is too much and fix a painful wound in their own hearts before they get what they plotted in their minds." The **φθονεροί** seem to be running a race, and wound themselves in the process of dragging the finish line.[41]

The story of Ixion warns against having aims that exceed one's abilities; unlike god, man cannot "come up to every mark on his hopes" (49). The echo **ἑλκόμενοι . . . ἕλκος** emphasizes that the envious men's desire, like Ixion's, in fact becomes their destruction. For the foxes too **κέρδος** will not prove **κερδαλέον** (78). Observers (like poets) of the achievements of others cannot praise without feeling some longing for the same approbation themselves. Like the fox in the fable, each of us longs for what the other has.

But the next lines return to a description of right behavior, in language used before to praise Hieron: "to bear lightly and take the yoke on one's neck lends strength. Kicking against the goads is a slippery road." The opening stanzas implied that the right relationship between man and god resembles that of domestic animal and man: Cinyras is priest ram of Aphodite (17); Hieron "tamed in gentle hands those mares with intricate reins" (8) and "yokes (**καταζευγνύῃ**) the strength of horses to the polished car and to the chariot that persuades the bit" (11-12). His boldness **ἀρήγει** in war (63-64). The poet bears song to his patron (3), and the straight-tongued man bears his right way forth into everything (86). The conventional **ποτὶ κεντρὸν λακτιζέμεν** derives additional force from the negative connotations of "feet" throughout the ode: Ixion's "limb-bonds" (41), the "four-legged" wheel (40), the wolf treading crooked paths (85). Ixion climbed high and fell (41); his two wrongs **φερέπονοι τελέθοντι** (31); now kicking against the goads **τελέθει ὀλισθηρὸς οἶμος**, as if mirroring "for gain how is (τελέθει) this so gainful" (78).

The final sentence of the ode "may I please and consort with good" is a wish for constructive conduct like "may it be (εἴη) mine to love a friend" (83). ἐν ἀγαθοῖς the deceitful citizen cannot throw out a word that wins (81). Pleasure (ἁδόντα) accompanies acts of reciprocation (17). This final wish is striking in its simplicity and contentment: "may I stay in such company, may I be satisfied with who I am." Stating this as a prayer rather than as a fact ends the ode on a note of tension. Nor do the repeated admonitions of this stanza reassure: "one must not fight with a god," "bearing the yoke lightly on one's neck lends strength, kicking against the goads is a slippery road." The conclusions of the preceding stanza were likewise tentative: "may it be mine to love a friend." The capacity to be a wolf remains.

So the poem ends, with much less complexity and excitement than it began. The shift from the second praise of the victor to a description of evil speaking in the last triad may also strike us as surprising: why should the poet discuss in such detail what he does not approve or practice? The answer may simply be that Pindar and his contemporaries tend to express complex totalities by means of opposites, to understand the good, we must also see the bad. Compared to the destruction a poet could have caused by being jealous and either flattering unduly or praising insufficiently, the poem will appear a greater gift, because it is honest and given without selfish motive.[42]

The analogies drawn to different animals in the last triad would seem incomprehensible out of context, but in their place have special meaning in a poem where earlier the right relationship between man and god was characterized in terms of animals. The victorious Hieron "tamed his mares in gentle hands" (8), King Cinyras is "priest ram of Aphrodite" (17), but Ixion in his greed for more than a man should have, begets a son who "mixed himself with the Magnesian mares" (45) and begot in turn a race of horse-men.

After the story of Ixion the right relationship between poet and patron is described similarly in terms of wild and tame behavior. Evil talk has a "close bite" (53). A man who listens to the "delusions" of whisperers is like an ape (72-75); "low speakings of slander" are like foxes (76-77); enemy acts like a wolf towards his enemy (84). The poet who is content with his role "bears the yoke lightly," (93), like the victorious horses that "Hieron yokes down" to his polished chariot (11).

The reference to fables and recollections of the Ixion myth give the poet's statement about his art application beyond himself to human conduct in general. There are perhaps hints of political dissension in the references to deceitful citizens and to the different people who watch a city (86-88), but whether Pindar has specific difficulties in Syracuse in mind, or the fast changing political climate of many other Greek cities, is impossible for us to ascertain, and not directly relevant. The comments Pindar makes about gratitude and ingratitude are deliberately general; perhaps we cannot see the direct application of many ambiguous lines and allusions in the ode because we are not meant to.

The long process of exegesis accordingly has not explained the meaning of every detail, but at least it has provided us with a sense of the ode's purpose and its contents: the ode praises the victor and in the process describes the potentials of the poet's art by descriptions of the victor's present success, by illustrations of past success and failure, and by examples of right and wrong behavior in fables and in simple maxims.

The concentration in the ode on wrong-doing serves not only by polarizing to demonstrate what is right, but also confronts directly the successful man's inevitable concern with failure. The value system of Greek athletic contests, where the winner takes all, offers the loser only disgrace. Envy accordingly is a natural by-product of failure to achieve one's goal, and Greek religion, which teaches that gods are jealous of the man of extraordinary achievement, reflects accurately the attitude of its adherents.[43] The successful man's apprehensiveness about the danger of his achievement determines the character of the topic's presentation in a song of praise: the possibility of failure is approached only indirectly, in general fable, in description of potential (but not historically identifiable) misconduct.

Abrupt changes of subject back and forth between positive and negative reflect the tension generated by the perception in victory of subsequent defeat. Reiterated words and structures, expanding and reflecting on one another, convey an impression of anguished preoccupation. Actions otherwise unrelated are described in similar language: Ixion's delusions and the children's (both "beautiful," 40, 72-73); Ixion's crimes, the foxes' greed, and the slippery road of envy (τελέθοντι/ει, 31, 78, 95). Pairing links Ixion's crimes (31, 33), the centaur's appearance (48), human success and failure (twice, 51-52, 89), and Hieron's military achievements (63).

What in other poetry might simply be descriptive, "Syracuse with your great city, of man and horses that rejoice in iron god-like nurse" (1-2), is elaborated over and over again, in the new adjective πεισιχάλινος ("persuading-the-bit," 11) that stresses willing cooperation, in the myth of the army of horse-men (46-48), in fuller statement of Syracuse's military power (58, 65), in the final advice "to bear lightly and take the yoke on one's neck" (93-94). The concentration is dramatic and intense. Anne Lebeck's description of the choruses of Aeschylus' *Oresteia* also fits *Pythian* 2: "there is little which fails to contribute to the unity of the work; the significance of each part can be appreciated only by reference to the whole."[44]

It is no coincidence that the very characteristics of style and content that make victory odes distinctive have proved most difficult for modern readers to understand. To appreciate this kind of poetry requires a trained ear, a retentive memory, and an instant acquaintance with mythology and literature, none of which any twentieth-century reader can readily possess. Is the struggle justified? *Pythian* 2 begins to provide an answer. Pindar, in his concern with the poet's role, concentrates on the workings of the mind, in what we would call the motivations for achievement. The processes that lead to success and joy (and their opposites) intrigue him. The myth describes not only crime and punishment, but its cause and effect on Ixion the individual. His contemporary, Aeschylus, explores the background that led to famous murders in his dramas about the Danaids and the houses of Laius and of Atreus. Describing such forces has a social function: understanding is a first means of control. Pindar's language, like Aeschylus', in its gyrations, expresses concerns that become progressively more articulated in later writing, especially in the connections it makes between human lust, greed, jealousy, and the world of animals. That the notion of human bestiality had continuing influence needs no documentation. Pindar realized what the ancient myths and fables implied; Plato, in the *Phaedrus*, relied on the analogy of the soul's good and bad horses to demonstrate to his audience the benefits of rational behavior.

But our analysis of *Pythian* 2 so far leaves much unresolved. Only by looking at what Pindar does in other odes will we be able to state with assurance that Pindar's preoccupation with failure and envy in *Pythian* 2 is not so much a determinant of date as characteristic of genre. Comparison of Pindar's work with his contemporary Bacchylides' will help us better to estimate the nature of his originality: how much, and for what purpose does Bacchylides alter myth and language? Reading Bacchylides' *Ode* 5 with its companion piece Pindar's *Olympian* 1 will provide preliminary insight on these questions.

NOTES

In November 1973, after the first draft of this chapter was written, I heard Prof. Hugh Lloyd-Jones read a paper on *Pythian* 2 ("Modern Interpretation of Pindar," Intr. n. 3) which anyone interested in this ode and in Pindaric studies will want to read. I was reassured to discover that quite independently we had agreed on many points of interpretation (see his p. 137, n. 142). The present chapter owes much to his criticism, and follows the outlines of his explanation of the function of the different subjects and sections of the ode; it was not his purpose, as mine is here, to try to describe also distinctive characteristics of style and language. I am grateful also for many specific improvements, to Profs. William M. Calder III and William J. Slater, and also to the late Prof. Douglas Young.

1. Thoreau's comments and translations were first published in *Dial* (Intr. n. 1) pp. 379-390; translations only may be found in *The Writings of Henry David Thoreau* (Boston, 1906) V, pp. 375-392. See also R.A. Brower, "The Theban Eagle in English Plumage," *Class. Philology* 43 (1948): 25.

2. Reducing the ode to a list of elements, as, e.g., in the coding suggested by Hamilton (Intr. n. 2) p. 91 or in the kind of model suggested by C.O. Pavese, "Semantematica della poesia corale greca," *Belfagor* 23 (1968): 389-430, will be of no more help to us in interpreting the whole of the ode than a catalogue of stones in the understanding of any archaeological site. Cf. Norman N. Holland's warning, *The Dynamics of Literary Response* (New York, 1968) p. 25: "It is not difficult to demonstrate that any verbal text, taken as a series of discrete words or events, can be recursively classified into a final, single 'meaning'. Any two things can be logically related: an elephant is like a Rembrandt in that neither is a wastebasket; they are both in the class of non-wastebaskets."

3. On increasing professionalism in athletics after the Persian wars, see E. Norman Gardiner, *Athletics of the Ancient World* (Oxford, 1930: reissue 1955) pp. 101-106. The athlete Astylus from Croton in Italy entered himself in the Olympic games of 480 as a Syracusan, as a favor to Hieron (Pausanias vi. 13.1).

4. On the research methods of the Alexandrian scholars see "The Influential Fictions" (Intr. n. 9). In addition to the political allegories in their interpretation of *Pyth.* 2 (see n. 5), we can find hypothetical geography, and the creation, according to established mythological patterns, of fictional persons, voyages, and houses.

5. In *Scholia Vetera in Pindari Carmina*, ed. A.B. Drachmann (Leipzig, 1910; reissue Amsterdam, 1964), see esp. *Pyth* 2. inscr., vol. II p. 31; 3-4, 6b, II 33; 97, II 47; 131bc, II 53; 132 abcdef, II 54-55; and 171c, II 60 on "dragging the yoke." On the interpretative distortions resulting from modern scholars' too eager acceptance of the scholiasts' "historical" information, see "Pindar's Lives" (Intr. n. 2) pp. 79-87, and on the dangers of biographical criticism in general, see esp. Harold F. Cherniss, *The Biographical Fashion in Literary Criticism* (*Cal. Publ. in Class. Philol.* 12. 15; Berkeley, 1943) pp. 279-292; David C. Young, "Pindaric Criticism" (Intr. n. 4) pp. 52-56; Köhnken (Intr. n. 3) pp. 1-18; and Lloyd-Jones (Intr. n. 3) pp. 109-117.

6. Cf. L.R. Farnell's King-Jamesian translation of *Pyth.* 2. 49, *The Works of Pindar* (London, 1930), "all things are brought to their destined end by God according as he planned." On the unconscious tendency to normalize the past into contemporary terms, see my article, "Cultural Conventions and the Persistence of Mistranslation," *Class. Journal* 68 (1972): 31-38.

7. On deliberate imitation in English of Pindar's seemingly abrupt and allusive style, see ch. IV n. 7.

8. Ready accessibility of printed material obviates the need for memorization regularly employed in any non-literate society. See James A. Notopoulos, "Mnemosyne in Oral Literature," *Trans. and Proc. of the Amer. Philol. Assoc.* 69 (1938): 491: "The oral mind is capable of memorizing with ease what seems incredible to us, and to remember the exact and specific ideas of a speaker was not unusual." Even in the fourth century A.D. audiences could remember what they heard to a degree that seems incredible to us, e.g., in the case of the orator Libanius' observation about an audience in Antioch: "how can I speak adequately about their tears during my prologue, which many also memorized before they left" (Oration 1. 88). On repetition in archaic poetry, see B.A. Van Groningen, *La Composition Littéraire Archaïque Grecque* (Ed. 2; Amsterdam, 1960) pp. 83-90, 330; Walter Stockert, *Klangfiguren und Wortresponsion bei Pindar* (European Univ. Papers Ser. 15. 2; Bern/Frankfurt, 1971) pp. 87-88. On associative techniques in epic, see James A. Notopoulos, "Continuity and Interconnexion in Homeric Oral Composition," *Trans. and Proc. of the Amer. Philol. Assoc.* 82 (1951): 81-101; and on repetition in primitive poetry, Franz Boas, "Stylistic Aspects of Primitive Literature," in *Language, Race, and Culture* (New York, 1940) pp. 491-502.

9. On Aeschylus' development of themes, see especially Anne Lebeck, *The Oresteia: A Study in Language and Structure* (Washington, D.C., 1971) p. 2; and Mae Smethurst, "The Authority of the Elders (The *Agamemnon* of Aeschylus)," *Class. Philology* 67 (1971): 93. On the eagles and the hare see Lebeck, pp. 13-16 and Froma I. Zeitlin, "The Motif of the Corrupted Sacrifice in Aeschylus' *Oresteia*," *Trans. and Proc. of the American Philological Soc.* 96 (1965): 463-508.

10. See James Olney, *Metaphors of Self: The Meaning of Autobiography* (Princeton, 1972) pp. 270-271 on how repetition in T.S. Eliot's *Four Quartets* serves both to unify the various sections of the poem and to express the poet's central concern with the action of memory and perception. In discussing the work of Pindar and Bacchylides I have avoided terms like symbol and image because they may imply to some readers that choice of metaphor on a poet's part is consistently a deliberately calculated and articulatable process. I would assert only that a poet's language is carefully chosen, even though the poet might not at any given moment be able (or want) to tell what went into the process of selection. See, e.g., Virginia Woolf's reaction to the suggestion that the Lighthouse had symbolic meaning: "I meant *nothing* by *The Lighthouse*. One has to have a central line down the middle of the book to hold the design together . . ." (cited in Quentin Bell, *Virginia Woolf* [New York, 1972] II, p. 129).

11. See B.A. Van Groningen, *In the Grip of the Past: An Essay on an Aspect of Greek Thought. Philosophia Antiqua Monographs* 6 (Leiden, 1953) pp. 18, 81, on the use of past tenses to describe what is still happening in the present.

12. For a survey of similar practice in early Greek prose and poetry, see G.E.R. Lloyd, *Polarity and Analogy* (Cambridge, 1966).

13. On the tendency of narrative in archaic poetry to proceed in circles rather than in straight lines, see Harry and Agathe Thornton, *Time and Style: A Pyscho-Linguistic Study* (London/Dunedin, 1962) pp. 1-50.

14. The predictability of these patterns can easily be estimated in Hamilton's abbreviated lists of repeated elements (Intr. n. 2), pp. 97-102, based on categories defined by Bundy (Intr. n. 3) and refined by Thummer (Intr. n. 2). The poet's variation of the placement and length of these elements within the odes sets up the desirable tension between free expression and control essential to effective poetry; see Holland (above, n. 2), pp. 132-133, who suggests that the artist's secret lies in "being able to take pleasure not only from the drives but also from the very defenses inherent in what he does."

15. As the owner of the victorious chariot went to claim his prize crown, the herald announced his name, his father, and his city; see E.N. Gardiner, *Athletics of the Ancient World* (above n. 3), pp. 227-228. The practice still survived in the first century A.D.; see H.A. Harris, *Greek Athletes and Athletics* (Indiana, 1966), pp. 130, 168-169. The use of athletic terminology to describe song is discussed by F.J. Nisetich, "The Poetry of Victory: A Study in the Occasional Nature of Pindar's Odes" (unpubl. diss. Harvard Univ., 1973).

16. See Greengard (Intr. n. 3) pp. 188-191 on the function of proems and subsequent development of themes.

17. See Greengard (Intr. n. 3) pp. 74, 212 on the word order of the proem to *Pythian* 2.

18. On the meaning of πεισιχάλινος ("persuading the bit"), see D.S. Robertson, "Bits and Chariots: A Note on Pindar *Pythians* II 9, Sqq.," *Studi in Onore di Luigi Castiglioni* (Florence, 1960) II, pp. 803-805.

19. By mentioning Apollo and Aphrodite's love for Cinyras, Pindar diverts attention from stories that would not suit his theme, such as Cinyras' daughter tricking him into committing incest and his promising Agamemnon fifty ships for the Trojan expedition, but sending instead along with one real ship forty-nine made of clay. See P.B. Katz, *The Nature and Function of Pindar's Poetic Persona in Nemean VII and Pythian II* (diss. Columbia University, 1968; U.M. order 69-20, 178) p. 61.

20. I have translated κτίλος as a substantive "ram" (cf. *Il.* 3. 196) better to preserve in English the word's association with the animal world. Pindar's contemporary Empedocles used it as an adjective to describe the gentleness of wild animals to man in the golden age (130. 1 D-K). Anna Morpurgo's suggestion that Pindar chose this term because the ram is sacred to Aphrodite on Cyprus "*Ktilos* (Pind. *Pyth.* II 17)," *Rivista de Cultura Classica e Medioevale* 2 (1960): 30-40 is questioned by Lloyd-Jones (Intr. n. 3) p. 119 n. 59, but in any case the use of this animal term for a man, especially a priest, seems unusual (cf. possibly Hesiod, frag. 323 M-W, but at least one word and the entire context are missing).

21. On the interpretation, "before her house" (rather than Hieron's), see Lloyd-Jones (Intr. n. 3) p. 119 n. 61, who suggests that Pindar may be describing a religious celebration. Unfortunately historical information about Locri is drawn not from a continuous account, but from passing references in many different authors. According to the scholia on this line, Hieron forestalled an attack on

Locri by Anaxilas, the tyrant of Rhegium, by threatening him with war. This incident, mentioned nowhere else, would have occurred between 478, when Hieron became tyrant of Syracuse, and 477 when Anaxilas died. According to Justin, the epitomizer of the Augustan historian Pompeius Trogus, Anaxilas' son Leophron, who ruled from 477 to 468 under a regent, and until 461 together with his brother, also threatened Locri, at which time the Locrian men vowed to offer their virgins as prostitutes to the service of Aphrodite, should they win the war (*Epitome* 21. 3).

Justin does not indicate when in Leophron's reign the Locrian vow was made, but the reference to Cinyras and Aphrodite in *Pythian* 2 may indicate that Pindar had this incident in mind rather than the unspecified troubles with Anaxilas mentioned in the scholia. Some confirmation of this possibility comes from the fact that either side technically could have won. The vow was a significant event in Locrian history, as Justin's account indicates, remembered a century later. But the evidence is too uncertain to be of any value in dating the ode; see Lloyd-Jones (Intr. n. 3) p. 120 and cf. C. Sourvinou-Inwood, "The Votum of 477/6 B.C. and the Foundation Legend of Locri Epizephyrii," *CQ* n.s. 24 (1974): 187, n. 4.

22. On the meaning of δέρκομαι ("look forth, shine"), see especially Bruno Snell, *The Discovery of the Mind* (1948), tr. T.G. Rosenmeyer (Cambridge, Mass., 1953) p. 2.

23. Another link which the ancient audience might have sensed between this statement and "joyful thanks . . . for his deeds" occurs in the collocation of "joy" and "good deeds" in the Homeric formula "there is no joy afterwards in good deeds" (χάρις . . . εὐεργέων), *Od.* 4. 695 and 22. 319. The notion of repayment for good deeds also occurs in epic. *Od.* 22. 235 (εὐεργεσίας ἀποτίνειν).

24. The practice of first summarizing the contents of a story or a poem in part performs the function of a chapter heading on a written page, see Van Groningen *In the Grip of the Past* (above, n. 11) pp. 66, 351. On the inductive reasoning process involved, see Lloyd (above, n. 12) pp. 421-423.

25. On the interpretation of line 34 ("one must always according to oneself see the measure of everything"), see esp. Basil Gildersleeve, *Pindar: The Olympian and Pythian Odes* (New York, 1890) p. 260.

26. My interpretation of this difficult passage is based on the connotations of ποτί later in the ode, where it consistently describes hostile confrontations (potential or actual: 66, 82, 84, 94). So in *Pythian* 1 Pindar appears to have used special compounds of σύν (σύνδικος, 2; συντυχία, 36; σύμφωνος, 71; συντανύω, 81) to denote close joining or cooperation; see ch. III.

27. Stockert (above, n. 8) pp. 36-37. On conscious juxtaposition of mortal/immortal in epic verse, see Howard N. Porter, "Repetition in the Homeric Hymn to Aphrodite," *Amer. Journal of Philology* 70 (1949): 249-272.

28. νόμος, originally an area bounded by δίκαι, by Pindar's time meant specifically a "right area" outside of which was chaos and disorder; see Martin Ostwald, *Nomos and the Beginnings of the Athenian Democracy* (Oxford, 1969) pp. 30-31 and "Cultural Conventions" (above, n. 6) pp. 32-34.

29. On Pindar's etymology of Centaurus, see Peter von der Mühll, "Weitere

pindarische Notizen," *Museum Helveticum* 25 (1968): 226-229.

30. My translation deliberately retains the ambivalence and generality of the Greek; Pindar wishes the statement to apply not just to himself (vs. Archilochus), but to the following stanza (cf. the several meanings intended in the simile of the eagle in Bacchylides' *Ode* 5. 16-30; see ch. II). Lloyd-Jones' rendering "to be wealthy while one attains one's proper fate is the best thing wisdom offers" (Intr. n. 3) p. 121, by construing πότμου with τύχᾳ and by adding the particularizing "attains," "proper," "offers," settles the meaning too precisely. Pindar, as so often at stanza end (cf. 33) wishes to leave us in suspense. σοφία, when the topic concerns poets, will seem to refer primarily to poetry (e.g., *Pyth.* 1. 12); when the topic is competition, σοφός can describe a victor's skill (*Pyth.* 1. 42; see p. 115).

31. Stockert (above, n. 8) p. 6.

32. In *Nemean* 3. 17, στόλος means the course of the pancration; in *Pythian* 8. 98, a journey or "send-off"; in Aeschylus' *Persians* 408-409, the "ram" of a ship; see J.S. Morrison and R.T. Williams, *Greek Oared Ships 900-322 B.C.* (Cambridge, Eng., 1968) pp. 95, 157, 339. Again Pindar chooses words with multiple connotations: ships, games (the preceding line refers to wrestling), and public speaking; ἀναβαίνω, "embark," also means mount the speaker's rostrum as well as the deck of a ship.

33. On the interpretation of Castoreion, see Lloyd-Jones (Intr. n. 3) pp. 123-124. The scholia interpreted lines 67-71 as referring to two different songs, a Castoreion sent as a bonus, along with the officially commissioned ode (127 II 52 Dr). Scholars since, accepting the notion that the Castoreion and victory ode are not identical, have suggested that the Castoreion was in fact the commissioned ode, and *Pythian* 2 a poetical epistle, or even a prospectus of the poet's wares for Hieron's consideration. See, e.g., John F. Oates, "Pindar's Second Pythian Ode," *Amer. Journ. of Philology* 84 (1963): 387-389; Bowra, *Pindar* (Intr. n. 2) p. 135; Ruck and Matheson (Intr. n. 6) pp. 136, 140. As David Young observed in a paper presented at the American Philological Assoc. meetings in Dec. 1971, "Pindar's Poetical Epistles: *Pythians* 2, 3, *Isthmian* 2: Occasion and Date," this genre was unknown in antiquity.

34. On the use of this type of admonition in other Greek literature, and on conventions of thought in the fourth triad, see Leonard Woodbury, "The Epilogue of Pindar's Second Pythian," *Trans. Amer. Philol. Assoc.* 76 (1949): 11-30. The rhetorical function within the ode of advice is catalogued by Erich Thummer, "Die zweite pythische Ode Pindars," *Rhein. Mus* 115 (1972): 293-307. Pindar in these lines and elsewhere proves not to be innovative in his philosophy, or in the choice of admonitions to suggest the greatness of his patron's achievement; here it is not what he says, but how he says it, that makes him worth reading.

35. Archilochus, frags. 185-187 W; Aesop, Fable 81 (Perry). Aesop 345 (Babrius 130) tells a similar story of a fox tricking a wolf, cf. also Aesop 568. Archilochus 81 begins to tell how the "greedy (κερδαλῆ) fox" encountered (συνήντετο cf. "see and meet," in the following stanza).

36. Hesiod, *Great Works*, frag. 286 MW. The moral to Aesop 345 (above, n. 35) is similar: the trapped wolf says to the fox "if you give such to your friends how

will a friend *encounter* you (συναντήσει, cf. "meet" in the preceding stanza, and Archilochus 82)?"

37. In Hesiod, *Theogony* 770-773, Cerberus has an "evil trick" (τέχνη, cf. Ixion's murdering "not without skill," (τέχνη): he fawns (σαίνει) on those entering the lower world, but eats (cf. "the close bite of evil speaking") those who try to leave.

38. Katz (above, n. 19) cites a recently discovered fragment of Archilochus (23. 14-16): "I know that I should love my friend (τὸν φίλεον ... φιλεῖν) and like an ant (?) hate and speak evil of my enemy." Cf. also Archilochus 66: "One big thing I know is to repay (ἀνταμείβεσθαι, cf. with gentle exchange, ἀμοιβαῖς) the man who does me wrong with fearful evil." For similar sentiments in other poets see David A. Campbell, *Greek Lyric Poetry* (New York, 1967) pp. 153, 235; and Douglas E. Gerber, *Euterpe* (Amsterdam, 1970) p. 29, who observes that Archilochus is not satisfied with equal repayment, but wishes punishment to exceed the wrong done to him. "Wolf-walking" may be a traditional way of designating an enemy, cf. Archilochus' invective directed at Lycambes ("wolf-gait"). See Gregory Nagy, "Iambos: Typologies of Invective and Praise," forthcoming in *Arethusa*.

39. On the usage and meaning of δίκη, see esp. L.R. Palmer, "The Indo-European Origins of Greek Justice," *Trans. of the Philol. Soc.* (1950): 149-168. In Aeschylus the phrase "like a . . . " (δίκην) occurs persistently throughout the *Oresteia*, as if to emphasize the trilogy's central theme.

40. On the meaning of νόμος and the translation of this passage, see Ostwald (above, n. 28). Although the position of δέ (unusually postponed until after the *second* word) cues the ear to separate ἐν πάντα from νόμον and προφέρειν is normally transitive, it is possible to argue that the line means something like "into every right (i.e. civilized) area the straight-tongued man bears himself forth (cf. the epic προφερέστατος, "foremost"). If νόμος is interpreted as "law" in the sense of government, serious misinterpretation can result; see "Cultural Conventions" (above, n. 6) pp. 32-34 and Swanson (Intr. n. 5) p. xxii.

41. The characterization of envy as a self-inflicted wound is proverbial, see Ernst Milobenski, *Der Neid in der griechischen Philosophie (Klassisch-philologische Studien* 29; Wiesbaden 1964) p. 4 and n. 16. But Pindar's association of wounding (ἕλκος) with dragging (ἑλκόμενοι) the finish line in the games is unique. It is difficult here and elsewhere (e.g., *Pythian* 1. 81-82: see ch. III n. 13) to get an exact idea of what Pindar has in mind in this description of measuring and wounding. "Fix a painful wound in their own heart" (ἐνέπαξαν ἕλκος ἑᾷ καρδίᾳ) echoes the Homeric phrase "fixed his spear in his heart" (δόρυ δ'ἐν κραδίῃ ἐπεπήγει, *Il*. 13.442)—does the finish line have a sharp end, like a plumb line? Cf. the references to hunting in Aeschylus' *Agamemnon*: as Lebeck observes, "these images are imprecise, their employment 'catachrestic'. They paint a picture drawn from fantasy, a blend of fishing and hunting which corresponds to no hunt in this world" (above, n. 9) p. 65.

42. On the function of the last triad, see Lloyd-Jones (Intr. n. 3) p. 125. Thummer classifies the closing triad as "praise of the poet and his art" (Intr. n. 2) pp. 89-90. See also Burnett (Intr. n. 2) p. 234: "for an epinician poet this [his sincerity as an artist] is a matter close to the conscience, and the passion and den-

sity, the evident seriousness of the poem, make its obscurities the more pressing."

43. Lloyd-Jones' suggestion (Intr. n. 3) p. 136, "the frequency in Pindar's poetry of the theme of envy and ingratitude is to be accounted for by the requirements of the religion in which he and his audiences believed," deals with the symptom rather than the cause, which is the value society places on success; see esp. Alvin W. Gouldner, *The Hellenic World.: A Sociological Analysis (Enter Plato,* Part I: New York, 1966) pp. 45-60. This study, which is essential for understanding the emphasis on envy in victory odes, deserves more serious attention than it has yet received from classical scholars; see Philip Slater, *The Glory of Hera* (Boston, 1968) pp. 36-37. On the disgrace felt by losers, see Pindar's *Pyth.* 8. 83-87, *Pyth.* 11. 34-35; and Swanson (Intr. n. 5) pp. xlix-l.

44. On the economy of image and motif in the *Oresteia,* see Lebeck (above, n. 9) p. 19.

Chapter II

Pindar was not the only poet who wrote victory odes. Two of his contemporaries were equally famous in their day, Simonides of Ceos and his nephew Bacchylides. Only small fragments of Simonides' work survive, and only one papyrus of Bacchylides' poems is still extant, but the fifth ode in the papyrus was written for the same victory as Pindar's *Olympian* 1: Hieron's victory in the horse race at Olympia in 476 B.C.[1]

Pindar's *Olympian* 1 has been read with admiration since antiquity. It stands first in the collection of Pindar's odes that has come down to us, and it has seemed, with its swift changes of ideas and its dramatic language, to be the most "Pindaric" of all odes. Bacchylides' ode was lost in late antiquity and rediscovered only at the end of the nineteenth century.[2] During the centuries when Bacchylides' text was lost, critics were forced to rely heavily on the estimation of his work by the ancient critics. We have already noted how the scholia on *Pythian* 2 find "evidence" in Pindar's lines about the beautiful ape, the whisperers, and the foxes that Bacchylides was slandering Pindar behind his back.[3] The ancient critics almost invariably interpreted fable as allegory: when Pindar speaks of two crows talking against an eagle or compares an eagle to jackdaws flying low, the ancient commentary observes that Pindar sees his talent as natural, while that of Bacchylides and Simonides is merely "learned."[4] As a result, Bacchylides acquired the reputation of being an imitator and a second-rate poet.

One wonders what would have happened if all manuscripts of Pindar's odes had been lost instead and one or two rediscovered only in recent years, while in the meantime texts of Bacchylides' works had continuously been preserved. The description in Bacchylides' *Ode* 5 of an eagle who is "bold and trusts in his strong might, and the shrill-voiced birds crouch in fear" (19-23) might then have been interpreted as a statement of Bacchylides' supremacy over the fearful, minor poets Pindar and Simonides.

In the case of *Pythian* 2, biographical criticism of the type recorded in the scholia has seriously hampered appreciation of the poem's function as a song of praise. Biographical criticism seems also to have kept us from giving fair evaluation to Bacchylides' real talents as a poet. Bacchylides was read and respected by intelligentsia until late antiquity.[5] Only accident has kept us from knowing his poems as well as we know Pindar's.

Reading Bacchylides' *Ode* 5 and Pindar's *Olympian* 1 together gives an immediate impression of the amazing potential of this apparently restricted form of art. The way the poets compose, and their evaluation of the events they celebrate seems remarkably divergent. Bacchylides' language, with its formal epithets, seems designed to recall the epic past; his story of Heracles and Meleager emphasizes the ultimate failure in all human achievement, and describes the irrational forces which lead men to destruction: Meleager was killed by his mother, Heracles by his wife, neither sees in time that what he does will ultimately destroy him. Pindar, by contrast, changes myth to affirm the value of human achievement: Pelops becomes a hero who wins by divine grace instead of treachery. Tantalus is doomed to live forever in fear of death because he cannot accept the limitations of mortality.

This evident disparity in the two poets' approach suggests that the audience expected adherence only to a basic format. Each ode begins with a complex praise, reference to the victor, his home, and the victory itself. Each tells a series of stories, elaborately interrelated to each other, and each in turn connected to the victory. Each concludes with a simpler, more discursive reference to the victor. In each, associations between the different subjects is made by repetition of words or themes. Praise is tempered by reference to envy, and the danger of failure or defeat. How any of these subjects are expressed, or how much space is devoted to them, seems to be a matter of free choice.

Bacchylides' *Ode* 5

After Pindar's *Pythian* 2, *Ode* 5 seems remarkably straightforward. Sentences are short and simple, the narrative proceeds in chronological order, there are no long statements about the destructive powers of poetry. Even in translation we can see how reiteration binds the different subjects of the poem together, because Bacchylides repeats words, where Pindar restates ideas. Bacchylides relies on traditional language to recreate for us a meaningful epic context; Pindar twists words and sentences into new configurations, to make us see the past with different eyes. Accordingly Bacchylides may seem to us less interesting, because he is less puzzling.

But although there are in Bacchylides' *Ode* 5 no Locrian maidens, apes, foxes, or corks, the poet's sequence of thought may not immediately appear coherent. The first antistrophe begins abruptly, with a description of an eagle cutting the deep air (16-30), with a reference to the bird's "light-haired mane" (28-29), a phrase that may appear to have little appeal or meaning. More disturbing still, in terms of our taste, is the choice of myth: the tragic tale of Meleager's death, and the promise of a similar fate for Heracles. In addition, to anyone used to epic, the portraits of the two heroes can hardly be reassuring. Each man ultimately fails, and Heracles' lack of understanding is portrayed with painful clarity.

Why did Bacchylides choose such a topic to celebrate a victory? If our assumptions about *Pythian* 2 are valid in this case also, the answer may again be that the poet is depicting the meaning of victory and of life by describing their antitheses, defeat and death. The problems these two odes present reveal why the victory ode as an art form intrigues us and repays our study. The odes do not concern only an athletic event, but include all the larger forces in life that games display in microcosm.

Εὔμοιρε [Σ]υρακ[οσίω]ν
ἱπποδινήτων στρατα[γ]έ,
γνώσηι μὲν [ἰ]οστεφάνων
Μοισᾶν γλυκ[ύ]δωρον ἄγαλμα, τῶν γε νῦν
5   αἴ τις ἐπιχθονίων,
ὀρθῶς· φρένα δ' εὐθύδικ[ο]ν
ἀτ'ρέμ' ἀμπαύσας μεριμνᾶν
δεῦρ' ⟨ἄγ'⟩ ἄθ'ρησον νόωι·
ἦ σὺν Χαρίτεσσι βαθυζώνοις ὑφάνας
10   ὕμνον ἀπὸ ζαθέας
νάσου ξένος ὑμετέραν
ἐς κλυτὰν πέμπει πόλιν,
χρυσάμπυκος Οὐρανίας
κλεινὸς θεράπων· ἐθέλει {δὲ}
15   γᾶρυν ἐκ στηθέων χέων
                           (1-15, strophe 1)

The first lines of Bacchylides' ode, for all their apparent simplicity, must have made an astounding impression on the audience.[6] Our contemporary familiarity with open praise of human beings keeps us from seeing what is unusual in "well-destined general of horse-whirling Syracusans." But the ancients would have remarked immediately how the poem is not addressed, like a traditional hymn, to a god or a divinity or to some continuing truth. *Pythian* 2 begins with an address to "Syracuse of men and horses god-like nurse"; *Olympian* 1, as we will see, with "best is water"; *Pythian* 1 with an address to "golden lyre"; Bacchylides' *Ode* 3 with an invocation to Demeter and Persephone.

Ode 5 begins instead with εὔμοιρε Συρακοσίων στραταγέ—an invocation to a man, the victor. This departure from tradition in itself constitutes a statement of theme. εὔμοιρος and ἱπποδίνητος are in fact both new words, modelled respectively on the traditional εὐδαίμων and the Homeric epithet of land ἱππήλατος ("for driving horses"). The opening lines of *Pythian* 2 would lead us to expect in Bacchylides' *Ode* also praise of Hieron's military success and of Syracuse's horses. But the new εὔμοιρος and ἱπποδίνητος also turn our attention to themes that will later be important in the poem: the problem of man's ignorance of his fate (μοῖρα) and the speed and violence of a horse race.

The next lines add new dimension to the unusually direct praise with which the ode began: "you know the brightness, sweet-gift of violet-crowned Muses, if any of today's men on earth know it, rightly." This is again a compliment: Hieron has been celebrated more in song than other men of his generation, because he has won more victories.

But the praise is hedged by a qualification αἴ τις ἐπιχθονίων. A recollection from Hesiod in the next lines expands on this inference that men partake only intermittently of the beautiful and the sweet: "make your heart that-marks-straight cease from sorrows, and look here in your mind." The new εὐθύδικος characterizes Hieron as the ideal king Hesiod describes in the *Theogony* judging ἰθείῃσι δίκῃσιν (86), in a passage where the bard makes a man "forget his troubles and remember his sorrows no longer" (99-103).

In *Ode* 5 the addition of ἀτρέμα combined with the insistent δεῦρ' ἄθρησον νόῳ implies that Hieron is so preoccupied with fears and cares that he must make a special effort to join in the celebration. ἄθρησον also calls attention to the colors and movement in the traditional epithets that accompany each name. The Muses are ἰοστέφανοι, and in the next lines the Charites are βαθύζωνοι, and the Muse Urania χρυσάμπυξ: "now with the deep-bound Charites he has woven a song of praise from the holy island, a friend to your famed city he sends it, the famed servant of gold-banded Urania."

The pun ὑφάνας ὕμνον makes explicit what the ordinary term for bard ῥάψῳδος ("song-stitcher") implies, that both the poets's work and the goddesses' presence together are needed to create song. "From the holy island" (i.e., Ceos) is a signature, like Pindar's "I bring you this song from shining Thebes" in *Pythian* 2. 3-4. But where Pindar introduces himself as a herald in the games, Bacchylides emphasizes again the poet's traditional role as the Muse's θεράπων (Hesiod, *Theogony* 100). By repeatedly associating human action with the presence of female divinity, Bacchylides establishes a theme that will be explored more fully in the ode's myth. The repeated κλυτὰν . . . κλεινός also implies that a close resemblance—not yet explicit—exists between poet and patron.

The last words of the strophe, like the concluding lines of many stanzas in *Pythian* 2, introduce an element of suspense. In epic, "pouring speech" denotes the nightingale's song, e.g., θρῆνον ἐπιπροχέουσα χέει μελίγηρυν ἀοιδήν (pours forth song honey-spoken," *Homeric Hymn* 19.18). The implied comparison is strange: why would the poet of a victory ode, that is intended to make the victory "cease from cares," talk of his song in language traditionally used to describe the nightingale's lamentation? The sentence is left tantalizingly incomplete until the next stanza.

> αἰνεῖν Ἱέρωνα. βαθὺν
> δ᾽ αἰθέρα ξουθαῖσι τάμνων
> ὑψοῦ πτερύγεσσι ταχεί-
> αις αἰετὸς εὐρυάνακτος ἄγγελος
> 20 Ζηνὸς ἐρισφαράγου
> θαρσεῖ κρατερᾶι πίσυνος
> ἰσχύϊ, πτάσσοντι δ᾽ ὄρνι-
> χες λιγύφθογγοι φόβωι·
> οὔ νιν κορυφαὶ μεγάλας ἴσχουσι γαίας,
> 25 οὐδ᾽ ἁλὸς ἀκαμάτας
> δυσπαίπαλα κύματα· νω-
> μαῖ δ᾽ ἐν ἀτ|ρύτωι χάει
> λεπτότ|ριχα σὺν ζεφύρου πνοι-
> αῖσιν ἔθειραν ἀρίγ|νω-
> 30 τος {μετ᾽} ἀνθρώποις ἰδεῖν·
>   (16-30, antistrophe 1)

". . . to praise Hieron" comes as a surprise, a startling contradiction in terms, since the sentence beginning with "pouring song from his heart" ought ordinarily to have ended with some reference to lamentation. By combining the terminology of the nightingale's song with the victory ode, Bacchylides reminds us both of the occasion of victory and the suggestion of unhappiness in "fearlessly make your heart cease from cares" in the first strophe (6-7). The ambivalence prepares the audience for the sentence that follows: "cutting the deep air with whirring swift wings high, the eagle, herald of Zeus, wide-ruler, loud-thunderer, is bold and trusts in his strong might, and the shrill-voiced birds crouch in fear."[7]

The ancient ear would have heard in the description of the eagle's flight reminiscence of the scene in the *Homeric Hymn to Demeter*, where Aidoneus' horses bring back Persephone to her mother from the world of the dead: "lightly they accomplished the long paths, and not the sea or the water of the rivers or the grassy valleys of crags held back the force of the immortal horses, but they cut the deep air above them (βαθὺν ἠέρα τέμνον) as they came" (*Homeric Hymn* 2. 380-383). Before we know who cuts the deep air we have associated whoever-it-is with deliverance, with a movement from sorrow to joy, darkness to light.

"With whirring" and "high with wings swift" still keeps us in suspense: divine horses like Aidoneus' (and, in *Olympian* 1. 87, Poseidon's) are winged: "the pair of horses not unwilling flew: (πετέσθην, *Homeric Hymn* 2.379). Only "whirring" (ξουθαῖσι), a word associated especially with nightingales, hints that what is cutting the air is not a team of immortal horses but a bird: "the eagle, herald (ἄγγελος) of Zeus, wide-ruler, loud-thunderer."

ἄγγελος designates also the poet's function: Pindar, in *Pythian* 2 brings "this song, an announcement (ἀγγελίαν) "of Hieron's victory" (3-4). "Is bold and trusts in his strong might" mirrors the poet's encouragement to Hieron in the first strophe: "fearlessly make your heart cease from cares and look here in your mind" (6-7).

Our impression that the eagle represents Bacchylides is strengthened in the following lines: "and the shrill-voiced birds crouch in fear." The comparison of eagle to weaker birds is a traditional expression of supremacy, but λιγύφθογγος, "shrill voiced" is the special epithet of heralds in Homer. Again Bacchylides has combined traditional terminology from different sources to say something new and relevant to his poem. The comparison also recalls, with the reiterative amplifications that we saw also in Pindar's language in *Pythian* 2, the opening lines of the first strophe, where Hieron is distinguished from other men: "general of Syracusans, you know, if any of today's men on earth knows it, rightly" (3-6). In stating his own supremacy over other poets, Bacchylides suggests at the same time the supremacy of Hieron. Syracuse and the "servant of Urania" were both designated "famed" (κλυτὰν . . . κλεινός, 12-14) in the first stanza. Praise of one suits both.

The next lines continue to emphasize the sense of deliverance, of transition to a better state, expressed in the reminiscence "cutting the steep air." οὔ νιν κορυφαὶ μεγάλας ἴσχουσι γαίας/οὐδ' ἁλὸς ἀκαμάτας/ δυσπαίπαλα κύματα, "the summits of great earth do not hold him nor the untiring sea's rough-turning waves" again recalls the description of Aidoneus' horses, οὐδὲ θάλασσα/οὔθ' ὕδωρ ποταμῶν οὐδ' ἄγκεα ποιήεντα /ἵππων ἀθανάτων οὔτ' ἄκριες ἔσχεθον ὁρμήν, "and not the sea or the water of rivers or the grassy valleys or crags held back the force of the immortal horses" (*Homeric Hymn* 2.380-382). In Bacchylides the addition of "great earth" (μεγάλας γαίας) and "rough-turning" (δυσπαίπαλα) sea stresses the sense of the eagle's power and freedom.[8] "He steers his light-haired mane in untouched emptiness with the West wind's breathings" distinguishes the eagle from Aidoneus' horses: no one guides the eagle. He is his own master, in air that is "untouched" (ἀτρύτῳ) by anyone else before him.

Why Bacchylides chose to add new emphasis on singularity to the traditional description of rescue is hinted at in the surprising phrase λεπτότριχα ἔθειραν. "Light-haired mane" might seem at first like an extraordinarily perverse way to speak of feathers, but the ancients would have been quicker than we to guess why Bacchylides chose this terminology rather than something more conventional. The reminiscence underlying this passage describes immortal horses; the victory that the ode celebrates was won by a single race-horse, Phereni-cus. By speaking of "mane" or "hair" instead of "feathers", Bacchylides makes us associate the eagle with the winning horse, in addition to himself and the victor Hieron. The effect is similar to Pindar's sudden description of Cinyras in *Pythian* 2.17 as ἱερέα κτίλον Ἀφροδίτας ("priest-ram of Aphrodite) or his remarkable characterization of Ixion's first crime, αἷμα ἐπέμειξε θνατοῖς ("mixed blood for mortals" 32). These strange phrases, initially obscure, become increasingly clear in retrospect.

The stanza closes once again with an explicit reference to vision; ἀρί-γνωτος μετ' ἀνθρώποις ἰδεῖν ("well-known among men to see"). Again there is emphasis on singularity: Hieron knows brightness, if any man on earth knows it (4-5). Acts of vision play an important role also in *Pythian* 2, but what is seen seems consistently less specific: the Locrian maiden looks forth in safety (on what? 20); joy for a friend's deeds shows admiration (18); one must see according to oneself the measure of everything (34); the poet saw from far off Archilochus blaming in helplessness (54-55). It is hard in all these cases to visualize directly what Pindar is describing. But Bacchylides tells us explicitly what he wants us to see: "look here in your mind: a friend has woven a song" (8-12). Where Pindar strives to state the universal significance of events, Bacchylides devotes his energies to detailed depiction. So far in the ode there has not been a single generalization about right and wrong behavior.

> τὼς νῦν καὶ ⟨ἐ⟩μοὶ μυρία πάνται κέλευθος
> ὑμετέραν ἀρετάν
> ὑμνεῖν, κυανοπ|λοκάμου θ' ἕκατι Νίκας
> χαλκεοστέρνου τ' Ἄρηος,
> 35 Δεινομένευς ἀγέρωχοι
> παῖδες· εὖ ἔρδων δὲ μὴ κάμοι θεός.
> ξανθότ|ριχα μὲν Φερένικον
> Ἀλφεὸν παρ' εὐρυδίναν
> πῶλον ἀελλοδρόμαν
> 40 εἶδε νικάσαντα χρυσόπαχυς Ἀώς,
>
> (31-40, epode 1)

"For me there are ten thousand paths," with the concluding formula (τὼς νῦν) of a Homeric simile, narrows the comparison: the eagle can take himself anywhere above and beyond the earth; the poet too can cross the sea from Ceos to distant Syracuse in his song. "To sing praise of your achievement," (ὑμνεῖν) restates the poet's initial description of his art, "he has woven a song of praise (ὑφάνας ὕμνον, 9-10). But like a Homeric simile, the picture of the eagle has a larger function than the specific line of comparison the poet designates.

The next lines indicate that the eagle also represents the victorious Hieron: "for the sake of dark-haired Victory and bronze-chested Ares, honored sons of Deinomenes." Ares is Hieron's patron; the birds crouch in fear before the eagle. Victory is **κυανοπλόκαμος**; the eagle has a "light-haired mane" (28). The traditional prayer against envy, "may the god who does good not tire (κάμοι)" is framed in the terminology of the eagle's flight above the "waves of the untiring (ἀκαμάτας) sea" (25-26). The eagle's wings, "yellow-whirring" like the nightingale's throat (17), and his "light-haired mane" (28) anticipate the dramatic initial description of Hieron's winning horse, "blonde-haired Pherenicus," where the new ξανθότριχα has the same metrical position as λεπτότριχα.

"Beside the broad-whirling Alpheus colt storm-runner" returns us to the opening praise of Hieron, king of "Syracusans with whirling horses" (ἱπποδινήτων, 1-2). The sudden ἀελλοδρόμαν, a new word modelled on Iris' epithet ἀελλόπους, connotes a violence absent in the "breathings of the West wind" in which the eagle flies (28-29). Every word in the last line of the epode echoes an earlier statement, uniting poet and victor and winning horse. εἶδε νικάσαντα χρυσόπαχυς Ἀώς, "gold-armed Dawn saw him victorious." The eagle is "well-known among men to see" (ἰδεῖν, 29-30); νικάσαντα repeats "victory," for the third time in the epode (νίκας, 33; Φερένικον, 37). The muse Urania is "gold-banded" (χρυσάμπυκος, 13). All the references to vision and color in the preceding lines prepare us for the final reference to the morning light of the day when the contest was won.

Looking back for a moment from *Ode 5* at the first triad of *Pythian 2*, we can see immediately basic similarities in method and content. In both odes there is allusion to the poet's homeland, "from shining Thebes" (3); "from the holy island" (10-11). In both there is praise of the victor's homeland and of her winning horses: "Syracuse of men and horses that rejoice in iron godlike nurse" (1-2); "Syracuse with whirling horses" (1-2). In both there is mention of Hieron's prowess in war: "Syracuse, precinct of Ares" (1-2); "well-destined general of Syracusans" (1-2). Both contain reference to the actual event of victory and its patron deities: Artemis guiding Hieron's chariot (7-8); Dawn watching Pherenicus victorious (40).

We can begin tentatively to identify what the poets considered the essential elements of the victory odes: praise of the victor's athletic and political achievements, description of the victory, statement about the powers of the poet himself.

We can also note similarities in style. Both odes open dramatically, with exciting descriptions of victory, without making explicit the connections among the topics they take up. In the first lines of both poems new words, Pindar's μεγαλοπόλιες and σιδαροχαρμᾶν, Bacchylides' εὔμοιρε and ἱπποδινήτων serve as first expressions of themes that become important later in the ode: civilization and joy in *Pythian* 2, destiny (μοῖρα) and violent, undirected motion in Bacchylides.

In both poems unusual verbs describe ordinary actions, making us sensitive to what will happen later in the myths. In *Pythian* 2 Hieron's crowning of Artemis' shrine is described as "binding" (6); we hear subsequently of Ixion chained to his wheel. In *Ode* 5 Bacchylides asks Hieron to turn his attention to rejoicing, "look here in your mind," and in subsequent lines the description of the poet's powers and the victory itself likewise depends on sight: the eagle "among men to see" (30); "Dawn saw him victorious" (40). We will find that in *Ode* 5 visual impression also determines the outcome of the myth.

But in other respects the two odes sound remarkably dissimilar. Pindar's sentences are elaborately interdependent; he makes his points by elaboration, reworking, adding. From an initial statement about Syracuse "nurse of men and horses" (1) he proceeds later in the stanza to a description of Artemis guiding Hieron to a chariot victory, in which Hieron "has tamed those mares with gentle reins" (7-8). Appositives are piled on appositives: Syracuse/precinct/nurse, this song/announcement, Ortygia/shrine.

Bacchylides, by contrast, composes in simpler clauses, like the Homeric bards, with one subject and object each, "general, you know the brightness of the Muses" (1-4); "make your heart cease from sorrows and look here" (6-8). Also significantly different is the way Bacchylides depends for effect on direct literary reminiscence. Full appreciation of his description of Hieron and of himself derives from the recognition of allusions to Hesiod and to Homer. In order to grasp the significance of the eagle's flight we must hear that it resembles the journey of Aidoneus' horses from death to life.

Bacchylides' use of traditional language would make his poetry readily comprehensible to an ancient audience. Pindar instead tries to break with previous associations, changing even traditional myth to establish a new and more constructive ethic.

The two poets' approaches differ in one other significant respect. Pindar constantly attempts to state in general terms what is implied in the specifics of his praise: "for other kings some other man has paid a sounding hymn of praise, requital for achievement" (13-14), "joyful thanks for one of their friends leads and shows admiration" (17-18).

Bacchylides links different themes together by more direct repetition than Pindar allows himself, the eagle's "light-haired mane" (28), "blonde-haired" Pherenicus (37). Like the epic bards he does not state in abstract terms the interrelationships he sets before us. We move from description of the poet's singing in praise of Hieron, without formal introduction to "cutting the steep air with whirring swift wings high the eagle" (16-19). A formal conclusion tells us that the eagle's flight represents the poet's ability to choose from many topics of praise. Only our ability to remember what we have heard tells us that the eagle also represents the poet's fame, his ability to transcend distance, Hieron's supremacy in war, and the speed and singularity of Pherenicus' winning race.

To return to *Ode* 5—the first epode ended in what seemed like a complete sentence: "colt storm-runner Dawn saw victorious." But the sentence is in fact continued in the second strophe:

> Πυθῶνί τ' ἐν ἀγαθέαι·
> γᾶι δ' ἐπισκήπτων πιφαύσκω·
> οὔπω νιν ὑπὸ π⌊ροτέ[ρω]ν
> ἵππων ἐν ἀγῶνι κατέχ⌊ρανεν κόνις
> 45 πρὸς τέλος ὀρνύμενον·
> ῥιπᾶι γὰρ ἴσος βορέα
> ὃν κυβερνήταν φυλάσσων
> ἵεται νεόκ⌊ροτον
> νίκαν Ἱέρωνι φιλοξείνωι τιτύσκων.
> 50 ὄλβιος ὧιτινι θεός
> μοῖράν τε καλῶν ἔπορεν
> σύν τ' ἐπιζήλωι τύχαι
> ἀφ⌊νεὸν βιοτὰν διάγειν· οὐ
> γά⌊ρ τις⌋ ἐπιχθονίων
> 55 π⌊άντ⌋α γ' εὐδαίμων ἔφυ.
>
> (41-55, strophe 2)

Phenenicus has won not only the present race at Olympia, but previously at the Pythian games. The phrase, "in holy Pytho," serves both as completion of the previous sentence and as introduction to what follows. By using the formal epic designation of Apollo's oracle, instead of referring to the games themselves, Bacchylides prepares us for the statement: "Striking the earth I reveal." Laying one's hand on earth connotes a solemn oath; we sense that what he will say will be otherwise incredible. Again, knowledge is expressed in terms of vision: Dawn "saw Pherenicus victorious" (40); the poet, through song will make others *see* him (**πιφαύσκω**) as well.

The description of Pherenicus' victory in the next lines again recalls the simile of the eagle: "that never in the contest did dust of horses before defile him, as he rushed toward the goal." The alliterative, κατέχρανεν κόνις, is emphatic. Pherenicus outdistances other horses as the brave eagle flies above the fearful birds. The reason why Bacchylides altered the description of Aidoneus' horses to stress the eagle's singularity now becomes apparent: Pherenicus is alone, untouched by the dust of horses before him, like the eagle who "steers in untouched emptiness" (26-27). The eagle flies on "swift wings" (18-19); Pherenicus "rushes toward the goal."

But suddenly a comparison "like the North wind's hurling" elaborates on the description of Pherenicus as "colt storm-wind runner" (30), setting the horse apart from the eagle who steers himself "in the West wind's breathings" (28-29). The phrase ῥιπᾶι ἴσος βορέα derives from a standard epic simile of sudden force, "just as when from the clouds snow or hail flies cold under the hurling of the North wind" (ὑπαὶ ῥιπῆς βορέαο, Il. 15. 170-172).

The next line also suggests the presence of danger, this time on the sea, "guarding his helmsman;" the eagle, by contrast, could fly beyond the "tireless sea's turning waves" (25-26). "He shot new-ringing victory, aiming for Hieron kind to friends," dramatically makes us compare Pherenicus' winning run to Odysseus' aiming and shooting (ἧκε τιτυσκόμενος) the fateful arrow through the axes in his contest with the suitors (Od. 21. 420-421). The alliterative νεόκροτον νίκαν echoes the references to victory clustered in the first epode (Νίκας, 33; Φερένικον, 37; νικάσαντα, 40). But there is a sense of danger in Pherenicus' triumph that is absent in the description of the eagle's flight.

Repeated reference in the epithet φιλόξεινος to the friendship between patron and poet (Bacchylides called himself "a ξένος from the holy island," 11) hints that the opening praise is drawing to an end. A generalization (the first in the ode) prepares us for a change of topic: "happy the man to whom the god gives a destiny of the beautiful, with luck to envy and a rich life to lead." The description suits the "well-destined" (εὔμοιρε, 1) Hieron, who knows the Muses' brightness (3-4). So does the negative qualification: "no, not anyone on earth was in all ways fortunate." τις ἐπιχθονίων echoes the opening αἴ τις ἐπιχθονίων (5).

The sentiment of the lines is reminiscent of Achilles' statement to Priam in Iliad 24: "there is no use in cruel lamentation: for so the gods have spun for poor men, to live in sorrow, and they themselves are free from care" (524-526). In Homer, this generalization is followed by specific illustration: Zeus has on his threshold jars of good and evil: to some men he gives all evil, to others a mixture, like Achilles' father Peleus, and Priam himself. Accordingly in Bacchylides' song, with its many recollections of epic, we listen for a story to follow. So in *Pythian* 2

Ixion's tale begins "At the god's command they tell that Ixion says this to mortals, come and repay a benefactor with gentle exchange" (21-24).

>   δῦναί π]οτ' ἐρειψιπύλαν
>   ἄνδρ' ἀνίκ]ατον λέγουσιν
>   ἔρνος Διός] ἀργικεραύ-
>   νου δώματα Φερσεφόνας τανισφύρου,
> 60   καρχαρόδοντα κύν' ἄ-
>   ξοντ' ἐς φάος ἐξ Ἀΐδα,
>   υἱὸν ἀπ¹λάτοι' Ἐχίδ¹νας·
>   ἔνθα δυστάνων βροτῶν
>   ψυχὰς ἐδάη παρὰ Κωκυτοῦ ῥεέθ¹ροις,
> 65   οἷά τε φύλλ' ἄνεμος
>   Ἴδας ἀνὰ μηλοβότους
>   πρῶνας ἀργηστὰς δονεῖ.
>   ταῖσιν δὲ μετέπ¹ρεπεν εἴδω-
>   λον θρασυμέμνονος ἐγ-
> 70   χεσπάλου Πορθανίδα·
>
> (56-70, antistrophe 2)

The narrative, like the eagle simile, unfolds gradually. It is not clear at first whom the story is about "once the gate-tearer . . . they say." The new word ἐρειψιπύλαν carries connotations of the violence of dying (ἔριπε, "fall down in death") from the *Iliad*, but has no associations with any particular hero. But in the next line, the traditional "white-lightning" (ἀργικέραυνος), Zeus' epithet, implies that the "tearer of gates" has some special relationship to Zeus, that perhaps was made clearer in the original, undamaged text. "To the halls of slim-ankled Persephone" begins to reveal who the hero is. "The sharp-toothed dog to bring back" (κύν' ἄξοντ') makes identification certain. The narrative concerns Heracles, whose shade tells Odysseus in the lower world:

> I was the son of Zeus Cronion, but I had boundless woe. For I was slave to a much worse man, who set hard trials on me. And he sent me here to bring back the dog (κύν' ἄξοντ'). He said there would be no stronger trial than this for me." (*Odyssey* 11.620-624).

The reminiscence of Heracles' sad journey adds dimension to Bacchylides' narrative. The epithets ἀργικέραυνος, τανίσφυρος, and the traditional Homeric καρχαρόδους seem in retrospect not merely decorative, but designed to set a consciously epic tone. The dog's formal genealogy, "son of Echidna unapproachable" maintains the sense of epic diction. It is not till later in the ode that we become aware of the full importance of parentage.

"There the souls of fallen mortals he learned" again suggests

Odysseus' journey to the world of the dead, to inquire from the soul of Tiresias, the means and distance of his return to Ithaca. δύστανος, the Homeric term for great misfortune, continues to set a somber tone. The scene is further detailed as "beside the streams of Wailing." Then a simile reveals that what Heracles "learned" is his mortality: "(the souls of mortals) like the leaves the wind whirls up along Ida's bright sheep-pasturing hills." οἴά τε φύλλ' echoes the opening of the famous simile in the *Iliad* where Glaucus tells Diomydes about his family:

> as is the generation of leaves (οἴη περ φύλλων γενέη) so is that of men; some leaves the wind pours on the ground, but the forest blooms and bears others, and the season of spring comes on; so of men one generation grows, another ceases. (*Il.* 6.146-149).

But Bacchylides' description of the leaves mirrors only the negative side of Homer's simile, "some leaves the wind." He puts new emphasis on the wind's force (δονεῖ), and implies with ἀνά that they have fallen from the trees, while by contrast the land along which the wind whirls them is explicitly "bright, sheep-pasturing," i.e., sustaining of life. These are also the hills specifically of Mt. Ida, where Paris grazed his sheep before the Trojan war. At the same time "headlands" (πρῶνας), which is also the word for ship's "prow," and the reference to whirling makes us think back to Phereticus "colt storm-(wind)-runner, beside the broad-whirling Alpheus" (38-39) "guarding his helmsman" (47). The eagle and the storm-wind-runner horse can set their own courses; dead souls, like leaves, are helpless, blown by the wind. Again recollection and ambiguity let the simple lines of Bacchylides' narrative convey many related ideas at once.[9]

Homeric reminiscences continue to add meaning to the concluding lines of the stanza: "and among them was seen the image of bold-willed spear-shaker Porthanides." It is important to note that Bacchylides does not say here "Porthanides came (ἦλθε) forth from among the shades," like Tiresias emerging from the crowd of gibbering souls in *Od.* 11. 90-91. Instead, the emphasis falls once again on vision: μετέπρεπεν ἔιδωλον. The application of θρασυμέμνων to Meleager is remarkable, since it is the special epithet of only one hero in Homer, and that is Heracles. The "image" Heracles sees is an analogue of himself, a rival. ἐγχέσπαλος, a traditional epithet of warriors, reinforces the impression that this is somehow an encounter on a battlefield. Suspensefully, only the last word in the stanza indicates who the hero is, the grandson of Porthaon, Meleager.

> τὸν δ' ὡς ἴδεν Ἀλκμή⟨ν⟩ιος θαυμαστὸς ἥρως
> τ[ε]ύχεσι λαμπόμενον,
> νευρὰν ἐπέβασε λιγυκ|λαγγῆ κορώνας,
> χαλκεόκ|ρανον δ' ἔπειτ' ἔξ

75   εἵλετο ἰὸν ἀναπτύ-
       ξας φαρέτ⟩ρας πῶμα· τῶι δ' ἐναντία
       ψυχὰ προφάνη Μελεάγ⟩ρου,
       καί νιν εὖ εἰδὼς προσεῖπεν·
       „υἱὲ Διὸς μεγάλου,
80   στᾶθί τ' ἐν χώραι, γελανώσας τε θυμόν
                                    (71-80, epode 2)

Recollection immediately charges these lines with excitement: "when Alcmena's wondrous hero saw him, shining in his weapons." Earlier in the ode Dawn saw (εἶδε) Pherenicus victorious (40); the eagle was "among men to see" (ἰδεῖν, 30). The designation of Heracles by his mother's name is unusual; Cerberus was also "son of Echidna" rather than of his father Typhaon (62). In the context of this ode the reiteration of mother's names has a special purpose: Meleager's mother, as the ancient audience knew, caused her son's death.

θαυμαστός denotes the "wonder" characteristic of first meetings: Achilles seeing Priam (Il. 24. 629-31), Nausicaa beholding Odysseus in fine clothes at the banquet in her father's palace (Od. 8. 459). τεύχεσι λαμπόμενον adds further significance to the confrontation: the same phrase in Homer describes Achilles at his most sinister, when the Trojans see him returning to battle to avenge Patroclus' death (Il. 20.46). Similarly, as Achilles comes to kill Hector, "the bronze shone (ἐλάμπετο) around him like the light of burning fire or the rising of the sun (Il. 22. 134-135).

These reminiscences prepare us for the violence of Heracles' response. In Meleager he sees not only himself, the θρασυμέμνων, but also the frightening Achilles τεύχεσι λαμπόμενον. He (and we) forget that he is not on the battlefield.

The description of Heracles' drawing his bow adds further dramatic tension: "he mounted the shrill-ringing cord of his bow and then a bronze-tipped arrow he chose, unfolding the lid of his quiver." The new words λιγυκλαγγής and χαλκεόκρανος bring connotations of combat from the opening stanzas of the ode: "the shrill-voiced (λιγύφθογγοι) birds crouch in fear" (22-23); "bronze-chested (χαλκεόστερνος) Ares" (34). In addition, the details ἒξ εἵλετο ἰόν and φαρέτρας πῶμα echo closely the scene in the Iliad where the Trojan Pandarus, during a truce, wounds Menelaus with an arrow and prevents the equitable settlement of the war by single combat (4.116-126). Pandarus similarly "rips back the cover of his quiver (πῶμα φαρέτρης) and chooses out an arrow (ἐκ δ'ἕλετ ἰον)." Bacchylides' λιγυκλαγγής suggests how Pandarus' "bow cried out (λίγξε) and the string screamed loudly, and the arrow leapt forth."

These recollections imply that Heracles' action, like Pandarus', is ill-advised and ultimately self-destructive. The next line reminds us why: "and opposite him the soul of Meleager appeared, and recognizing him, spoke." This is not a confrontation in battle, but an encounter with the dead, where ordinary response is meaningless, and where souls can "appear" calmly before weapons which the living would have fled. The lines deliberately bring to mind Odysseus' description of the prophet Tiresias in the world of the dead: "and the soul of Theban Tiresias came forth, holding a golden rod, and recognized me and spoke" (*Od.* 11. 90-91). In Bacchylides, "come" (ἦλθε) has been replaced by **προφάνη**, again placing emphasis on vision. Heracles *sees* Meleager, but does not yet fully understand what he has seen; Meleager, by contrast appears with the authority of the seer Tiresias. We recall that Odysseus went to the world of the dead to learn from Tiresias how he could return home, and that Tiresias also prophesies to him how he will end his life. Again Homeric reminiscence adds special meaning to Bacchylides' narrative: we wait to learn from Meleager some analogous prophecy about Heracles' life and fate.

"Son of great Zeus, stand your ground, and making your heart laugh," the epode ends, suspensefully, at the beginning of Meleager's speech. Like Tiresias, he begins with genealogy: "son of great Zeus"; "Zeus-descended Laertiades, Odysseus of many wiles." But where Tiresias takes time to ask why Odysseus has come (*Od.* 11. 93-94), Meleager immediately tells Heracles to stop, confirming our impression that this is somehow a battlefield, and that the danger of death is somewhere present. His next words make it clear that his concern is not for himself but for Heracles, "and making your heart laugh." The line ends in mid-sentence, leaving us expecting a second command to match "stand your ground."

The closing reference to laughter suggests that the story might in fact have a happy continuation: the jolly Heracles, hero of comedy, enjoyed his trip to the dead. But the somber associations with which the story began are not dispelled: Meleager as Heracles, Achilles, and Tiresias; Heracles as Odysseus. Reminiscences from the ode's introduction linger in our minds, comparing the singular Meleager to the eagle and Pherenicus. What these complex associations together imply is not yet fully clear. References to sight in the opening only hint at the outcome of the narrative. The full significance of an event is revealed only slowly, and each participant beholds it differently. We are told twice of Pherenicus' winning race: "Dawn saw him victorious" (40); "striking the ground I reveal" (42); and this only after we have heard of the eagle, "well-known among men to see" (29-30).

>   μὴ ταΰσιον προΐει
>   τραχὺν ἐκ χειρῶν ὀϊστόν
>   ψυχαῖσιν ἔπι φθιμένων·
>   οὔ τοι δέος." ὣς φάτο· θάμβησεν δ' ἄναξ
> 85 Ἀμφιτρυωνιάδας,

εἶπέν τε· „τίς ἀθανάτων
ἢ βροτῶν τοιοῦτον ἔρνος
θρέψεν ἐν ποίαι χθονί;
τίς δ' ἔκτανεν; ἦ τάχα καλλίζωνος Ἥρα
90 κεῖνον ἐφ' ἁμετέραι
πέμψει κεφαλᾶι· τὰ δέ που
Παλλάδι ξανθᾶι μέλει."
τὸν δὲ π'ροσέφα Μελέαγ'ρος
δακ'ρυόεις· „χαλεπὸν
95 θεῶν παρατ'ρέψαι νόον
(81-95, strophe 3)

Meleager had begun his speech with "stand your ground, and making your heart laugh" (80), but what he continues to say in the third strophe only confirms our first impression that there is little to laugh about. "Do not send forth a vain jagged arrow from your hands," dramatically characterizes "arrow" with the word Homer uses to describe the "vain journey" (τηυσίην ὁδόν) that Telemachus might have made had he not returned home to keep the suitors from taking his property (*Od.* 3.316, 15.13). In addition, the arrow is "jagged" (τραχύς) like a "rocky path" (*Od.* 14.1), instead of the conventional "bitter." These connotations endow the unsent arrow with the significance of a hero's travels. The words are linked by emphatic alliteration, **ταῦσιον τραχὺν ὀϊστόν**. Pherenicus' winning race also resembled an arrow's flight: "he shot aiming new-ringing victory for Hieron" (48-49). In *Pythian* 2 events in the myth (the trap Zeus' hands set for Ixion, 39-40) are set in antithesis to the event of victory (the mares Hieron tamed "in gentle hands," 8).

In the lines following, recollections from Homer and from earlier in the ode itself continue to emphasize death: "(do not send a vain jagged arrow) upon souls of the dead; do not fear. So he spoke." When Heracles first came to the lower world he saw **δυστάνων βροτῶν ψυχάς** (63-64). **οὔ τοι δέος** adds to the tension: the phrase in Homer always connotes fear of death (e.g., *Il.* 1. 515). Then Heracles is described by the name of his mortal father, Amphitryon, rather than, as he was earlier "son of Zeus" (58): "and the lord Amphitryonides was amazed." **Θάμβησεν** describes the reaction also of Achilles and his friends when they first see Priam coming to Achilles' tent to claim his son Hector's body:

> as when close delusion seizes a man, who has killed a person in
> his homeland, and comes to the country of others, to the house
> of a rich man, and amazement (**θάμβος**) holds all who look on
> him, so Achilles was amazed (**θάμβησεν**) when he saw godlike
> Priam, and the others were amazed (**θάμβησαν**), and looked at
> one another (*Iliad* 24. 480-484).

In Priam's case, the effect he has on others derives not only from his being "godlike" but from the presence of delusion and death around him. The recollection implies that a similar aura surrounds Meleager.

Heracles' first question to Meleager maintains the tension established in these sinister reminiscences: "who of immortals or mortals raised so strong a plant, in what land? who killed you?" In contrast to Meleager, who "recognized" Heracles immediately, just as Tiresias recognized Odysseus, whom he had never seen in life, Heracles does not know who the amazing image is. His first two questions conform to the standard pattern of inquiry in Homer: "who are you among men, where is your city, and your parents?" But again careful substitution of phrases adds painful dimension to what Heracles says. "Who of immortals or mortals raised (θρέψεν) so strong a plant (ἔρνος)" recalls Thetis' description of Achilles, "he grew up like a plant (ἔρνεϊ ἴσος), him I raised (θρέψασα), a shoot from the high ground of the vineyard . . . and I shall never receive him back again, returning to his home." (*Il.* 18.56-60).

Bacchylides' narrative gains force from compression: the more leisurely comparison in Homer, "like a plant . . . a shoot from the high ground of the vineyard" becomes the brief, arresting "who raised so strong a plant?" Heracles' next question explains why he still seems afraid. "Who killed you?" replaces the conventional inquiry "where is your city, and your parents?" Heracles lives in constant fear of death: "yes, soon Hera beautifully-bound will send that man on our head." The epithet καλλίζωνος contrasts strangely with Hera's murderous hatred of Heracles. The Charites who accompanied Bacchylides with his song are similarly βαθύζωνοι (9). The epithets imply that the god's beauty is constant, but that their attitude toward men changes. In the next lines, Pallas is ξανθά, like ξανθότριξ Pherenicus (37), but in Heracles' case the outcome is uncertain: "yet somehow blonde Pallas will care for this."

Meleager's reaction to Heracles' question heightens our sense of foreboding. At the end of the previous stanza he urges Heracles to make his heart "laugh" (80). Now "Meleager answered him weeping." The Greek audience would know who killed Meleager: when he was born, the fates had told his mother that he would live as long as the log in the fire. His mother took the log from the fire and put it in a chest, but years later when Meleager killed her two brothers in battle, she took the log from the chest and put it back in the fire, killing her son.

The audience would be intrigued to learn how Bacchylides would tell Meleager's story. Why has he brought Meleager and Heracles together? Why does Meleager suddenly weep? The importance of feminine divinities, the recollections of short-lived Achilles in this stanza, hint at the shape the narrative is to take. Suspense is maintained by ending the strophe with a generalization that has yet no specific application: "it is hard to change the god's mind." We recall that the story of Heracles' journey to the world of the dead began, also at the end of a strophe, with the general "no, not anyone on earth was in all things fortunate" (53-55).

> ἄνδρεσσιν ἐπιχθονίοις.
> καὶ γὰρ ἂν πλάξιππος Οἰνεύς
> παῦσεν καλυκοστεφάνου
> σεμνᾶς χόλον Ἀρτέμιδος λευκωλένου
> 100 λισσόμενος πολέων
> τ' αἰγῶν θυσίαισι πατήρ
> καὶ βοῶν φοινικονώτων·
> ἀλλ' ἀνίκατον θεά
> ἔσχεν χόλον· εὐρυβίαν δ' ἔσσευε κούρα
> 105 κάπρον ἀναιδομάχαν
> ἐς καλλίχορον Καλυδῶ-
> ν', ἔνθα πλημύρων σθένει
> ὄρχους ἐπέκειρεν ὀδόντι,
> σφάζε τε μῆλα, βροτῶν
> 110 θ' ὅστις εἰσάνταν μόλοι.
> (96-110, antistrophe 3)

The first words of the third antistrophe set the tone of the story: "for men on earth." Before Meleager added this qualifying phrase, we might have assumed that the last lines of the third strophe, "it is hard to change the gods' mind" simply reiterated what Phoenix says to Achilles in the *Iliad*, when he tries to get Achilles to resume fighting for the Greeks: "even gods can be turned aside" (*Il.* 9.497). He supports this assertion by telling a version of Meleager's story, in which Meleager, angry at his mother, was finally persuaded by his wife to help defend his city.

In Bacchylides' ode ἄνδρεσσιν ἐπιχθονίοις implies instead that prayers avail little. The phrase echoes "no, not anyone on earth (τις ἐπιχθονίων) was in all things fortunate" (53-55) at the close of the second strophe, and "you know the brightness of the Muses, if any of today's men on earth (τις ἐπιχθονίων) knows it, rightly" at the opening of the ode (4-6). Each time a reference to "men on earth" serves as an introduction to a description of some particular man on earth: Hieron, the poet, Heracles, Meleager, Oeneus. The repetition links Hieron to Heracles and Heracles to Meleager, suggesting that the life of each has bearing on the others, at the same time reinforcing the distinction in our minds between god and man.

The following lines continue to develop these associations between the victor and the heroes of the myth. "Since horse-smiter Oeneus too would have made bud-crowned Artemis' anger cease, holy goddess white-armed." The traditional πλάξιππος does more than establish an epic tone: Hieron himself was "general of Syracusans with whirling horses" (ἱπποδινήτων, 2); the eagle had a "mane" (29); the colt Pherenicus was untouched by the dust from other horses (ἵππων, 44). Also significant is the fact that Oeneus' antagonist, like Heracles', is female. The new καλυκοστέφανος matches the ἰοστέφανοι Muses of the introduction (3), but beauty, as in the case of "Hera beautifully-bound" (89) goes hand-in-hand with destructiveness: σεμνά suggests that "bud-crowned Artemis" inspires not joy but awe.

A final epithet λευκώλενος confirms these sinister possibilities, surprisingly designating Artemis by Hera's special attribute "white-armed." We begin to see why Meleager began his story weeping: he foresees that Heracles' death, like his own, will ultimately be caused by a goddess' anger.

The next lines "imploring her with sacrifices of many goats, my father, and of red-backed cattle" make explicit what Meleager already implied in the introduction to his story, "it is hard for men on earth to change the gods' mind," denying the more positive message of Phoenix' tale to Achilles in *Iliad* 9. πατήρ dramatically interrupts the description of the sacrifices. Again emphasis is placed on parentage: Heracles has been called by the name of each of his parents, Zeus (58, 79), Alcmena (71), and Amphitryon (85). After the yellow of the eagle's wings (17) and Pherenicus' and Pallas' hair (37, 92), the new φοινικονώτων seems especially sinister, denoting the color of blood in the sacrifice, the death that accompanies the feasting.

Violence and slaughter is in fact the subject of the following lines: "but the goddess held her anger victorious." In contrast to the repeated references to victory in the introduction (33, 37, 40, 49), νίκα here is seen from the point of view of the defeated: "the maiden shook a wild boar with wide force, shameless in battle, into Calydon with its beautiful dances."

Set against the description of violence, the traditional καλλίχορος has special poignancy. Now we see force from the point of view of the birds who crouch in fear and of the horses defiled by Pherenicus' dust, to whom he appears "like the North wind's hurling" (46). "There with the strength of flood tides, he cut off the fruit trees with his teeth and slaughtered sheep, and mortals, whoever came to oppose him" adds frightening new detail.

A striking metaphor πλημύρων σθένει places Meleager in a storm at sea: in *Odyssey* 9, the wave that almost brings Odysseus' ship back to the Cyclops is a πλημυρὶς ἐκ πόντοιο (485-486). Pherenicus, by contrast, "could guard his helmsman" (47), and the eagle could fly above "the untiring sea's rough-turning waves" (25-26).

Each word in the description of the damage done by the boar has a previous association with death. Phoenix' account in *Iliad* 9 the "wild-toothed boar did much harm to Oeneus' vineyard, and threw on the ground the long trunks of trees with their own roots and flowers of apples" (540-542). In Bacchylides' narrative the boar more violently ὄρ-χους ἐπέκειρεν ὀδόντι. Heracles called Meleager "so strong a plant" (87); Heracles learned the souls of men like leaves (65); Cerberus was καρχαρόδους (60).

This boar (unlike the boar in the *Iliad*) kills sheep and men; Oeneus also slew goats and cattle in unavailing sacrifice (101-102); the hills along which the leaves are whirled are "sheep-pasturing" (65-67). βροτῶν echoes Heracles' learning the souls of mortals (βροτῶν, 63), and his question to Meleager, "who of immortals or mortals raised you" (βροτῶν, 87-88), in repeated reference to human death. The confrontation of Heracles and Meleager (τῷ δ'ἐναντία ψυχὰ προφάνη, 76-77) was described in language similar to the present encounter with the boar: εἰσάνταν μόλοι. By characterizing the boar's attack in terms simultaneously reminiscent of Pherenicus' victory and of Heracles' meeting with Meleager, Bacchylides gradually reveals the relevance of Meleager's story, both to Heracles and to the victor Hieron himself.

> τῶι δὲ στυγερὰν δῆριν Ἑλλάνων ἄριστοι
> στασάμεθ' ἐνδυκέως
> ἓξ ἄματα συνεχέως· ἐπεὶ δὲ δαίμων
> κάρτος Αἰτωλοῖς ὄρεξεν,
> 115 θάπτομεν οὓς κατέπεφ'νεν
> σῦς ἐριβ'ρύχας ἐπαΐσσων βίαι,
> Ἀ[γκ]αῖον ἐμῶν τ' Ἀγέλαον
> φ[έρτ]ατον κεδ'νῶν ἀδελφεῶν,
> οὓς τέ]κεν ἐν μεγάροις
> 120 .....]ς Ἀλθαία περικ'λειτοῖσιν Οἰνέος·
>
> (111-120, epode 3)

In the third epode, the focus shifts from the goddess' anger to her human victims. We hear directly of the reactions of these "men on earth" to the destruction they have experienced. "Against him the best of us Hellenes stood hateful strife, carefully for six days continuously."

The Greek audience would have perceived immediately a remarkable change from Phoenix' version of the story. There "the son of Oeneus, Meleager killed (the boar), collecting hunters from many cities, and dogs" (*Il*. 9.543-545). In Bacchylides, the initiative of the individual hero Meleager is replaced by the hesitation of a group. ἐνδυκέως, with the rhyming συνεχέως emphasizes their weakness. Victory comes not through human achievement, but because god "gave strength to the Aetolians," where the phrase δαίμων ὄρεξεν used in epic to disclaim responsibility, further conveys the impression of the powerlessness of the men involved in the fighting.

The account of Heracles' meeting with Meleager has prepared us for this absence of traditional heroism: Heracles afraid, drawing his bow against a dead man, Heracles cautiously questioning, Meleager weeping. Instead of hearing how Heracles captures Cerberus, we are told that Heracles "learns the souls of the dead" (64). So Meleager's account of the slaying of the boar concerns not the triumph but the losses: "we buried the men whom the loud-roaring boar killed, rushing on in force." Noise again connotes fear: the "shrill-voiced birds" crouched in fear before the eagle, messenger of ἐρισφαράγου Zeus (20-23).

Reiteration in the alliterative σῦς ἐριβρύχας ἐπαΐσσων βίᾳ of the story's opening reference to εὐρυβίαν κάπρον ἀναιδομάχαν (104-105) indicates that the narrative is reaching a conclusion. At the epode's close we learn that the dead are "Ancaeus and Agelaus, best of my dear brothers, whom Althaea bore in Oeneus' famous palace." Their relationship to Meleager is doubly emphasized; they are both his brothers and sons of his mother and father. Oeneus' palace, like Hieron's city (12, and his friend the poet, 14) is "famous." Does "horse-smiter" Oeneus bear some resemblance to the victor Hieron from Syracuse "with whirling horses?"

These last lines of the third epode both state the conclusion of the action which the third triad describes, and hint at the dominant motifs of the fourth triad, the importance of parentage, the relation of Meleager's fate to Hieron's and Heracles'. The second triad ends similarly with reflections and predictions, contrasting Meleager's omniscience to Heracles' ignorance, and suggesting that Heracles stop fighting and be happy, themes illustrated in the poet's opening command to Hieron "make your heart cease from cares and look here" (6-8). The first triad also ends with a description of Pherenicus "colt storm-runner, victorious" (39-40), that both recalls the description of the eagle in the stanza preceding, and presages the destructive significance of victory expressed in the second and third triads.

> . . . . . ὤ]λεσε μοῖρ' ὀλοὰ
> . . . . . .]ς· οὐ γάρ πω δαΐφ'ρων
> παῦσεν] χόλον ἀγ'ροτέρα
> Λατοῦς θυγάτηρ· περὶ δ' αἴθωνος δορᾶς
> 125 μαρνάμεθ' ἐνδυκέως
> Κουρῆσι μενεπτολέμοις·
> ἔνθ' ἐγὼ πολλοῖς σὺν ἄλλοις
> Ἴφικλον κατέκτανον
> ἐσθλόν τ' Ἀφάρητα, θοοὺς μάτρωας· οὐ γὰρ
> 130 καρτερόθυμος Ἄρης
> κρίνει φίλον ἐν πολέμωι,
> τυφ'λὰ δ' ἐκ χειρῶν βέλη
> ψυχαῖς ἔπι δυσμενέων φοι-

τᾶι θάνατόν τε φέρει
135 τοῖσιν ἂν δαίμων θέληι.

(121-135, strophe 4)

"Destructive destiny destroyed" whom? At least Meleager's brothers, in the struggle against the wild boar. But in the context of the ode, this brief reiterative phrase has intense impact. ὤλεσε, with the echoing ὀλοά emphasizes the difference between this μοῖρα and εὔμοιρος Hieron (1), and the summary statement that concluded the first praise, "happy the man to whom god gives a destiny (μοῖρα) of the beautiful" (50-53). The renewed reference to μοῖρα serves as introduction to a new theme: "no, somehow the sharp wild daughter of Leto . . . her anger."

Meleager's story began with a description of how his father could not make Artemis' χόλον cease (98-99). There Artemis' epithets "bud-crowned" and "white-armed" suggested a possibility of growth and life. But now in the continuation of her anger, the goddess is ambiguously designated δαΐφρων. The word's root meaning is "knowledgeable" (from δάω, "learn"), but its frequent use in epic as an epithet for fighting men associates its sound with δαΐ, "in the fire of war." Artemis' cult title ἀγροτέρα stresses violence. Once again a matronymic is used, "daughter of Leto" (Cerberus was son of Echidna, 62). As before, the result of her anger is fighting "about the blazing skin." αἴθων, the epithet used in Homer to describe the tawny skin of lions, horses, and an eagle, is the destructive antithesis of the bright color that denoted success in the ode's introduction, the eagle's yellow wings (17), "blonde-haired" Pherenicus (37), and that characterized "blonde" Pallas (92). Together with δαΐφρων, αἴθων associates Artemis' anger with burning.

Earlier in the ode force was associated with the wind, storms, and the sea: Pherenicus "storm-runner" (39), "like the North wind's hurling, guarding his helmsman" (46-47), and the boar "with the strength of flood-tides" (107). Now destructive force takes on the aspect of fire. The significance of this shift in terminology will soon become clear.

The battle over the boar's skin is told in language that recalls the caution and the slow progress of the battle against the living boar: "we fought carefully against the Curetes steadfast in war" echoes "we stood hateful strife carefully (ἐνδυκέως) for six days continuously" (111-113). Again two deaths occur: "and I along with many others killed Iphiclus and good Aphuretes, my swift uncles." The boar had killed "Ancaeus and Agelaus, best of my dear brothers" (117-118). But now Meleager himself does the killing, indiscriminately, as the boar had slaughtered "whoever came to oppose him" (110). The traditional epithet θοός, used in Homer of Ares himself, ironically characterizes Meleager's uncles at the moment when their speed did not help them. Pherenicus too is swift ("storm-runner," 39), and the eagle has "swift" (ταχείαις) wings (18-19).

As in the case of the first battle, where victory came only when "god gave might to the Aetolians" (113-114), the outcome of events is determined not by men but by divinities: "No, Ares strong-heart does not distinguish a friend in war." καρτερόθυμος is an epithet in Homer of both Achilles and Heracles; "bronze-chested" Ares accompanied Hieron's victory (34). Every event in the myth has reference to some earlier event in the ode.

The concluding lines of the strophe derive their remarkable impact from continued reminiscence of the ode's introduction and of Heracles' first confrontation with Meleager: "blind weapons from our hands go against the souls of the enemy, and bring death on whom the god wills." Weapons are τυφλά; earlier in the ode sight denoted victory and its celebration: "look here (i.e. at my song) in your mind" (18); the eagle is "well-known among men to see" (30); "Dawn saw Phrenicus victorious" (40); Heracles "saw" Meleager (71). Now it becomes clear that what we do not see also matters.

ἐκ χειρῶν βέλη ψυχαῖς ἔπι δυσμενέων echoes Meleager's command to Heracles "do not send forth a vain jagged arrow from your hands upon souls of the dead" (ἐκ χειρῶν ὀϊστόν ψυχαῖσιν ἔπι φθιμένων, 81-83). Pherenicus' winning race was like a bow shot (48-49). But in the fight against the Curetes, weapons bring not victory but death. τοῖσιν ἂν δαίμων θέλῃ grimly reiterates the conclusion of the second strophe, which introduced Heracles' story: "(no man) was in all things fortunate" (πάντα γ' εὐδαίμων ἔφυ, 55). This close correspondence, along with the almost verbatim repetition of Heracles' bow shot from the beginning of the myth, suggests that Meleager's tale may be drawing to a close.

>   ταῦτ' οὐκ ἐπιλεξαμένα
>   Θεστίου κούρα δαΐφρων
>   μάτηρ κακόποτ|μος ἐμοὶ
>   βούλευσεν ὄλεθ|ρον ἀτάρβακτος γυνά,
> 140 καῖέ τε δαιδαλέας
>   ἐκ λάρνακος ὠκύμορον
>   φιτ|ρὸν ἐξαύσασα· τὸν δὴ
>   μοῖρ' ἐπέκ|λωσεν τότε
>   ζωᾶς ὅρον ἁμετέρας ἔμμεν. τύχον μὲν
> 145 Δαϊπύλου Κλύμενον
>   παῖδ' ἄλκιμον ἐξεναρί-
>   ζων ἀμώμητον δέμας,
>   πύργων προπάροιθε κιχήσας·
>   τοὶ δὲ πρὸς εὐκτιμέναν
> 150 φεῦγον ἀρχαίαν πόλιν

(136-150, antistrophe 4)

The patterns already established in Meleager's story help us grasp immediately the significance of the next lines, without formal introduction. "This she did not consider, daughter of Thestius, sharp mother, evil fate for me, she planned my destruction, fearless woman."

The many references earlier in the ode to parentage, to destructive destiny, to evil female presences have led up to this part of Meleager's story. His mother resembles at once Ares, who "does not distinguish a friend in war" (130-131), and Artemis who is also δαΐφρων (122). The new κακόποτμος is the antithesis of Hieron's special epithet εὔμοιρος (1). In contrast to Heracles, who is afraid of what he sees (84), and who reacts without thinking, Althaea "planned" Meleager's death, "fearless." κούρα, μάτηρ, and γυνά stress all aspects of her feminity: yet Heracles in his ignorance thought that Meleager was killed by a man (90).

The familiar story of Althaea's putting in the fire the log that matches her son's life is now recounted in words already charged with significance: "she burned from the ornate chest the fast-destined branch, screaming—this Destiny had spun to be the boundary of our life." The emphatic first word, καῖε, makes explicit the sinister implications of the "blazing" boarskin, for which Meleager killed his mother's brothers (124). δαιδαλέας echoes the sound of δαΐφρων; ὠκύμορος, standard epithet of heroes in Homer, derives new force from the connotations of the μοῖρα that destroyed Meleager's brothers (121), and that has granted Hieron's success (1, 50-53).

By speaking of the charred log Althaea saved in the chest as a φιτρόν, i.e., a living thing, Bacchylides recalls Heracles' initial designation of Meleager as a "plant" (ἔρνος, 87), the comparison of the souls to the leaves whirled by the wind (65-67), and the fruit trees cut down by the boar (108). Althaea "weeping" matches Meleager "weeping" (δακρυόεις, 94) at the beginning of the tale. The traditional epic formula μοῖρ' ἐπέκλωσεν again attributes determining power to a feminine divinity, Destiny; at the triad's opening "dread Destiny destroyed" Meleager's brothers (121). Pherenicus in victory rushed toward the goal (τέλος, 45); Meleager's life is marked by a "boundary." The language of these lines ensures that we regard what Meleager here describes as the ultimate defeat, the inverse of triumph in games or war.

The relentless pace of the narrative stops for a moment, while Meleager explains where he was when his mother put the branch back into the fire. "By luck Clymenus, Daipylus' brave son, his blameless body, I was stripping. I had come on him before the towers. Toward the well-built city they had fled." The myth began with a reference to "luck (τύχᾳ) to envy and a rich life to lead" (52); now Meleager happens (τύχον) to be at what also seems to be a moment of triumph, stripping the armor that is the victor's prize from his dead adversary. Homeric words, ἄλκιμος, ἀμώμητον, εὐκτιμένα, set a heroic tone. But in the context of the ode the dead Clymenus' father's name Daipylus ("gate in war") also echoes the sound of Althaea's and Artemis' sinister epithet δαΐφρων (122, 137).

The deaths of Patroclus and Hector also took place "before the towers" of Troy. But the last line "they had fled to the old, well-built city" deliberately postpones mentioning the actual name of the town which the audience would recognize as the site of Meleager's death, until the next stanza.

> Πλευρῶνα· μίνυθεν δέ μοι ψυχὰ γλυκεῖα·
> γνῶν δ' ὀλιγοσθενέων,
> αἰαῖ· πύματον δὲ πνέων δάκ'ρυσα τλά[μων,
> ἀγ'λαὰν ἥβαν προλείπων.
> 155 φασὶν ἀδεισιβόαν
> Ἀμφιτ'ρύωνος παῖδα μοῦνον δὴ τότε
> τέγξαι βλέφαρον, ταλαπενθέος
> πότ'μον οἰκτίροντα φωτός·
> καί νιν ἀμειβόμενος
> 160 τᾶδ' ἔφα· ,,θνατοῖσι μὴ φῦναι φέριστον
> (151-160, epode 4)

The first word in the epode is the name of the fatal city, Pleuron. The account of Meleager's death follows immediately: "my sweet soul grew weak. I knew I had little strength, aiai, and breathing my last I wept suffering, leaving behind my bright youth." Like the log in the fire, Meleager diminishes in size, **μίνυθεν, ὀλιγοσθενέων. προλείπων**, which can connote abandoning in battle, marks the difference between this impersonal wasting away and a hero's death in combat. The dramatic cry **αἰαῖ** and the statement of realization, **γνῶν**, resemble a recognition statement in tragedy, like Oedipus' "iou, iou, all could come out clear" (O.T. 1182). Hieron, in the ode's proem, "knows the brightness (**γνώσῃ ... ἄγαλμα**) of the Muses" (3-4); now Meleager in death leaves behind his **ἀγλαάν** youth.

The lines derive additional impact from Homeric reminiscence. The deaths of Patroclus and Hector are both followed by "his soul (**ψυχά**) flew from his limbs and went to Hades, lamenting his fate, leaving manhood and youth" (**λιποῦσ' ἀνδροτῆτα καὶ ἥβην**, Il. 16.856-857, 22. 362-363). The resemblance becomes more sinister as we remember that Patroclus and Hector each die predicting the death of the man who has killed him. The implication is that Meleager's death will also presage the death of the man that he is speaking to, Heracles.

φασίν marks the end of Meleager's story, and like **λέγουσιν**, which introduces the myth (57), turns our attention to Heracles: "they say that only then the man who feared no shout wet his eyes." Meleager wept as he began his story (94) and at the moment of his death (153); now Heracles "wets his eye" at the story's end. The new **ἀδεισιβόας** reminds us of the traditional sound of battle to which Meleager's death and the two heroes' weeping bear so little likeness. Meleager is now described with the epithet which Odysseus uses to describe his attitude toward death to Calypso, "if one of the gods wrecks me on the wine-dark sea, I shall endure it, since I have a heart enduring grief (ταλαπενθής, *Od.* 5. 221-222). Heracles' descent to the lower world sounded like Odysseus' meeting with Tiresias; now Heracles applies to Meleager Odysseus' special epithet. But what he says to Meleager indicates that he understands the relevance of Meleager's tale only in a general way: "and answering him, he said, for mortals not to be born is best." His answer is a cliché of consolation. Whether or not he sees the implications for himself in Meleager's fate is held in suspense till the next triad.

>   μηδ' ἀελίου προσιδεῖν
>   φέγγος· ἀλλ' οὐ γάρ τίς ἐστιν
>   πρᾶξις τάδε μυρομένοις,
>   χρὴ κεῖνο λέγειν ὅτι καὶ μέλλει τελεῖν.
> 165   ἦρά τις ἐν μεγάροις
>   Οἰνῆος ἀρηϊφίλου
>   ἔστιν ἀδ|μήτα θυγάτ|ρων,
>   σοὶ φυὰν ἀλιγκία;
>   τάν κεν λιπαρὰν ⟨ἐ⟩θέλων θείμαν ἄκοιτιν."
> 170   τὸν δὲ μενεπτολέμου
>   ψυχὰ προσέφα Μελεά-
>   γ|ρου· "λίπον χλωραύχενα
>   ἐν δώμασι Δαϊάνειραν,
>   νῆϊν ἔτι χ|ρυσέας
> 175   Κύπ|ριδος θελξιμβρότου."

(161-175, strophe 5)

The first words of the fifth strophe, "not to see the light of the sun," restate what Heracles said in the last line of the fourth epode: "for mortals not to be born is best." This reaffirmation of the futility of human existence conflicts directly with the bright colors of the ode's introduction, of the victory which Pherenicus won at dawn (40). "Not to see" vitiates the importance placed earlier on vision (30, 40, 71). Heracles seems instead to accept Meleager's characterization of the world, in which "blind from our hands weapons go against the souls of the enemy" (132-133). ἀελίου προσιδεῖν φέγγος recalls what the soul of Heracles says in *Odyssey* 11 to Odysseus when they meet among the dead: "ah poor man, now are you too the leader of some evil destiny, which I myself bore as a burden beneath the rays of the sun?"(αὐγὰς ἠελίοιο, 617-619). In Bacchylides' poem, the living Heracles, who first resembled Odysseus on his journey to the world of the dead, now seems more like his own soul in death, pessimistic, reflective.

His next words also imply, through reminiscence, that he has acquired the close knowledge of death which in the *Iliad* only Achilles seems to possess, through loss of Patroclus and through his awareness of the imminence of his own death. Heracles' "it is no use for us to mourn this" (οὐ γάρ τίς ἐστιν πρᾶξις τάδε μυρομένοις), echoes Achilles' consolation to the grieving Priam "there is no use in cruel lamentation (οὐ γάρ τις πρῆξις πέλεται κρυέροιο γόοιο), for so the gods have spun for poor mortals, to live in sorrow, while they themselves are without care" (*Il.* 24. 524-526).

In the context of *Ode* 5, Heracles' association to Achilles has special poignancy: we recall that at the beginning of the story, Heracles "was amazed" (84) when Meleager first spoke to him, as was Achilles when he first saw Priam, both because of Priam's courage and the extent of Priam's bereavement (*Il.* 24.480-484). What Heracles first sees in Meleager is a likeness to himself "bold-willed" (69) and then a resemblance to Achilles "shining in his armor" (71-72). The Homeric echo "it is no use for us to mourn this" subtly reinforces our impression that Heracles and Meleager, like Priam and Achilles, share a common fate.

But where Achilles in the *Iliad* proceeds to explain to Priam first that all men suffer, and that in particular both Achilles' father Peleus and Priam himself, though fortunate in other respects, have lost what mattered most to them, their sons, Bacchylides' Heracles turns instead to action: "it is no use for us to mourn this, we must say that which we can complete." Unlike Achilles, Heracles still believes that something positive can be "done." He will return to the world of life, he will marry Meleager's sister. But the pattern of his words is ominous: in his first speech to Meleager Heracles began in epic style "who among immortals or mortals raised such a plant? who killed you," concluding with direct reference to himself "yes, soon Hera beautifully-bound will send that man (κεῖνον) on our head" (86-91). Now in his second speech, the Homeric οὐ γάρ τίς ἐστιν πρᾶξις is also followed by "we must say that which (κεῖνο) we can complete."

Against this recollection of his concern that the man who killed Meleager will kill him, his next words strike with greater irony: "is there in the palace of Oeneus, Ares' friend, a daughter unwed like you in growth?" The simple question "do you have a sister?" is stated in language with increasingly negative overtones. Earlier in the ode the phrase ἐν μεγάροις Οἰνέος accompanied a reference to Meleager's brothers, the first of his family to die in the long struggle with the boar (120). Oeneus is ἀρηΐφιλος but Ares is the god who "does not distinguish a friend (φίλον) in war" (129-131). The other "daughters" in the poem are Artemis (124) and Althaea (137). The terminology of growth has so far connoted death: Heracles compared Meleager to a plant (86-88); Meleager's life is measured by a "branch" (142).

After words with these associations, Heracles' final statement "her I would make my shining wife" can only seem ambiguous in meaning. Meleager's youth that he leaves behind in death was "bright" (154),

Pallas' and Pherenicus' have blonde hair (92, 37), the eagle's wings are yellow (17), Hieron knows the "brightness" of the Muses (4). But at the same time, the emphasis placed throughout Meleager's story on the destructiveness of Artemis and Althaea, suggests that the "shining wife," like "bud-crowned Artemis" (98), in time could prove "sharp" (122), and "wild" (123), for Heracles.

The Greek audience knew the outcome of the story: Heracles married Daianeira, Meleager's sister, who would later cause his death by sending him what was supposed to be a love charm, but in fact turned out to be poison, the blood of the centaur Nessus who tried to rape her, but whom Heracles had killed. Bacchylides only hints at this final outcome, selecting the details that best illustrate his central themes. "Him Meleager's soul steadfast-in-war answered: I left pale-necked Daianeira at home, not yet knowing golden Cypris who charms mortals."

Virtually every word in these lines has dual significance. τὸν δὲ ψυχὰ προσέφα Μελεάγρου virtually repeats the formal introduction to Meleager's story τὸν δὲ προσέφα Μελέαγρος δακρυόεις (93-94), but now it is Meleager's "soul" that speaks, emphasizing death, and the order of words mirrors Heracles' final, ominous statement τάν κεν λιπαρὰν ἐθέλων θείμαν ἄκοιτιν. μενεπτόλεμος, earlier the epithet of Meleager's enemies the Curetes (126), now describes Meleager himself. Meleager's answer begins with λίπον, where his last speech ended, ἀγλαὰν ἥβαν προλείπων (154). Bacchylides' uncle Simonides used the epithet χλωραύχην to describe a nightingale (586.2) but χλωρός in Homer is the color of fear.[10] The alliterative ἐν δώμασι Δαϊάνειραν continues the ambivalence: Artemis and Althaea are both δαΐφρων (122, 137), Meleager's enemy was the son of Daipylus (145). Will Daianeira also prove to be what her name says she is "learner/destroyer of men?"

The last lines of the strophe sketch the outline of the story to come: "not yet knowing golden Cypris who beguiles mortals." "Golden Cypris," like "bud-crowned Artemis" (98) is beautiful to look at, but will also cause Heracles' death. The new θελξίμβροτος hints at the reason why Daianeira sent the fatal poison, Heracles' passion for the princess Iole. -βρότου at stanza end implies that the process of beguiling affects not only the characters in the story: all men are ignorant of their fates, dazzled by the beauty of what they see, the light of the "blazing" boar skin (124), of the "shining" wife (169), and perhaps also by the brightness of victory.

Here the story of Heracles and Meleager ends, at the end of a stanza, without formal summation or statement about its meaning. We are left to infer for ourselves what Bacchylides has suggested all along through reminiscence and echo, that what Heracles has in common with Meleager, although he does not realize it, is dying an unheroic death at a woman's hands.[11] The correspondence is brought out in many ways at once, by making characters seem like each other, or two characters resemble a third, by repetition of words, by recollection of Homer. Association builds upon association, so that by the story's end in the fifth strophe, virtually every word seems charged with multiple meaning, ostensibly saying something hopeful, simultaneously promising death.

In its capacity to make different events seem related, Bacchylides' method of telling the story resembles Pindar's account of Ixion in *Pythian* 2. Pindar made Ixion's lust for Hera become Ixion's punishment, and live on in his son Centaurus' "mixing" with the Magnesian mares (45), which itself resembles Ixion's "mixing" of blood in a kinsman's murder (32). Pindar's story also ends without explicit reference to its beginning: we must infer from what he has said before that the "army wondrous, like both parents, the mother below, above the father" (46-48) will continue to pursue their grandfather Ixion's deeds of lust and violence. The Greek audience would know the story of the horse-men's rape of the Lapith women, and the bloody battle that ensued. Both poets tell their stories with excursions back and forward from strict chronological order: in *Pythian* 2 Ixion's lust, crime, previous crime, lust, crime, punishment, offspring: in *Ode* 5 Heracles meets Meleager, Meleager tells the story of his past, then Heracles and Meleager discuss the future. What makes Bacchylides' narrative easier for us to follow is its more leisurely pace, and the fact that movement back and forward in time is contained within separate formal speeches.

As in the case of the story of Ixion, repetition and reiteration connect the details of the myth to the ode's introduction. In *Pythian* 2, Ixion is made to seem a negative illustration of the gratitude shown by Hieron to the gods, and of Pindar to Hieron. In *Ode* 5, we see in Meleager the antithesis of the "well-destined" (1) Hieron, in Heracles the antithesis of the confident eagle and the horse who aims and shoots on target. But the description of the boar also reminds us of the destructive side of Pherenicus' victory, the dust on the other horses (44), the birds crouching in fear before the eagle (22-23).

Since Heracles' hope for a "shining wife" (169) and trust in "blonde Pallas" (92) are belied by what we know will be his fate, we begin to question the promise in the introduction of Pherenicus' "blonde" hair (37) and the gold and brightness brought by song. In *Pythian* 2 the story of Ixion similarly suggests that in moments of triumph lies the greatest danger. If association becomes too close with the forces that bring victory, the iron weapons of war and the horses that pull the winning chariot, victory can turn to violence, the way Ixion's "sweet life" (26) turned to "beautiful pain" (40).

Victory bears close resemblance to destruction: Hieron tames his colts in gentle hands and wins the race (7-8); Centaurus mixes himself with the mares and begets the violent horse-men (44-48). Hieron and Pherenicus are singular in triumph, like the eagle; we meet Heracles as he is about to complete his greatest labor, but his chance meeting with Meleager en route will cause his death; Meleager's achievements in battle destroy him, at a moment when yet another victory seemed near.

        λευκώλενε Καλλιόπα,
        στᾶσον εὐποίητον ἅρμα
        αὐτοῦ· Δία τε Κ⌐ρονίδαν
        ὕμνησον Ὀλύμπιον ἀρχαγὸν θεῶν,
180   τόν τ' ἀκαμαντορόαν
        Ἀλφεόν, Πέλοπός τε βίαν,
        καὶ Πίσαν, ἔνθ' ὁ κ⌐λεεννὸς
        πο]σσὶ νικάσας δρόμωι
        ἦλθ]εν Φερένικος ⟨ἐς⟩ εὐπύργους Συρακόσ-
185   σας Ἱέρωνι φέρων
        εὐδ]αιμονίας πέταλον.
        χρὴ] δ' ἀλαθείας χάριν
        αἰνεῖν, φθόνον ἀμφ[οτέραισιν
        χερσὶν ἀπωσάμενο͞ν,
190   εἴ τις εὖ πράσσοι βροτῶ[ν.
                      (176-190, antistrophe 5)

"White-armed Calliope, stand your well-made chariot here." Every word in the fifth antistrophe draws significance from earlier lines. λευκώλενε could seem for a brief moment to be a continuation of the myth, an address to λευκώλενος Artemis (as in 99), or even Heracles' divine enemy Hera, to whom the epithet properly belongs. But then the Muse's name marks a transition to a new theme. Again song is characterized as a road down which the poet travels, as in the introduction "so now for me too there are ten thousand paths everywhere to sing praise of your achievements" (31-33). στᾶσον... αὐτοῦ echoes Meleager's command to Heracles, στᾶθί τ' ἐν χώρᾳ (80), as if to imply that further progress down the road of myth would be like Heracles' "vain jagged arrow" (81-82). εὐποίητον instead calls attention to the craftman's skill.

Repetition of ὕμνησον, as at the end of the eagle simile (31-33), turns our attentions to the victory: "of Zeus Cronides sing, leader of gods, the Olympian, and of the tirelessly-flowing Alpheus, and of Pelops' might and of Pisa, where famed for his feet, victorious in running, Pherenicus came to towered Syracuse, bringing to Hieron the leaf of good fortune."

The subject of this later praise is no longer Hieron; but rather the enduring divinities and landmarks of Olympia. Where before Hieron was "general" (2), Zeus is ἀρχαγόν. The Alpheus, before εὐρυδίνας (38) like the ἱπποδίνητοι Syracusans (2), has become ἀκαμαντορόας, like the ἀκαμάτας sea that the eagle flies above (25). Only after this tribute to divinity do we return to Pherenicus' victory, described first in language that derives from the introduction; κλεενός, like Syracuse and the poet (12, 14); with the echoing νικάσας ... Φερένικος ... φέρων, like Φερένικον ... νικάσαντα (37-40); with reference to his δρόμῳ, as in ἀελλοδρόμαν (39).

But the conclusion of the sentence is framed in the language of the myth. Pherenicus ἦλθεν ἐς εὐπύργους Συρακόσσας; Meleager died πύργων προπάροιθε κιχήσας (148). In the battle over the boar's skin, blind weapons θάνατον φέρει (134); now the horse brings (φέρων) not the traditional olive crown of Olympian victory, but instead a single leaf—the souls of the dead are like leaves (65), Meleager is a "plant" (87), a "branch" measured his life (142). The myth has caused us to see victory not at the moment of celebration, but in the context of a lifetime.

The poet's role is redefined accordingly in the stanza's closing lines: "for truth's joy (i.e., for the sake of truth) one must praise, thrusting envy aside with both hands, if any mortal does well." The first antistrophe began "to praise (αἰνεῖν) Hieron" (16). But this final statement omits the bright ornamental epithets of the ode's introduction. The poet's duty is not to celebrate but to defend. Reference to "hands" suggest that envy must be repelled like an attacking army, as "blind weapons from our hands" brings death to the souls of enemies in the battle over the boar's skin (132). "If any mortal does well" restates tentatively "happy the man to whom god gives a destiny of the beautiful with luck to envy and a rich life to lead" (50-53). After a myth of failure, the achievement of victory appears the more remarkable.

This antistrophe, with its sudden transition from myth, and the sharp distinctions that it draws between mortal and immortal capability, and its emphasis on the role of envy, has a function similar to that of the third strophe of Pindar's *Pythian* 2, which also follows the myth. There Pindar marks the end of the story of Ixion with a description of the distinction between god and man, "a god comes up to every mark on his hopes" (49), continues with a description of the dangers of envy, "I must keep escaping the close bite of evil talk" (52-53), and concludes with a restatement of the possible, "to have wealth with luck is the best of a fate of skill" (56). A reminder to the victor of the difference between his achievement and the lasting perfection of god must have seemed essential, along with reassurance that the poet will not use his powers to reduce victory's value, out of envy for his patron's success.

Βοιωτὸς ἀνὴρ τάδε φών[ησεν, γλυκειᾶν
Ἡσίοδος πρόπολος
Μουσᾶν, ὃν ⟨ἂν⟩ ἀθάνατοι τι[μῶσι, τούτωι
καὶ βροτῶν φήμαν ἔπ[εσθαι.

```
195  πείθομαι εὐμαρέως
     εὐκλέα κελεύθου γλῶσσαν οὐ[__ᴗ_
     πέμπειν Ἱέρωνι· τόθεν γὰ[ρ
     πυθ'μένες θάλλουσιν ἐσθλ[ῶν,
     τοὺς ὁ μεγιστοπάτωρ
200  Ζεὺς ἀκινήτους ἐν εἰρήν[αι φυλάσσοι.
```
(191-200, epode 5)

The first line of the epode seems suddenly to move in a new direction: "a Boeotian man said here [ ]." We think of Pindar, the Theban poet, commissioned to compose an ode for the same occasion. But the next lines indicate that Bacchylides is in fact returning to the theme of the ode's opening strophe. Not Pindar, but Pindar's countryman Hesiod, "priest of the Muses." Bacchylides called himself "servant (θεράπων) of Urania," in the first strophe (14), quoting Hesiod's description of the bard, "servant of the Muses" who can make a man forget his troubles (*Theogony* 100). This recollection helps us recognize immediately the context of the lines Bacchylides is about to quote. It is the same passage that Bacchylides reminded us of when the ode began, the description of the just king, whose heart "marks straight" (6). "The man the immortals honor, talk of men also follows" states in general terms that could describe either victory or government, what Hesiod says more specifically in *Theogony* 81-93:

> The man among Zeus-raised kings the daughters of great Zeus (the Muses) honor . . . All the people look at him as he judges with straight markings . . . and when he comes to a trial people welcome him as a god with sweet respect, and he stands out among them as they gather, such is the Muses' gift to men.

The repetition of a theme long suspended indicates that the poem is drawing to a close.

"I submit with good skill my famous tongue, not far from the path . . . to send Hieron" again returns to the opening description of the famous poet who "sends" (πέμπει) Hieron a song (10-14), and who has many paths (κέλευθος, 31) to praise him. But now the elaborate "he has woven a song of praise" (9-10) has become briefly εὐμαρέως, the traditional εὐκλέα encapsulates the reiterated "famed city . . . famed servant" (12-14) and "song of praise . . . speech" (10-15), and the direct πείθομαι replaces the terminology of the nightingale's "pouring from his heart" (15).

Gone are the brightness of the violet-crowned Muses, the Joys deep-robed, the holy island, gold-banded Urania. The emphasis in the final epode falls on the actions of men, as they are ordinarily known: "Boeotian" (not, "from the holy island," 10-11), "Hesiod" (not, "a friend," 11), πρόπολος, the god's interpreter to men (not θεράπων, human servant to god, 14), the "talk of mortals" (not a nightingale's song, 15). The last lines of the ode hold human achievement in the perspective established in the myth "from there the roots of good flourish, which greatest father Zeus unmoved in peace . . . " All through the ode men have been associated with trees and leaves, but πυθμένες, in contrast to the single "leaf of good fortune" conferred by victory (186) connote stability and the possibility of renewal: Odysseus' bed, built on the base (πυθμήν) of an olive tree, cannot be moved unless a man cuts the roots which grow above ground at the tree's base and puts the bed elsewhere (*Od.* 23.204). The new μεγιστοπάτωρ denotes both power and masculinity, as if in counterbalance to the destructive femininity of the myth.

Like *Pythian* 2, *Ode* 5 ends without fanfare, or a reprieve of the exciting diction of the opening lines. Had we begun by looking first at its last stanza, we would have seen little remarkable in it: a quotation from Hesiod, a statement in the conventional terminology of roads that the poet's praise is true, a prayer for continued success in the traditional language of growth. But read in proper sequence, the lines serve as a coda, reminding us briefly of the major themes that we have heard. In the opening strophes, Hieron, like Hesiod's king, was honored by the Muses, the poet's obligation to give true praise to Hieron was easy to fulfill in "ten thousand paths." The final sentence of the last epode stands as response to the myth: the roots of good flourish for Hieron, while Meleager's life has been cut down; Zeus greatest father will protect these roots, where Meleager and Heracles were killed by females, Artemis, Althaea, Hera and Daianeira.

Reiteration, or more simply, memory, as in the case of *Pythian* 2, is the key to understanding how this poem works. If we stock our unretentive minds with constant recollection of what has gone before, we can begin to imagine what the ancient audience, who could remember, must have heard in this poem. The range of language, characters, and action in the poem is in fact carefully limited. The poet and victor are accompanied by feminine deities; each section of the myth has a male protagonist and a female antagonist. Throughout, much of the important action consists of seeing and recognizing. Negative forces are described as storm winds, seas; man, like the trees, is their victim. Through memory, echoes of Hesiod and Homer add historical dimension: we can compare Hieron and Bacchylides to the portrait of the ideal king and bard in the *Theogony*. Shifting reminiscences of Homer make Meleager resemble Heracles, Achilles, Tiresias, Patroclus, and Hector; and Heracles seems variously like Odysseus, Pandarus, and Achilles. Through these momentary likenesses we glimpse a past whose achievements seem negated in Meleager's failure and Heracles' consistent lack of perception. The heroes' shortcomings, the souls of the dead like leaves, and the unnamed victims of the boar, form the reverse image of the ode's dramatic address to an individual man and his achievements.

We can conclude that as in *Pythian* 2, every word in *Ode* 5 has a vital function. Nothing is purely decorative, or an accidental survival of some forgotten convention. Both poets follow the same general pattern of exposition. The opening stanzas are packed with descriptions and statements that will later be elaborated in more detail: gradually within the myth the same words and events recur, and they in turn influence the restatement of opening praise that ends the poem. Without Ixion we could not see the purpose of the apes and foxes. Without the story of Heracles and Meleager we could not understand why the second praise in *Ode* 5 seems so much sparer than the first.

Both odes, for all their differences in style and content, have the same basic format: a first praise, a myth, a second praise. The praises include reference to the victory's name and family, the circumstances of the victory, and commentary on the poet's function. But this formal similarity guarantees identity no more than the nineteenth century convention that concertos have three movements. Even on the basis of these two odes it is possible to perceive the wide range of variation possible within the established form. The amount of time the poet will spend on any topic varies considerably. The introduction of *Ode* 5 and its myth are far longer than the corresponding sections in *Pythian* 2. Pindar devotes two triads to the second praise in *Pythian* 2; Bacchylides in *Ode* 5 concludes in an antistrophe and an epode. The audience must have judged when the myth or the poem would end by what the poet said, not by the length of time he spent in total. Length is rather a sign of emphasis: Pindar in *Pythian* 2 places most stress on his role as a poet; Bacchylides in *Ode* 5 on the narration of a myth about man's ignorance of the true nature of his fate. This ability to vary the amount of space given to any theme permits great freedom within a format that is otherwise rigidly constricted both by metrical structure and the demands of traditional content.

From our point of view, *Ode* 5 is certainly the more accessible of the two odes. Its language and the pacing of its narrative simulate epic; emphasis on ignorance, and sudden reversal of fortune make its myth seem like an excerpt from a tragedy. This comparative familiarity may make us undervalue the originality of Bacchylides' approach. In Syracuse in 476 B.C., where Attic tragedy was just being discovered, his work would have seemed more innovative. His new adjectives and reapplication of traditional epithets would have struck the ancient ear as remarkable in a way that we can barely appreciate. There is nothing ordinary about aiming and shooting a victory, learning souls, the strength of flood tides, the roots of good. The setting of the meeting of Heracles and Meleager, and Meleager's story into a Homeric framework would have seemed impressive: Heracles like Odysseus, Meleager like Achilles, and then Patroclus and Hector, the log put back from the fire, dead, like the fallen leaves, reset traditional material into interesting new configurations. The Greek audience would have enjoyed the suspenseful endings of his stanzas, with sentences left incomplete, the sudden addition to Pherenicus' winning run of the fact that he means an earlier victory "at holy Pytho" (41), the "Boeotian man" left for a little while unidentified (191).

Modern criticism, based on tales in the scholia of Bacchylides' rivalry with Pindar, has done much to keep us from giving this great poet the credit he deserves. Bacchylides used the capabilities of his audience to best advantage—their close knowledge of Homer, their awakening interest in drama. Pindar, in *Pythian* 2 and elsewhere, deals with larger questions of morality, and changes standard forms of speech. Bacchylides would have been more easily understood by his contemporaries. Pindar seems more interesting to us because he tries to break with, rather than use tradition, and in so doing, presages the major literary trends of the next generation.

Pindar's *Olympian* 1

To return to Pindar's *Olympian* 1 after reading Bacchylides' *Ode* 5 is for the modern reader something of a shock. We can easily understand the plot of Bacchylides' gently paced narrative; his praise and statements about poetry are less abstract than Pindar's. He speaks of individuals, the patron, and the poet, while Pindar in *Pythian* 2 speaks of men in groups, nameless whisperers, men who drag markers too far and wound themselves, other men who complete songs of praise for other kings, all with seemingly unlimited application in space and time. We will see analogues in *Olympian* 1: "there are many wonders and somewhere somehow, too, men's talking beyond the true account . . . stories deceive" (28-29); "it is right for a man to speak what is beautiful about the gods: the blame is less" (35).

Then, too, where Bacchylides describes the Muses, the Charites, and Victory in their traditional Homeric trappings, "violet-crowned" (3), "deep-bound" (9), "dark-haired" (33), Pindar gives animation also to "low speeches of slanders" (*Pythian* 2. 76-77), and in *Olympian* 1, turns the "days that are left" into "witnesses most wise" (33-34).

Bacchylides describes poet and patron both as "famous" (12, 14), and uses a simile of an eagle's flight to characterize simultaneously the different powers of poet, victor, and winning horse. But in *Pythian* 2 categories overlap, so that the same advice about repaying one's benefactor applies to all involved in the achievement and celebration of victory: Hieron tames his mares in gentle hands (8), the poet will bear the yoke lightly on his neck (93). In *Olympian* 1 also, song, like a victor's wreath, surrounds not Hieron, but the poet (8-9, 18-19).

Where Bacchylides' metaphors follow along lines already established in epic, e.g., the souls of the dead like leaves (65), the horse swift as the north wind (46), Pindar makes associations that would have seemed arresting even to an ancient audience. In *Pythian* 2, murder and sexual intercourse are both "mixing" (32, 45); in *Olympian* 1, right conduct involves "digesting" (55). These new clusters of ideas make Pindar's poetry distinctive, difficult, and the more valuable, in that it tells us what would otherwise not be known.

> Ἄριστον μὲν ὕδωρ, ὁ δὲ χ'ρυσὸς αἰθόμενον πῦρ
> ἅτε διαπ'ρέπει νυκτὶ μεγάνορος ἔξοχα πλούτου·
> εἰ δ' ἄεθ'λα γαρύεν
> ἔλδεαι, φίλον ἦτορ,
> 5 μηκέτ' ἀελίου σκόπει
> ἄλλο θαλπνότερον ἐν ἀμέρᾳ φαεν-
>   νὸν ἄστρον ἐρήμας δι' αἰθέρος,
> μηδ' Ὀλυμπίας ἀγῶνα φέρτερον αὐδάσομεν·
> ὅθεν ὁ πολύφατος ὕμνος ἀμφιβάλλεται
> σοφῶν μητίεσσι, κελαδεῖν
> 10 Κρόνου παῖδ' ἐς ἀφ'νεὰν ἱκομένους
> μάκαιραν Ἱέρωνος ἑστίαν,
>
>   (1-11, strophe 1)

"Best is water, and gold like blazing fire, shines out at night beyond great man's wealth." We sense that somehow this statement concerns supremacy, but why did Pindar choose water out of all the things in man's experience that might be called ἄριστον? Why does he talk of gold like fire at night, rather than gold like sun reflected in water by day? The poem itself reveals the answers: as if anticipating our reaction, that these opening statements seem to have no relation to each other, or to the games, the poet interjects, "and if you want to talk of prizes, my heart, look no longer for some other star bright through the empty air hotter in day than the sun: we will not speak of a contest greater than Olympia."

The opening lines had described ultimates, the water that was best, the gold beyond other wealth. So also the subject of song is ἄεθλα, end result rather than process. The poet too has reached his goal: Olympia, the hottest star in day is like the gold that shines beyond other wealth at night. In each case the degree of excellence is expressed by contrast: any metal can shine in day, but only gold remains untarnished, so it can shine in the dimmer light of torches. Similarly, any star can shine at night, but all save one are invisible at noontime. So Olympia surpasses other contests. Speaking of the ἀγών rather than the whole of the festival (ἑορτά) keeps the emphasis on competition. Supremacy is relative: one man's victory is made possible only by another man's defeat. These impressive opening lines concern not only success, but the testing and competition by which success is measured.

"We will not speak of a contest greater than Olympia." By referring to himself the poet introduces a new topic: "from where the song men talk of is thrown around the plans of poets to sing the son of Cronus after they come to the rich blessed hearth of Hieron." The ancient audience might have anticipated the shift of focus from the fact of victory to its celebration. In *Pythian* 2 the poet's announcement of victory similarly leads up to a brief description of a festival in Syracuse: "to you (Syracuse) I come, this song from shining Thebes I bear, an announcement of the four-horse-rig earth-shaking, in which Hieron with his chariot won and bound Ortygia high with far-beaming crowns, the shrine of Artemis of the river, not without whom did he tame in gentle hands those mares with intricate reins" (3-8).

In both odes, though the nature of the celebration differs, tribute is paid immediately to a god: in *Olympian* 1 the poets come "to sing the son of Cronus." In *Pythian* 2 Hieron "bound high the shrine of Artemis with crowns." In both odes the description of celebration elaborates on the themes already introduced. In *Pythian* 2, which began with an invocation to "Syracuse, of men and horses who rejoice in iron, godlike nurse," Pindar speaks of Hieron's gentle control of horses. In *Olympian* 1 where the subject is success in competition, the poet's arrival at Hieron's house resembles the victor's coming (ἰκομένους) before the judges who give him his prize crown of olive and bind his head (ἀμφιβάλλεται) with a ceremonial fillet.[12] The poet's task is somehow synonymous to the victor's: in *Pythian* 2 also jealous speakers are like defeated athletes wrestling empty thoughts (61) and dragging markers that are too long (90-91). The ode began with reference to gold and fire; now the poets come to the "rich hearth of Hieron." But, as we might expect at stanza end, new ideas are introduced that will be elaborated later. The song celebrates Zeus specifically as "son of Cronus"; Hieron's house is μάκαιρα, a term used to describe the happiness of the gods. Why this last line concentrates on celebration in the home rather than at the site of the games becomes increasingly apparent as the ode continues.

Our study of *Pythian* 2 and *Ode* 5 shows that the meaning of the opening stanza of *Olympian* 1 will be revealed gradually, in retrospect. The brightness of the gold will recur in references to Hieron's bright fame (23), Pelops' radiant shoulder (27), Hieron bright in song (14), Pelops mixed in bright blood sacrifices (91). The mysterious water turns up later in the ode in a way we would not have expected: boiling over fire, with Pelops in the caldron (48). The connection between these two references to water will seem less surprising when we think of *Pythian* 2, where the meaning of good response to god's gifts is explained by the examples of the greedy Ixion and "low speeches of slander" (76).

In *Ode* 5 Hieron's present good fortune is described by inverse image, the fates of Meleager and Heracles. Comparison with the first stanzas of *Pythian* 2 and *Ode* 5 makes the juxtaposition of images in the opening lines of *Olympian* 1 seem less sudden and confused. *Olympian* 1 and *Ode* 5 both begin with assertions: "best is water"; "general, you know the brightness of the Muses." Both proceed from there to a statement about poetry. In *Olympian* 1 "and if you want to talk of prizes, my heart, look no longer," has its analogue in "look here in your mind: now with the Joys deep bound he has woven a song of praise from the holy island" in *Ode* 5. 8-11. In *Pythian* 2 Pindar similarly says, after the invocation to Syracuse, "to you I come, this song from shining Thebes I bear" (3-4).

Each of the three odes begins with a staccato series of closely related statements: in *Pythian* 2 "Syracuse . . . precinct . . . nurse," in *Ode* 5 "you know, make your heart cease from care . . . look here in your mind," in *Olympian* 1 "water . . . gold . . . prizes . . . Olympia." *Ode* 5 begins, surprisingly, with praise of the victory, while Pindar's two odes reach Hieron only in the concluding lines of their first strophes, through a series of intricately dependent clauses: in *Pythian* 2 "rig *in which* Hieron bound . . . the shrine of Artemis . . . not *without whom* did he tame," in *Olympian* 1 "Olympia *from where* the song is thrown about the plans of poets . . . *after* they come to the hearth of Hieron." These underlying structures would have instinctively prepared ancient ears for what seem to us like sudden and inexplicable transitions.

> θεμιστεῖον ὃς ἀμφέπει σκᾶπτον ἐν πολυμήλῳ
> Σικελίᾳ δρέπων μὲν κορυφὰς ἀρετᾶν ἄπο πασᾶν,
> ἀγ'λαΐζεται δὲ καί
> 15 μουσικᾶς ἐν ἀώτῳ,
> οἷα παίζομεν φίλαν
> ἄνδρες ἀμφὶ θαμὰ τράπεζαν. ἀλλὰ Δω-
>   ρίαν ἀπὸ φόρμιγγα πασσάλου
> λάμβαν', εἴ τί τοι Πίσας τε καὶ Φερενίκου χάρις
> νόον ὑπὸ γλυκυτάταις ἔθηκε φροντίσιν,
> 20 ὅτε παρ' Ἀλφεῷ σύτο δέμας
> ἀκέντητον ἐν δρόμοισι παρέχων,
> κράτει δὲ προσέμειξε δεσπόταν,
>
>   (12-22, antistrophe 1)

In *Pythian* 2 the first antistrophe praises the victor and describes his victory with continued emphasis on cooperation among gods, men, and horses. In *Olympian* 1 also, traditional praise in the antistrophe is phrased in the language of the strophe, with emphasis on superlatives, light, and celebration in the home: "who grasps his righteous sceptre in

Sicily of many apples, and he is made bright in the height of music (songs), which we men often play in friendship round his table."

The Homeric formula about the king "to whom Zeus entrusts a staff and right directions (θέμιστας) so that he may give counsel to his people (*Il.* 9.98-99) has been amalgamated into a new statement about excellence. The crop the king harvests in Sicily of many apples is, remarkably, *areta*.[13] The κορυφαί of this excellence are matched in the ἄωτος ("top") of music.[14]

Bacchylides describes Hieron's impressive patronage of the arts in *Ode* 5: "you know the brightness, sweet gift of violet-crowned Muses, if any of today's men on earth knows it, rightly," suggesting what he will elaborate later about the limitations of human perception. In *Olympian* 1, stress falls instead on the close relationship between poet and patron. Conventional ξενία (e.g., *Ode* 5. 11) becomes a description of poets like παῖδες in Hieron's house, playing rather than laboring at their songs; Pindar spoke also in the strophe of his eagerness to sing (ἔλδεαι, 4). The poets were first seen coming to Hieron's hearth (11); now the scene is explicitly the banquet table, τράπεζα.

"But the Dorian lyre from its peg take once again, if the joy of Pisa and Pherenicus have placed your mind beneath thoughts most sweet." The herald in Alcinous' palace pulls a shrill lyre from its peg (ἐκ πασσαλόφιν φόρμιγγα), so the bard can sing to the assembled company (*Od.* 8. 105). But now the song is Dorian, for the Corinthian colony Syracuse, and continuous: λάμβανε ("keep on taking"), though the victory itself is only a single occurrence, ἔθηκε. As in the opening stanza, the theme is expressed conditionally, "if the joy . . . has placed," "if you want to sing" (3-4), with a resultant emphasis on the poet's ability to create and choose. Again song seems to surround, placing the mind beneath thoughts, as earlier it was thrown around the plans of poets" (8-9). A superlative (γλυκυτάταις) marks the description of successful competition, "when he (Pherenicus) beside the Alpheus rushed holding his body unspurred in the race and mixed his master with strength." The poet wants to sing (3-4); men play like children for Hieron (16); so Hieron's horse also runs "unspurred."

This singular race is described by Bacchylides in *Ode* 5 with emphasis instead on danger, "never did dust from other horses defile him as he rushed toward the goal" (43-45); he ran "like the North wind's hurling" (46), and a winning arrow shot (48-49). But Pindar states dramatically that Pherenicus κράτει προσέμειξε δεσπόταν, as if to remind us of the table (17) and the mixing of wine and water for the victory banquet. What in Pythian 2 was a sinister characterization of unlawful combination (ἐμφύλιον αἷμα ἐπέμειξε, 32; ἵπποισι ἐμείγνυτο, 45) in *Olympian* 1 expresses a positive communion.

Συρακόσιον ἱπποχάρ-
μαν βασιλῆα· λάμπει δέ οἱ κλέος
ἐν εὐάνορι Λυδοῦ Πέλοπος ἀποικίᾳ·
25 τοῦ μεγασθενὴς ἐράσσατο Γαιάοχος
Ποσειδάν, ἐπεί νιν καθαροῦ λέβη-
τος ἔξελε Κλωθώ,
ἐλέφαντι φαίδιμον ὦμον κεκαδ'μένον.
ἦ θαύματα πολλά, καί πού τι καὶ βροτῶν
φάτις ὑπὲρ τὸν ἀλαθῆ λόγον
δεδαιδαλμένοι ψεύδεσι ποικίλοις
ἐξαπατῶντι μῦθοι.

(23-29, epode 1)

The epode begins by returning specifically to the victor Hieron, "the king of Syracuse who rejoices in horses." This phrase, by reiterating themes already stated, indicates, much like a musical coda, that the opening section of the ode is drawing to an end. What was stated elaborately earlier is now stated in almost elemental form: "who grasps his rightful staff in Sicily of many apples" has become simply "Syracusan king"; "the joy of Pisa and Pherenicus" is now a single epithet, **ἱπποχάρ-μαν**.

The many references to light in the strophe and antistrophe are recapitulated here in "his fame shines (**λάμπει**)." So also in *Pythian* 2 reference to Hieron preceded the narration of the story of Ixion: "of you, son of Deinomenes, the Zephyrian Locrian maiden sings before her home, out from helpless weariness of war, through your power she looks forth in safety. At the gods' command they tell that Ixion says this to mortals" (18-22). In *Olympian* 1 the transition to the myth is equally swift: Hieron's fame "shines in the new home with her good men of Lydian Pelops." On the most direct level the phrase means that Hieron is famous in the Peloponnesus, site of Olympia. But at the same time **Λυδοῦ Πέλοπος ἀποικίᾳ** constitutes a summary of the hero Pelops' life story: his exile from his birthplace in Asia Minor, his settling in Mycenae, and giving his name to the south of Greece. In *Pythian* 2 the story similarly begins with a précis of its contents: "Ixion says this to mortals as he is spun round everywhere on his winged wheel: a benefactor repays those who come up to him with gentle exchange" (21-24).

The story of Pelops was of course familiar to Pindar's audience: his father Tantalus killed him and served him to the gods for dinner. Zeus restored him to life, replacing with ivory a portion of his shoulder, which Demeter had eaten by mistake.[15] But no one could have expected what Pindar says next: "for whom the Earth-holder great in strength lusted, Poseidon, when Clotho seized him from a pure caldron, surpassing with his shoulder radiant with ivory." Poseidon's love for Pelops is

Pindar's own invention; so is the idea that Pelops was born with an ivory shoulder.[16]

In *Pythian* 2 also Pindar changed the traditional story of Ixion's punishment to illustrate that greed is self-destructive. He states the revision cryptically at first: "they tell that Ixion says this to mortals as he is spun round everywhere on his winged wheel: a benefactor repays those who come up to him with gentle exchange" (22-24). The reference to wheels, "gentle," and "benefactor" indicate that the story has something to do with the description of Pindar and of Hieron in the opening stanzas, but the exact interrelationships become clear only later in the ode.

So in *Olympian* 1 the description of Pelops' "radiant shoulder" reminds us of Hieron, whose "fame shines" and the light in the water, gold, fire, and sun in the ode's opening lines. **κεκαδμένον** connotes preeminence: so gold is valued over other wealth, sun over other stars, Olympia over other contests, Phrenicus beyond other horses. To the ancient audience φαίδιμον ὦμον would bring to mind Odysseus carrying his oar inland on his φαιδίμῳ ὤμῳ at the conclusion of his journeying (*Od*. 11. 128): the recollection marks Pelops as a hero from his birth. "From a pure caldron" (λέβης, a large bowl also used for cooking), provides a first indication of the significance of the water whose excellence was established in the opening line, i.e., its power to cleanse.

"There are many wonders, and somewhere somehow too men's talkings beyond the true account, ornate with intricate lies, are stories that deceive." **ἦ θαύματα πολλά** anticipates our surprised reaction to the lines preceding, with the new story about Poseidon: Pindar's explanation is simply that the traditional myth is a lie men have "somehow" invented. The compressed language describing the lies hints at but does not fully explain the process. "Talkings," (φάτις) are "stories" (μῦθοι). In contrast to the single true account (ἀλαθῆ λόγον) these talkings are many in number and "ornate" (δεδαιδαλμένοι, "worked over") with intricate (ποικίλοις, varied) lies beautiful and carefully put together, like a painting. "How" and "where" the lies were devised is left in suspense to be described in the next triad.

As modern readers, rather than ancient listeners, it is only natural that we might feel at this point rather dazed. So much has been suggested in so few words, so many ideas associated that in ordinary life have no logical relation. The ancient audience, more accustomed than we to making connections between similar words and actions on first hearing, would have more readily understood the juxtaposition of absolutes in the ode's opening lines, and the emphasis on competition expressed in repeated comparatives and superlatives. "Hearth" to them would have connoted instantly the fires and cooking so often disassociated in today's electric kitchens; table would mean specifically dinner table: they would not have to think why it was unusual for a race horse to run unspurred. But startling juxtaposition like "gold blazing fire" (1) in the opening line and metaphors like "mixed his master with strength" (22) bear little resemblance to the more leisurely character of conventional hexameter verse. For the ancients too the ode, with its short, excited meters, and its confident assertions, must have seemed a tour-de-force.

> Χάρις δ', ἅπερ ἅπαντα τεύχει τὰ μείλιχα θνατοῖς,
> ἐπιφέροισα τιμὰν καὶ ἄπιστον ἐμήσατο πιστόν
> ἔμμεναι τὸ πολλάκις·
> ἁμέραι δ' ἐπίλοιποι
> μάρτυρες σοφώτατοι.
> 35 ἔστι δ' ἀνδρὶ φάμεν ἐοικὸς ἀμφὶ δαι-
> μόνων καλά· μείων γὰρ αἰτία.
> υἱὲ Ταντάλου, σὲ δ' ἀντία προτέρων φθέγξομαι,
> ὁπότ' ἐκάλεσε πατὴρ τὸν εὐνομώτατον
> ἐς ἔρανον φίλαν τε Σίπυλον,
> ἀμοιβαῖα θεοῖσι δεῖπνα παρέχων,
> 40 τότ' Ἀγλαοτρίαιναν ἁρπάσαι,
>
> (30-40, strophe 2)

The first lines of the second triad continue to discuss the power of the spoken word: "and joy who makes all things sweet for mortals brings honor and many times plans that unbelievable be believable, and the days that are left are witnesses most wise." τεύχει characterizes Χάρις as a craftsman; falsehood, too, as we have just heard in the last lines of the first epode is the product of skilled hands, δεδαιδαλμένοι ψεύδεσι ποικίλοις μῦθοι (29).

But as the sentence continues, it turns out that while χάρις and stories both use artifice, the end result differs. χάρις brings honor on men (ἐπιφέροισα), like a judge placing a wreath on the victor's head; earlier the χάρις of Pisa and Pherenicus placed the poet's mind beneath sweetest thoughts (18-19), and song was described as a fillet thrown around the μητίεσσι of poets (8-9). Now Χάρις herself "has planned" (ἐμήσατο) that the unbelievable be believable. But songs or crowns or stories, because they are man-made, have limitations: θνατοῖς falls emphatically at line end; joy has planned not always but πολλάκις that the unbelievable be believable, and only time will tell whether or not the transformation has been successful.

Time is characterized as ἁμέραι σοφώτατοι; the sun of the opening lines is radiant ἐν ἁμέρᾳ (6), the poets whose plans the song surrounds are σοφοί (9). The days are also μάρτυρες, and the next lines describe song as if it were testimony: "it is right for a man to speak what is beautiful about the gods; the blame is less." In contrast to φάτις ὑπὲρ τὸν ἀλαθῆ λόγον (28b), φάμεν καλά is to tell the truth. But again the man's powers are restricted: speaking what is beautiful about the gods results in "less blame," not in "no blame," as if to imply that because of our mortality we will not be able to say or know the beautiful completely.

The general statement about φάμεν καλά prepares us for what follows: "son of Tantalus, I shall sing of you opposite from my predecessors." By calling the son by his father's name, Pindar indicates that Tantalus will play an important role in the story. Direct address also marked the poet's repeated singularizing references to himself in the first triad, "if you want to sing, my heart" (3-4), "look no longer" (5); "take your Dorian lyre from its peg" (17-18). ἀντία προτέρων separates the poet from other poets; gold shines out beyond other wealth, the sun is hotter than other stars, Olympia is greater than other contests. The attainment of singularity and preeminence will continue to be a major theme in the new myth.

After the condensation of this allusive introduction, the myth unfolds in an almost leisurely fashion, first by recapitulating the revisions of the myth already stated in the first epode: "when your father called the gods to a most lawful banquet in his own Sipylus, holding for the gods a dinner in exchange, then the Bright Trident god seized you." εὐνομώτατον ἐς ἔρανον brings out what was implied earlier in the careful description of Pelops' ivory shoulder: the horrible banquet of tradition never took place. Reference to Tantalus as πατήρ and to φίλαν Σίπυλον indicates that Tantalus' relationship to Pelops was normal and loving, like that of Hieron and the poets who play like children around Hieron's φίλαν τράπεζαν (16-17). Tantalus' dinner was held to repay the gods for a previous invitation, reminding us that the present separation between god and man did not then exist. Poseidon's title Ἀγλαοτρίαινας, coined by Pindar, reinforces our first impression that the abduction was as much an occasion of joy as the celebration of victory, where Hieron ἀγλαΐζεται in song (14).

> δαμέντα φ⟨ρένας ἱμέρῳ, χρυσέαισί τ' ἀν' ἵπποις
> ὕπατον εὐρυτίμου ποτὶ δῶμα Διὸς μεταβᾶσαι·
> ἔνθα δευτέρῳ χρόνῳ
> ἦλθε καὶ Γανυμήδης
> 45 Ζηνὶ τωὔτ' ἐπὶ χ⟨ρέος.
> ὡς δ' ἄφαντος ἔπελες, οὐδὲ ματρὶ πολ-
>   λὰ μαιόμενοι φῶτες ἄγαγον,
> ἔννεπε κ⟨ρυφᾷ τις αὐτίκα φθονερῶν γειτόνων,
> ὕδατος ὅτι τε πυρὶ ζέοισαν εἰς ἀκμάν
> μαχαίρᾳ τάμον κατὰ μέλη,
> 50 τραπέζαισί τ' ἀμφὶ δεύτατα κρεῶν
> σέθεν διεδάσαντο καὶ φάγον.
>   (41-51, antistrophe 2)

In the introduction, the joy of Pisa and Pherenicus placed the poet's mind (νόον) beneath thoughts most sweet (18-19); now he describes how Poseidon seized Pelops "his heart (φρένας) mastered by desire, and on his golden horses went to the highest hall of wide-honored Zeus." In an ode that began with reference to gold, and where the victor harvests the "summits" of achievements, Poseidon's golden horses and Zeus' highest home confirm that Poseidon's love for Pelops is another instance of the beautiful that men should sing about the gods (35). "There at a second time Ganymede came also to Zeus for the same debt."

In *Pythian* 2 also maintaining right relationship with god involves repayment. But suddenly our attention is brought back to earth and the narrative is related from the human point of view. "When you were not seen, and men searching many times did not bring you back to your mother, someone straightway said in secret, an envious neighbor, that into the water's peak boiling with fire, with a knife they cut you limb by limb, and at the table into portions of meat they divided you and ate you." By describing Pelops' seizure in terms of visibility (ἄφαντος), Pindar turns from the bright world of the gods to a mortal existence characterized by separation and jealousy. Pelops does not come back to his mother, stories are told in secret, neighbors are envious, like Archilochus, the low speeches of slander, and the standard-draggers in *Pythian* 2 (54-56, 76, 90-91).

The careful detail with which the story is related illustrates how "men's talk beyond the true account" can in fact become "ornate with intricate lies, stories that deceive" (28b-29). The standard procedures for sacrifice of smaller animals are followed: cutting into pieces (cattle are roasted in sections), grouping of the cooked pieces, division into portions. The water and heights that marked supremacy at the ode's opening are transformed dramatically into the "boiling water's peak" into which Pelops is cast, without the prayers that accompany all pious sacrifices (e.g. *Od.* 3. 430-446). The table (τράπεζα) about which the poets played for Hieron (16-17) is now the scene of a cannibal feast.

Pindar's language helps us understand that the false story of Pelops represents the antithesis of the achievement celebrated in the opening lines of the ode. So in *Pythian* 2, Ixion is the egregious example of ingratitude that demonstrates why due thanks must be paid to benefactors, and in *Ode* 5, Meleager and Heracles are foils for Hieron's "destiny of the beautiful" (1, 51). The stanza ends emphatically with φάγον, without ever specifying who in fact did the eating.

> ἐμοὶ δ' ἄπορα γαστρίμαρ-
> γον μακάρων τιν' εἰπεῖν· ἀφίσταμαι·
> ἀκέρδεια λέλογχεν θαμινὰ κακαγόρους.
> εἰ δὲ δή τιν' ἄνδρα θνατὸν Ὀλύμπου σκοποί

55 ἐτίμασαν, ἦν Τάνταλος οὗτος· ἀλ-
λὰ γὰρ καταπέψαι
μέγαν ὄλβον οὐκ ἐδυνάσθη, κόρῳ δ' ἕλεν
ἄταν ὑπέροπ'λον, ἅν τοι πατὴρ ὕπερ
κρέμασε καρτερὸν αὐτῷ λίθον,
τὸν αἰεὶ μενοινῶν κεφαλᾶς βαλεῖν
εὐφροσύνας ἀλᾶται.
(52-58, epode 2)

The traditional story, that Demeter ate Pelops' shoulder, is never told. The right course of action, "speaking what is beautiful about the gods" (35) prevents the poet from relating the shameful story even if it is untrue: "for me there is no way to say one of the blessed is stomachmad. I stand aside." The new γαστρίμαργος does not connote cannibalism so much as ordinary greed. μάκαρος describes also Hieron's hearth, where poets willingly sing of their friend's achievement (11). From a tradition that would equate the world of the blessed with that of men, the poet stands apart as if in political revolt (ἀφίσταμαι), reiterating the separation expressed earlier, "I shall sing of you opposite from my predecessors." (36). The poet's actions are no less singularizing than the victor's.

A general observation then makes the association between greed and ungodlike behavior explicit: "many losses (literally, un-gains) reward speakers of evil." The syndrome of evil repaying evil is, of course, a theme that Pindar develops in more detail in *Pythian* 2, where Archilochus fattens on hatred (54-56), and low speeches of slander are an evil unconquerable, for gain not gainful (κέρδει ... κερδαλέον, 76-78). Pindar continues instead with his own "true" version of the story: "if the watchers of Olympus honored any mortal man, it was this Tantalus," stressing the close relation that once existed between man and god in the language that earlier described victory, the joy that brings honor (31), the days that are witnesses of success (34).

We speculate now about the role of "this Tantalus" in Pindar's story. If the dinner Tantalus held for the gods was "most lawful" (37) and not a cannibal feast, why was Tantalus ultimately excluded from the gods' company, and condemned to eternal suffering, as the old story tells? The description of the jealous neighbor and of the speakers of evil leads us to expect how Pindar will characterize Tantalus' crime and punishment: man's greed leads to his own destruction.

Pindar dramatically phrases his new story in the language of the old false tale: "but he could not digest his great prosperity and seized in his satisfaction high delusion." Tantalus himself, instead of one of the gods, becomes "stomach mad," not for human flesh, but for ὄλβος. The details of his greed are left mysteriously unexplained until we hear of its consequences: Tantalus seized high delusion, "which the father hung high above his head, a strong stone, which he strives ever to throw from his head and wanders from contentment."

In *Pythian* 2 Ixion embraces a "sweet falsehood that Zeus made as a trap for him" (37-39), fitting punishment to the crime. That Tantalus' ἄτη is a strong stone indicates that his wrong-doing did not consist of mere gluttony for food—if that were so, Pindar would have retained Homer's story that Tantalus was eternally condemned to hunger for food and thirst for water that he could see but never touch (*Od.* 11. 582-592).

Instead Pindar tells another ancient tale, that Zeus placed a stone above his head that follows him wherever he goes and always threatens to fall upon him.[17] The purpose of this punishment is constantly to threaten death: as long as he fears that pain and death are imminent his existence will lack the εὐφροσύνα that the blessed gods enjoy, and that the poet himself feels when singing of Hieron's victory ("if Pisa and Pherenicus placed your mind beneath thoughts most sweet," 18-19). The words which describe Tantalus' punishment provide a clear contrast with the happier scenes described earlier in the ode: "high delusion" has replaced "the summits of all achievements" (13) and the "highest home" of Zeus (42); Zeus πατήρ hangs a stone above the head of Tantalus who as πατήρ had invited the gods to a banquet (37); Tantalus wanders as he tries to throw (βαλεῖν) the stone from his head, but song is thrown (ἀμφιβάλλεται) around the plans of poets as they come to Hieron's hearth (8-9).

> ἔχει δ' ἀπάλαμον βίον τοῦτον ἐμπεδόμοχθον
> 60 μετὰ τριῶν τέταρτον πόνον, ἀθανάτους ὅτι κλέψαις
> ἁλίκεσσι συμπόταις
> νέκταρ ἀμβροσίαν τε
> δῶκεν, οἷσιν ἄφθιτον
> θέν νιν. εἰ δὲ θεὸν ἀνήρ τις ἔλπεταί
> ⟨τι⟩ λαθέμεν ἔρδων, ἁμαρτάνει.
> 65 τοὔνεκα {οἱ} π'ροῆκαν υἱὸν ἀθάνατοί ⟨οἱ⟩ πάλιν
> μετὰ τὸ ταχύποτμον αὖτις ἀνέρων ἔθνος.
> πρὸς εὐάνθεμον δ' ὅτε φυάν
> λάχναι νιν μέλαν γένειον ἔρεφον,
> ἑτοῖμον ἀνεφρόντισεν γάμον
>
> (59-69, strophe 3)

The third strophe explains why Zeus chose the hanging stone as punishment for Tantalus: "he has a life he cannot handle, this, fixed in toil, among three a fourth suffering, because he stole from the immortals for his drinking companions, nectar and ambrosia he gave them, with which they had made him deathless." ἀπάλαμος describes in Homer the condition of the poor, useless, and weak. The new ἐμπεδόμοχθος emphasizes that he is deprived of joy and movement; he has continuing life but without the control which brings pleasure: unlike Poseidon, he cannot go at will to the high home of Zeus (42), unlike the poet he cannot stand aside (52), instead he "wanders from contentment, trying ever to throw from his head" the stone that threatens pain and death (58).

"Among three a fourth punishment" alludes to Ixion on his winged wheel, lustful Tityus having his liver eaten by vultures, greedy Sisyphus forever pushing a stone uphill. For these men continued life is accompanied by desires that ensure continued suffering.[18] So Tantalus' punishment fits his crime of wishing to give man immortality. As in the traditional story, the crime in Pindar's revised version concerns what was eaten at a banquet, but with emphasis that the gods were not participants, ἀθανάτους κλέψαις.

But the disparity between man and god cannot be overcome: "if a man hopes that what he does can escape god, he errs." The word order stresses the contrast, θεὸν ἀνήρ. Gods live forever young and know all things; men grow old and die and know only in part. Tantalus' attempt to deceive the gods ends for his son also association with divinity: "so the immortals sent back his son again to the swift-dying race of men." In contrast to αθάνατοι, ταχύποτμον ἔθνος expresses the basic conditions of mortal life: death, brevity, anonymity, which are then described more fully in the brief description of Pelops' maturing: "and when on his well-flowered growth the hairs sheltered his dark chin." Human life has the transience and beauty of vegetation, εὐάνθεμος φυά. The transition from youth to manhood takes place in an instant: his chin is dark before hairs roof it over (ἔρεφον); immediately "he thought of a marriage ready." The gods live forever, and Tantalus' existence is "fixed-in-suffering," but Pelops' life is marked by insistent change.

Again the stanza ends at the beginning of a new story: we know the traditional tale of how Pelops won Hippodameia from her covetous father Oenomaus, who insisted that only the suitor who beat him in a chariot race would win his daughter as bride. In the conventional story Pelops wins by bribing Oenomaus' charioteer to tamper with the wheels of Oenomaus' chariot. Reference to the mind's action, ἀνεφρόντισεν, brings the stanza to a close without resolution: did he think up a plot, as in the old story, or will his thought, like the poet's sweetest φροντίσι about Pisa and Pherenicus (18-19), concern instead achievement won through excellence?

70 Πισάτα παρὰ πατ⌐ρὸς εὔδοξον Ἱπποδάμειαν
    σχεθέμεν. ἐγγὺς {δ᾽} ἐλθὼν πολιᾶς ἁλὸς οἶος ἐν ὄρφνᾳ
    ἄπυεν βαρύκτυπον

Εὐτρίαιναν· ὁ δ' αὐτῷ
πὰρ ποδὶ σχεδὸν φάνη.
75 τῷ μὲν εἶπε· 'Φίλια δῶρα Κυπ¹ρίας
ἄγ' εἴ τι, Ποσείδαον, ἐς χάριν
τέλλεται, πέδασον ἔγχος Οἰνομάου χάλκεον,
ἐμὲ δ' ἐπὶ ταχυτάτων πόρευσον ἁρμάτων
ἐς Ἆλιν, κράτει δὲ πέλασον.
ἐπεὶ τρεῖς τε καὶ δέκ' ἄνδρας ὀλέσαις
80 μναστῆρας ἀναβάλλεται γάμον
(70-80, antistrophe 3)

The story begins with the familiar details "to have from her father Pisatas famous Hippodameia." The unusual Pisatas (instead of Oenomaus) reminds us that the home of Pelops is Olympia. But the account of Pelops' contest with Oenomaus breaks completely with tradition: "and going near the grey sea alone at night he called on the Deep-thunderer, the Good-trident, and he was seen before him close at his feet." Instead of plotting with his charioteer to tamper with Oenomaus' chariot, Pelops asks aid from his divine lover, much as Achilles in the *Iliad*, "weeping sat away from his comrades, set apart, on the shore of the grey sea (ἁλὸς πολιῆς) looking out on the dark ocean, he prayed to his mother" (*Il.* 1. 348-351).[19]

In *Olympian* 1 especially isolation connotes supremacy, the gold shining beyond great men's wealth (1-2), the sun hotter than other stars. Rather than tell a story of treachery and deception, Pindar continues to speak "what is beautiful about the gods" (35). Poseidon comes to Pelops as quickly as Thetis comes to Achilles in the *Iliad* (1. 359-362). New epithets, βαρύκτυπος and Εὐτρίαινας, convey both his power and his special role as benefactor in this story: he was Ἀγλαοτρίαινας when he first saw Pelops (40). Again emphasis falls on vision, φάνη, just as Pelops in the false story was ἄφαντος (46). The poet asked himself at the beginning of the ode, "if you want to talk of games, dear heart" (3-4), "if the joy of Pisa and Pherenicus placed your mind beneath thoughts most sweet" (18-19).

Accordingly, Pelops' request to Poseidon implicitly anticipates an enthusiastic response: "if Cypris' gifts of friendship grow in any way to joy, shackle the bronze spear of Oenomaus, and bring me to Elis in your swiftest chariot, and be close in your strength, since he has killed thirteen men, her suitors, and throws off the marriage." Friendship is characteristic of Pindar's song (φίλον ἦτορ, 4) and the victory celebration (φίλαν τράπεζαν, 16-17); χάρις is the reward of victory (18, 30).[20] Like the poet in the proem Pelops moves from a questioning "if" to a series of commands. He asks Poseidon to bring him to Elis with his swiftest chariot, as he once took him to Zeus' highest home with "his golden horses" (41).

κράτει πέλασον takes us back again to Hieron and Pherenicus, who in victory κράτει προσέμειξε δεσπόταν (22). By contrast, Oenomaus' fate will be "shackled" (πέδασον, "bind the feet"), as Tantalus received a punishment ἐμπεδόμοχθον ("with suffering fixed at his feet," 59). Tantalus' punishment was μετὰ τριῶν τέταρτον, fourth with three other men (60); the deaths of Hippodameia's suitors are also specifically numbered, τρεῖς τε καὶ δέκα. Oenomaus ἀναβάλλεται his daughter's marriage; Tantalus strives to βαλεῖν the rock from his head (58). "Marriage" (γάμον) falls at line end, as at the end of the third strophe, contrasting Pelops' wishes ἀνεφρόντισεν γάμον (69) with Oenomaus', ἀναβάλλεται γάμον.

    θυγατ'ρός. ὁ μέγας δὲ κίν-
      δυνος ἄναλκιν οὐ φῶτα λαμβάνει.
    θανεῖν δ' οἷσιν ἀνάγκα, τά κέ τις ἀνώνυμον
    γῆρας ἐν σκότῳ καθήμενος ἕψοι μάταν,
    ἁπάντων καλῶν ἄμμορος; ἀλλ' ἐμοὶ
      μὲν οὗτος ἄεθ'λος
85 ὑποκείσεται· τὺ δὲ πρᾶξιν φίλαν δίδοι.'
    ὣς ἔννεπεν· οὐδ' ἀκράντοις ἐφάψατο
    ἔπεσι. τὸν μὲν ἀγάλλων θεός
    ἔδωκεν δίφρον τε χ'ρύσεον πτεροῖ-
      σίν τ' ἀκάμαντας ἵππους.
                              (81-87, epode 3)

The first word of the epode, θυγατρός, switches the emphasis from Oenomaus to the prize of victory, Hippodameia. Her importance depends in large measure on the fact that she must be won in competition, and not just acquired in negotiation, like an ordinary bride: "great risks take no one without courage. Since we must die, why should one sit in darkness, stewing one's nameless old age, with no share in all that's beautiful. This prize will lie before me; in friendship give me its accomplishment."

As in the ode's introduction, achievement involves movement. The poet tells himself "take (λάμβανε) your Dorian lyre from its peg" to sing of Pherenicus' victory at Olympia (18). So Clotho "seized" (ἔξελε) the baby Pelops from a pure caldron (26), and Tantalus, unable to digest his great prosperity, "seized (ἔλεν) high delusion" (56). As in the case of Tantalus, a fixed existence denotes failure: ἐν σκότῳ καθήμενος, is like the condition of the other wealth that does not shine out at night, like gold (1-2).

The dramatic ἕψοι ("stew") firmly connects the dark, static anonymous old age with Tantalus and his inability to καταπέψαι ("digest") his great prosperity (55-56). Stewing was Pelops' fate in the false story of his sacrifice: "into the water's peak boiling with fire they cut you limb by limb" (48-49). The significance of stewing Pelops, rather than roasting him in the traditional manner, now is manifest. Slow, confining, it is the antithesis of all that goodness and achievement promise.

To the neighbor's false story we can now compare the true Pelops, hero and victor. ἁπάντων καλῶν matches Hieron's ἀρετᾶν πασᾶν (13). In the proem, the poet sings of ἄεθλα (3-4); Pelops' marriage also is ἄεθλος. ὑποκείσεται again characterizes achievement in terms of height: Hieron harvests the summits of achievement (13); his victory places the poet's mind "beneath (ὑπὸ ... ἔθηκε) sweetest thoughts" (18-19). Like the poet, Pelops can imagine great achievement, but others must help make his visions realities.

φίλαν δίδοι, in a speech that began φίλια δῶρα (75), signals a conclusion. Pelops' speech is brief, the language compressed and metaphorical, but reminiscence makes it immediately comprehensible and contributes to its remarkable effect. The link between Hieron and Pelops implied at the start of the myth, "his (Hieron's) fame shines in the new home of Lydian Pelops" (23-24), is elaborated, and the interrelation of victory with poetry, first stated in the characterization of song as victors' wreaths (8-9), becomes associated in our minds with the glory man wins through god's help and love.[21]

"So he spoke, and he did not lay hold of words without fulfillment." The formal conclusion, ὣς ἔννεπεν, evokes the epic setting with which Pelops' speech began. The negative οὐκ ἀκράντοις again suggests the possibility of failure: "great risks seize no one without courage" (81). In Homer the phrase ἔπε' ἀκράαντα occurs only once, in the description of false dreams coming out through the gate of ivory (*Od.* 19.565). But ἐφάψατο has clear affirmative associations with the taking and seizing that mark constructive change in the ode, "great risks take (λαμβάνει) no one without courage" (81), in contrast to Tantalus' "life he cannot handle" (ἀπάλαμον, 59).

The concluding lines, "the god honored him and gave him a gold chariot and horses with wings untiring," immediately imply success: Hieron the victor "is honored" (ἀγλαΐζεται) in the height of music (14-15); Poseidon, when he seized Pelops, had golden horses (41); gold's preeminence is the subject of the poem's opening line. Pherenicus held himself "unspurred in the running"; Poseidon's horses are "tireless." The language in which the golden chariot is described, with the emphatic conclusion πτεροῖσίν τ'ἀκάμαντας ἵππους conveys the antithesis of the static, dark old age Pelops rejects, and the punishment of Tantalus described at the end of the second epode.[22]

ἕλεν δ' Οἰνομάου βίαν παρθένον τε σύνευνον·
ἔτεκε λαγέτας ἓξ ἀρεταῖσι μεμαότας υἱούς.
90   νῦν δ' ἐν αἱμακουρίαις
ἀγ'λααῖσι μέμικται,
Ἀλφεοῦ πόρῳ κλιθείς,
τύμβον ἀμφίπολον ἔχων πολυξενω-
τάτῳ παρὰ βωμῷ· τὸ δὲ κ'λέος
τηλόθεν δέδορκε τᾶν Ὀλυμπιάδων ἐν δρόμοις
95   Πέλοπος, ἵνα ταχυτὰς ποδῶν ἐρίζεται
ἀκμαί τ' ἰσχύος θρασύπονοι·
ὁ νικῶν δὲ λοιπὸν ἀμφὶ βίοτον
ἔχει μελιτόεσσαν εὐδίαν

(88-98, strophe 4)

In comparison to the long contemplation in his speech of his contest with Oenomaus, the story of Pelops' life, like the description of his growing up, is brief. His youth took place in a moment, "and when on his well-flowered growth the hairs sheltered his dark chin" (67-68); his maturing is also described in the space of two lines: "he seized Oenomaus' power and the maiden to share his bed; he begot six rulers who strove for achievement, his sons."

Language again joins past to present: Pelops seized (ἕλεν) the might of Oenomaus and his daughter as bride, while his father instead ἕλεν his delusion (56). Clotho also seized (ἔξελεν, 26) Pelops from a pure basin: the repetition signifies that the narrative is drawing to an end. Pelops' sons are rulers; Hieron is king (23). The sons strive for achievements, **ἀρεταῖσι μεμαότας**; Hieron harvests the summits of **ἀρετᾶν** (13), but Tantalus instead strives (**μενοινῶν**) to throw the stone from his head (58).

The story began by addressing Pelops as υἱὲ **Ταντάλου**; now it ends with his own **υἱούς**. Pelops' shrine at Olympia is described in terms that earlier described Hieron's triumph: "and now he is mixed in glorious blood sacrifice, near the path of the Alpheus, he has a tomb beside an altar with many visitors; his fame looks far out in the races of the Olympiads of Pelops, where the speed of feet is contested and the peak of might bold in suffering." Pelops **ἀγλααῖσι μέμικται**, as Hieron is "made bright" (**ἀγλαΐζεται**) in song (14) and as Pherenicus mixed (**προσέμειξε**) his master with might (22).

The ode began with feasting, Pelops' story began at a banquet (37-38), now he is celebrated in sacrifices. He is buried **Ἀλφεοῦ πόρῳ κλιθείς**; Pherenicus in victory rushed **παρ' Ἀλφεῷ** (20). His tomb has many visitors; poets come to the rich hearth of Hieron. **κλέος τηλόθεν δέδορκε** virtually echoes the description of Hieron's fame at the beginning of the myth (**λάμπει κλέος**, 23-24); Pelops is celebrated **ἐν δρόμοις** (94); Pherenicus held his body unspurred ἐν δρόμοισιν (21).

Again there is the emphasis on vision with which the ode began (5). The ἀκμαί of contests have replaced the ἀκμάν of water in the false story (48). The new θρασύπονοι associates the pain involved in winning with the power that has brought all accomplishment so far in the ode, as opposed to the helpless πόνος of Tantalus (60). Tantalus ἔχει ἀπάλαμον βίον (59), but the winner for what's left of his life has (ἔχει) sweet bright weather. The joy of victory makes τὰ μείλιχα for mortals; ἁμέραι ἐπίλοιποι judge success (30, 33-34). Without these previous statements, this concluding sentence about bright weather would seem truistic, but in the context of the ode reference to εὐδία connotes achievement: the brightness of gold, Pelops' movement from the grey sea at night to a fame that looks far out beyond Olympia.

> ἀέθ'λων γ' ἕνεκεν· τὸ δ' αἰεὶ παράμερον ἐσλόν
> 100 ὕπατον ἔρχεται παντὶ βροτῶν. ἐμὲ δὲ στεφανῶσαι
> κεῖνον ἱππίῳ νόμῳ
> Αἰοληΐδι μολπᾷ
> χρή· πέποιθα δὲ ξένον
> μή τιν' ἀμφότερα καλῶν τε ἴδ'ριν †ἅ-
> μα καὶ δύναμιν κυριώτερον
> 105 τῶν γε νῦν κλυταῖσι δαιδαλωσέμεν ὕμνων πτυχαῖς.
> θεὸς ἐπίτροπος ἐὼν τεαῖσι μήδεται
> ἔχων τοῦτο κᾶδος, Ἱέρων,
> μερίμναισιν· εἰ δὲ μὴ ταχὺ λίποι,
> ἔτι γ'λυκυτέραν κεν ἔλπομαι
>
> (99-109, antistrophe 4)

In the final antistrophe our attention is turned from contest to victory: "(the winner has sweet bright weather) because of his prizes." The ode opened with reference to ἄεθλα (3), and Pelops bravely asserted, "this prize (ἄεθλος) belongs to me" (84). Another generalization reaffirms that success to be meaningful must endure beyond the instant of victory. Poseidon took Pelops to Zeus' "highest (ὕπατον) home" (42); now ὕπατον (in the same exact metrical position) again defines an ultimate: "the good that lasts day after day comes highest to every mortal."

The ode began with a description of the sun ἐν ἁμέρᾳ (6), and ἁμέραι ἐπίλοιποι were said to be wisest witnesses of success (33). In contrast to *Pythian* 2, where the myth concluded with resounding praise of god (49-52), the second praise in *Olympian* 1 concentrates on man's capacity for achievement, and its meaning within his lifetime.

A reference to the poet himself, the first since the second epode, brings us back to Hieron: "and that man I must crown in a horseman's measure in an Aeolic rhythm." The song itself is a victor's crown, as in the opening stanza song "is thrown around the plans of poets" (8-9). Close repetition of familiar themes hints that the song is ending. The poet sings ἱππίῳ νόμῳ Αἰοληῒδι μολπᾷ, in the introduction Hieron was ἱπποχάρμας (23) and the poet sang to a Dorian lyre (17).

In the introduction the poet used words of deep commitment to describe his song (ἔλδεαι, 4), and stated his praise in terms of competition; so now also Hieron is singled out from other men, as one can look for "no star hotter in day than the sun" (6): "I believe I shall ornament no other friend who knows beauty more or is more masterful in power of today."[23] ἴδριν καλῶν attributes to Hieron the existence Pelops set out to achieve, the antithesis of sitting in darkness ἁπάντων καλῶν ἄμμορος (84). The same compliment in Ode 5 places particular emphasis on Hieron's patronage of song (3-5).

Reference to Hieron's military strength (δύναμιν), celebrated in more detail in Pythian 2, draws added significance in its contrast to the unsuccessful Tantalus "who could not (ἐδυνάσθη) digest his great prosperity (56).

The dramatic δαιδαλωσέμεν ὕμνων πτυχαῖς reminds us of the power of δεδαιδαλμένοι μῦθοι and their power to please and beautify (28b-29). But where men, like the neighbor or the evil speakers, ornament stories with lies in envy, in order to make other men's fortunes seem less favorable than their own, the poet's song both crowns and ornaments, like a judge honoring the victor at the games.[24] The ornamenting encloses Hieron ὕμνων πτυχαῖς, as the πολύφατος ὕμνος ἀμφιβάλλεται σοφῶν μητίεσσι (8-9), and the joy of victory puts the poet's mind beneath thoughts most sweet (19).

The next lines contain even greater praise for Hieron, "a god is turned toward your cares and plans, having them as his concern." The god, remarkably, takes on Hieron's problems as his own. Poseidon also came as Pelops called him, "and he was seen before him, close at his feet" (73-74). What is noteworthy about this description is that the god assumes powers traditionally assigned to poets: in Hesiod bards, as Bacchylides reminds us in Ode 5.7, by singing the famous deeds of men and of gods can make men forget their grief (κήδεα, Theogony 98-103).[25]

God "plans" (μήδεται) for Hieron, song is thrown around the μητίεσσι of poets (8-9), and χάρις ἐμήσατο that the unbelievable be believable (31). But the possibility of failure is still present, "if he does not leave swiftly, still I hope to sing." The swiftness (ταχυτάς) in competition at Olympia (95) is a quality also of life among the ταχύποτμον ἀνέρων ἔθνος (66).

Departure (λίποι) is inevitable: days are numbered (ἐπίλοιποι, 33), the victor's life limited (λοιπὸν βίοτον, 97). The beauty of the gods' presence, as in the case of Poseidon with Pelops, cannot remain long among men. The stanza ends without completing the sentence: ἔτι γλυκυτέραν κεν ἔλπομαι. A sweeter what? victory or song or both? And, in a poem so charged with comparison, what is it sweeter than?

> 110 σὺν ἅρματι θοῷ κλεΐ-
> ξειν ἐπίκουρον εὑρὼν ὁδὸν λόγων
> παρ' εὐδείελον ἐλθὼν Κρόνιον. ἐμοὶ μὲν ὦν
> Μοῖσα καρτερώτατον βέλος ἀλκᾷ τρέφει·
> ἄλλοισι δ' ἄλλοι μεγάλοι· τὸ δ' ἔ-
> σχατον κορυφοῦται
> βασιλεῦσι. μηκέτι πάπταινε πόρσιον.
> 115 εἴη σέ τε τοῦτον ὑψοῦ χρόνον πατεῖν,
> ἐμέ τε τοσσάδε νικαφόροις
> ὁμιλεῖν πρόφαντον σοφίᾳ καθ' Ἕλ-
> λανας ἐόντα παντᾷ.
>
> (110-117, epode 4)

The ode rushes to a conclusion with the same density and confidence with which it began. "With a swift chariot I'll make known" first makes us think γλυκυτέραν, left rootless in the preceding stanza, refers to a future chariot victory (νίκαν). Poseidon's "golden chariot and tireless horses with wings" came as reinforcement for Pelops (87), and before that to the "highest home of Zeus" (42). But suddenly the sweeter thing that Pindar will make known turns out to be ὁδόν, and then not an ordinary road, but a "road of speech." Separating adjective from noun by stanza break gives this simple sentence the widest possible range of meaning, again linking the achievement of victory and of song.

"When I go to far-seen Cronion" once again puts emphasis on vision, the steep hill rising conspicuously from the plain of the Alpheus. Poets also "come" to Hieron's hearth to sing the son of Cronus (9-10). "So for me the Muse cherishes her strongest weapon, with courage" (ἀλκᾷ) compares the poet's ambitions to Pelops, who states "great risks seize no one without courage" (ἄναλκιν, 81), and calls upon Poseidon for support. But a generalization, "different men are great in different ways," immediately acknowledges that the achievements of victor and poet, while similar, are not the same.

Each superlative in the opening lines was distinctive—water, gold at night, sun in day, Olympia. Now "the last summit is scaled by kings; look no longer beyond." The ultimate praise is due the victor; Hieron earlier harvested the κορυφὰς ἀρετᾶν (13); he is the βασιλεύς of Syracusans (23). μηκέτι πάπταινε πόρσιον, as if in mirror image, reiterates the command that marked the final comparison in the ode's first stanza "look no longer (μηκέτι σκόπει) for some other star radiant through the empty air in day hotter than the sun" (5-6).[26] Hieron, too, has achieved a singularity. But παπταίνειν in Homer connotes looking around in anxiety, glancing toward someone quickly.

The concluding prayer "may you through this time walk high" acknowledges impermanence, ὑψοῦ again describes human success in terms of height. Song also has hills and valleys, μουσικᾶς ἀώτῳ (15), ὕμνων πτυχαῖς (105). In the false story Pelops was thrown into the water's peak (ἀκμάν, 48); Tantalus lives below the stone Zeus "hung high above his head" (57-57b). There are no level stretches in man's life.

But in contrast to *Pythian* 2, which explores at length men's jealousies and failures, and *Ode* 5, which stresses the possibility of failure unforeseen, *Olympian* 1 concentrates on success. *Pythian* 2 ends with a quiet prayer of acceptance, "may I please and consort with the good"; *Ode* 5 with "may Zeus guard unmoved in peace." But in *Olympian* 1 the final prayer returns to the opening theme of competition, "may I stay so long with winners of victory, and be seen first in poetry among Greeks everywhere." The poet too is πρόφαντος, like the water, gold, and the sun. Vision again denotes success: Poseidon "is seen" (φάνη) before Pelops (74); Pelops is "unseen" (ἄφαντος) in the false story (46). The last word of the ode παντᾷ, keeps the emphasis where it began, on universals.

This final triad, in comparison to the complexities that preceded it, is comfortingly comprehensible. Each word reiterates or clarifies a theme that has previously been introduced; implicit associations are made explicit, Hieron with Pelops, poetry with victory, success with failure, so that in retrospect the intricate introduction seems to have presaged the contents of the ode. Heard out of context, many of the lines in this final triad would seem like ordinary proverbs ("different men are great in different ways," 113; "the good that lasts day after day comes highest to every mortal," 99-100) or would appear to be merely routine elements of praise ("the last summit is scaled by kings," 113-114); "I believe there is no other friend . . . more masterful," 103). But reminiscence from previous stanzas endows even these conventional ideas with new meaning.

To appreciate the effects of this reflection back and forth through reminiscence requires the kind of memory our society has long since lost, but Pindar's audience could easily have made the associations we must reconstruct by rereading. In recovering thus artificially some of the ancients' powers of memory, we can begin to see that Pindar's celebrated obscurity, like Bacchylides' celebrated simplicity, is a product of our own creation. Seemingly precipitous transitions or interjections follow established conventions of praise or narration; ostensibly sudden summary statements about human behavior are set in words that already carry or will acquire significance. This is not to say that *Olympian* 1 is or was as readily comprehensible as a prose or epic narrative, but that it could and did communicate its principal ideas on a first hearing to a Greek audience.

This is not to deny, however, that much of what Hieron and his friends heard in *Olympian* 1 would have seemed strikingly innovative: for example, Pindar's method of building up suspense at the end of strophes and antistrophes by leaving sentences incomplete, and his use of figurative rather than purely descriptive language, so that Pherenicus' winning run seems like an illustration of victory in general rather than a single remarkable event. More startling still would have been the way Pindar changes myth. Bacchylides in *Ode* 5 recreated a traditional encounter and conversation between Meleager and Heracles, skillfully emphasizing the similarities in their fates. Pindar changes both the sequence and actors in narratives, for an explicitly moral purpose. But he must have seemed most truly avant-garde in the stress he places on human achievement, man's competition, and striving for success. Like Bacchylides, Pindar saw and related in detail the reality of death and failure, but he chose to celebrate the moments of man's best resemblance to the gods rather than the limitations of mortality.

It is natural for us to speculate which of the two odes Hieron liked better: the remarkable economy of Bacchylides' recreation of the epic past and his recreation of the themes and tensions of drama, or Pindar's equally remarkable ability to express more contemporary concerns by restructuring traditional myth and language. Perhaps the question was for him, as it is for us, irrelevant. Each ode seeks to elicit a different response and to suit a different mood. Calling Pindar better than Bacchylides is like saying that Beethoven is better than Schubert, on the grounds that Schubert is not Beethoven.

Yet if a mark of greatness in art is the ability to foresee the concerns and patterns of the future, *Olympian* 1 would surely qualify as a masterpiece.[27] The abstractions of the ode's introduction, to which the specific occasion of Pherenicus' victory and the story of Pelops are subordinated, were to be reconstituted in Thucydides' prose, where narrative of selected events follows speeches concerning general patterns of human behavior. The potential destructiveness of the forces that move men toward achievement, portrayed in *Olympian* 1 in the opposition of Tantalus and Pelops, was to become a major subject of drama: for example, Oedipus, whose quick wits and desire to understand lead him to uncover his own ignorance and guilt, and Hippolytus, whose striving for virtue leaves him vulnerable to attack by evil. Pindar's efforts to make myths conform to contemporary standards of human morality were continued by the sophists and Socrates, and found their ultimate expression in Plato's condemnation of traditional Greek education in the *Republic*. The association of light and height with success was developed in drama and finally realized in the careful structuring of Plato's cave, where the progress toward knowledge of the good is depicted as a slow journey up from darkness toward the sun. The implication throughout that knowledge derives from vision was to become a principal feature of Plato's theory of cognition.

The only aspects of this famous ode which seem not to have been the subjects of continuing interest are the references to the customs of the games, the crowning, and the judging. It is no accident that we find "the song is thrown around the plans of poets" (8-9) and "days are witnesses most wise" (33-34) hard to understand. Virtually all the other images and ideas in Pindar's odes have long since become part of our literary inheritance.

For our purposes, reading the two odes in conjunction has at least brought into clearer focus some of the generic characteristics of diction in the victory ode. What we have learned should help us better understand still other odes which have continued to cause difficulties for modern readers. Of these problem odes I have selected for discussion Pindar's *Pythian* 1, Bacchylides' *Ode* 3, and Pindar's *Pythian* 3. *Pythian* 1 (for Hieron's chariot victory at Delphi in 470) has a long narrative section at the beginning of the ode, before praise of the victor, and seems to concern a variety of issues extraneous to a victory celebration. Bacchylides' *Ode* 3, for Hieron's chariot victory at Olympia in 468, conforms to the conventional sequence of praise-myth-praise, but contains a myth about death, and what seems to be a seriously distorted recollection of the opening of *Olympian* 1. *Pythian* 3, like *Pythian* 1, begins with an extended narrative, and seems to refer to no specific victory celebration.

I would like to show that language and myth are as closely related in these odes as they are in the three odes we have already read, and again to attempt to estimate what Hieron and his friends would have heard in the changing polarities and analogies that these other odes present. The results, I hope, will help us gain a better understanding of the possible function of a victory ode, and of the type of information the poet was expected to give about the victory the ode celebrates. These more precise definitions of scope and content, along with what else we can learn from these odes about Hieron, should help us propose some answers to the questions we left unresolved in the first chapter about *Pythian* 2.

NOTES

1. On the surviving scraps of Simonides' victory odes, see Campbell (ch. I, n. 38) p. 379. We can tell at least that like his nephew Bacchylides Simonides used Homeric epithets e.g. "storm-foot," (515), "end-bringer." (511. 1b. 5), and devised compound adjectives resembling Homeric epithets, "golden-lyre" (511. 1a. 5), "mountain-runner" (519. 35. 7), "child-raiser" (508. 6). Of Bacchylides' fourteen surviving victory odes and Pindar's forty-five, Pindar's *Nemean* 5 and

Bacchylides' *Ode* 13 were both written for Pytheas of Aegina in the pancration, and Bacchylides' short processional *Ode* 4 was composed for Hieron's chariot victory at Delphi in 470, celebrated also in Pindar's *Pythian* 1 (see p. 104).

2. The papyrus of Bacchylides was smuggled out of Egypt by Sir Wallis Budge under the auspices of the British Museum; see John A. Wilson, *Signs and Wonders upon Pharaoh* (Chicago, 1964) pp. 89-91.

3. On ancient misinterpretation of *Pythian* 2, see ch. I, particularly nn. 4 and 5.

4. For allegorical interpretation of eagle similes in Pindar, see the scholia on *Ol.* 2, I 154, 157a, 158d, I 98-99 and on *Nem.* 3. 143, III 62; the scholiasts' methodology is discussed in "The Influential Fictions" (Intr. n. 9) and in "Pindar's Lives" (Intr. n. 2).

5. In the fourth century of the Christian era, the emperor Julian read Bacchylides for moral edification; see Ammianus Marcellinus xxv. 4. 3. But before he was able to examine the contents of the newly discovered papyrus of Bacchylides, Gilbert Murray was prepared to be disappointed: "it would be an ungracious reception to a new-comer so illustrious in himself to wish that he had been someone else"; *A History of Greek Literature* (London, 1897) p. 109. Sir Richard Jebb, who later wrote what has become the standard edition of Bacchylides' poems, was more enthusiastic. He told Budge that the papyrus "was worth more than all the other things [Budge] had acquired for the Museum put together"; see E.A. Wallis Budge, *By Nile and Tigris: A Narrative of Journeys in Egypt and Mesopotamia on Behalf of the British Museum Between the Years 1886 and 1913* (London, 1920) II, p. 355. But Jebb also tended to underestimate the force and originality of Bacchylides' language; see my article "Cultural Conventions, etc." (ch. I, n. 6) pp. 34-36. On criticism since see "Bacchylides' *Ode* 5" (Intr. n. 9) pp. 45-46.

6. The following discussion is based on documentation and bibliography cited in my article "Bacchylides' *Ode* 5, etc." (Intr. n. 9) pp. 45-95. My interpretation has since been supported by P.T. Brannan, S.J., "Hieron and Bacchylides: An Analysis of *Ode* 5," *Classical Folia* 26 (1972): 185-278, who emphasizes the importance of repetition, see esp. pp. 267-273. Cf. also G. K. Galinsky, *The Herakles Theme* (Oxford 1972) 25-28.

7. For example, Carl Ruck's recent observation: "Bacchylides' metaphor is nothing but a thoroughly lovely extension of commonplace ideas; the passage functions as a somewhat extraneous ornament, adding only its elegant coloration to the total meaning of the ode," in "Marginalia Pindarica," *Hermes* 100 (1972): 161-162; but see Brannan (above, n. 6) pp. 52-54 on the unifying function of the description of the eagle.

8. On δυσπαίπαλος see M.S. Silk, *Interaction in Poetic Imagery* (Cambridge, Eng., 1974) p. 152.

9. Vergil's comparison of the dead to fallen leaves (*Aeneid* 6. 309-312) seems to have been influenced by this passage; see my article "Cultural Conventions, etc." (ch. I n. 6) pp. 34-36. But a version of the same simile may also have occurred in a recently recovered papyrus of lyrics describing Heracles and Meleager's meeting in the lower world, perhaps part of a lost dithyramb ascribed to

Pindar; see Hugh Lloyd-Jones, "Heracles at Eleusis: P. Oxy. 2622 and PSI 1391," *Maia* 19 (1967): 206-229 and Raymond J. Clark, "Two Vergilian Similes and the *Herakleous katabasis*," *Phoenix* 24 (1970): 244-255. Suggestions of death in these lines are conveyed primarily by the echo of the Homeric simile comparing men to leaves, since "whirl" (δονεῖν) can also refer to whirling in place, in the case of the olive shoot "which breezes from every sort of wind whirl," but a sudden wind finally "turns out and stretches out on the ground" (*Iliad* 17. 53-58); and in a Hellinistic epigram describing a plane tree "whose leaves the west wind whirls (δονεῖ) with soft breath" (1943–1944 Gow-Page).

10. Eleanor Irwin, in an attempt to assign a consistent connotation to χλωρός translates χλωραύχην, "with throbbing throat," suggesting that Bacchylides chooses this epithet to bring to mind the beauty of a live voice in comparison to the squeaking voices of the dead: see *Colour Terms in Greek Poetry* (Toronto, 1974) pp. 72-74. But this interpretation ignores the context and Bacchylides' own emphases, and the fact that the nightingale, like Daianeira herself, has reason to be *afraid* as well as sad or beautiful.

11. Bacchylides, in *Dithyramb* 16. 23-35 describes how Daianeira deliberately plans Heracles' death: "then uncontrollable fortune wove for Daianeira a plan of many tears, thought upon, when she learned the message suffering sorrow, that Zeus' son fearless in battle was sending Iole home, his white armed shining bride. O evil destiny, O, in suffering, what a deed she planned. Envy wide in force destroyed her, dark veil of what was to come, when on the rosy Lucormas (river) she received from Nessus the destined wonder." The style of the narrative bears close resemblance to *Ode* 5: δαίμων ("fortune") and Δαϊάνειρα in succession stress the sound of her name. The message, like Meleager in *Ode* 5 is "suffering sorrow" (ταλαπενθής); Iole, like Artemis is "white armed" (λευκώλενος) like Daianeira in *Ode* 5. Envy, like the boar, is "wide in force" (εὐρυβίας). Sophocles in the *Women of Trachis* changes the emphasis of the story by making Daianeira act in ignorance: she believes the Nessus' blood is in fact a love charm, and sends it to Heracles to win him back; see Galinsky (above, n. 6) 28-29.

12. "Throw around" (ἀμφιβάλλειν) in Pindar connotes crowning with a victor's wreath, e.g., *Ol.* 3. 13, *Pyth.* 5.31), *Nem.* 3. 65; cf. also *Pyth.* 8. 57 "I throw (βάλλω) crowns on Alcmeon." F. J. Nisetich, "*Olympian* I. 8-11: An Epinician Metaphor," *Harvard Stud. in Class. Philol.* 79 (1975): 55-68 and Gardiner, *Athletics of the Ancient World* (ch. I n. 3) pp. 227-228 and fig. 208, which depicts a judge placing a crown on a victor whose head is bound with a long fillet (or band of wool) and who has garlands around his wrists with long fillets hanging to the ground. Since "throw around" is used by other poets to describe clothing, Pindar's phrase "the song of praise is thrown around" is often interpreted as, e.g., "the mantle of poesy"; see Robert Renehan, "Conscious Ambiguities in Pindar and Bacchylides," *Greek, Roman and Byz. Studies* 10 (1969): 219-221. As the ode progresses Pindar seems to develop the idea of poetry as something wrapped around the participants in a victory celebration: victory puts the poet's mind beneath sweetest thoughts (109); the poet ornaments the victor in sounding folds of praise (105); the phrase "in the height (ἀώτῳ) of music" (15) is modelled on the Homeric "in tufts (ἀώτῳ) of wool." As in the case of the envious men in *Pythian* 2 "who drag a standard that is too much and fix a painful wound in their own hearts" (90-91), the metaphors are suggestive rather than precise; see ch. I n. 41.

13. I prefer to read "of many apples" (πολύμαλος) rather than "sheep" (-μηλος) because "apples" makes explicit the idea of harvest in δρέπων; see Silk (above, n. 9) p. 153 n. 2. "Apple-bearer" (μαλόφορος) is a formal epithet of Demeter, patron goddess of Sicily; see William M. Calder, III, *The Inscription from Temple G at Selinus (Greek, Roman, and Byz. Studies* Monograph 4; Durham, 1963) p. 31.

14. In Homer the word ἄωτος, here translated "height" always occurs in the formulaic phrase οἰὸς ἀώτῳ "in the tufts of wool"; its cognate ἀωτέω means to "extend" sleep (*Il.* 10. 159, *Od.* 10. 548). Pindar uses ἄωτος in connection with various aspects of victory (song, crowns, horses, hands) and also to describe the "best" among groups of men, which seems to imply that the word has for him a fairly abstract meaning. πεῖραρ ("boundary") also seems always to have had abstract connotations: see Ann L. Bergren *The Etymology and Usage of* πεῖραρ *in Early Greek Poetry* (American Classical Studies 2; Amer. Philological Assoc., 1975) pp. 40-43.

15. Greek myths of death by cooking have antecedents in shamanistic mythology: reduction to skeleton condition, return to life with one part missing to mark successful transcendance of the ordeal. The shoulder bone especially has significance in Asian divination ritual; see Mircea Eliade, *Shamanism: Archaic Techniques of Ecstasy* (New York, 1964) pp. 62-66, 161-164. On the relation of Pelops' story to his cult at Olympia, see F.M. Cornford in Jane Harrison, *Themis* (Cambridge, Eng., 1912) pp. 212-259. V.E.G. Kenna's suggestion that Pelops' ivory shoulder may simply represent a shoulder-shaped Cretan seal worn around the arm as identification seems unnecessarily rationalistic; "The Return of Orestes," *Journal of Hellenic Studies* 81 (1961): 100, n. 10.

16. On Pindar's revisions of the traditional myth of Pelops, see A. Köhnken, "Pindar as Innovator: Poseidon Hippios and the Relevance of the Pelops story in *Ol.* 1," *Class. Quart.* n.s. 24 (1974): 199-206. Pindar implies that he has modelled his story of Pelops and Poseidon on the myth of Ganymede and Zeus, but Pelops' son Chrysippus was also carried off by Laius, Oedipus' father. Cannibalism also recurs among Pelops' descendants: Pelops' son Atreus cooks his brother Thyestes' children and serves them to their father; Atreus' son Agamemnon sacrifices his daughter Iphigenia. The repetition of these motifs indicates that the myth of Tantalus' family attempts to confront some basic truths about generational conflict: homosexuality is one means of escape from the destructive syndrome. On myths as "mediation" of experience, see Claude Lévi-Strauss, "The Structural Study of Myth," in *Myth: A Symposium,* ed. Thomas A. Sebeok (Bloomington, Ind., 1958) pp. 209-211.

17. Archilochus knew the story of the stone of Tantalus. He seems to use it to express political danger, "may the stone of Tantalus not hang over this island" (frag. 55). Pindar in *Isthmian* 8 alludes to the Persian invasion as "a stone of Tantalus above our heads, a burden inescapable for Hellas" (9-11).

18. "He has a life he cannot handle, this fixed in toil, among three a fourth suffering." "Among three" (μετὰ τριῶν) seems most directly to refer to three other "lives that cannot be handled" (ἀπάλαμον βίον), which are, like Tantalus' life, "suffering" (πόνον). This sentence, like the sentence about the stone in the preceding stanza, builds up gradually, adding appositive to appositive "he seized in his satisfaction *high delusion=which* the father hung high above his head=a

strong stone=which he strives ever . . .;" "he has *a life he cannot handle*=this= fixed in toil=among three a *fourth suffering.*" (See above, pp. 13-14 on the opening sentence of *Pythian* 2).

"Among three" has also been interpreted as a reference to three other punishments for Tantalus (e.g., hunger, thirst, standing) among which the rock is a "fourth suffering." The translation would then read "he has a life he cannot handle, this, among his three sufferings a fourth." This interpretation seems to me to disregard the apposition of equivalencies so characteristic of Pindar's style and of this poem in particular (e.g., the opening strophe), since "the life he cannot handle" must be read as equivalent to one fourth of rather than to all of his sufferings. In the context of the ode it would seem more natural to think of Tantalus here in the company of his peers: Ixion, Sisyphus, and Tityus; before this he had banqueted with the gods: "if the watchers of Olympus honored any man it was this Tantalus." Being singled out gives opportunity for supremacy (gold beyond other wealth, etc.); in defeat one returns to an undifferentiated group. Pelops later distinguishes himself from the "three and ten" (again a specific number) of suitors whom Oenomaus killed; Pindar will "be seen first in poetry among Greeks everywhere."

19. On the significance of the hero's solitary visit to the sea shore, see Charles P. Segal, "God and Man in Pindar's First and Third *Olympian* Odes," *Harvard Stud. In Class. Philol.* 68. (1964): 226.

20. On the interrelationship of the several statements about "joy" (χάρις) in this ode, and the meaning of χάρις in Pindar's poetry in general, see Segal (above, n. 19) p. 225.

21. Segal (above, n. 19) pp. 212-228 sees as the principal subject of this ode a polarity between the divine (expressed primarily in repeated reference to light) and human world, e.g. "into [the poem's] atmosphere of unmitigated superlatives, the divine enters the human world suddenly and violently, obeying its own impulses, as incomprehensible to men as the eternal essence of water or gold" (p. 212). This perhaps states the case too much in the spirit of a mysticism in which divinity reveals itself through inspiration. In the ode divinity is comprehensible: man's problem lies in his inability to attain or to retain it. Humans like Hieron and Pelops can briefly aspire to or share divinity; Pelops can talk to Poseidon, his old lover, directly; the rest of us can look on and remember what we have seen. But the gods' participation in the brightness lasts, while ours is momentary.

22. Douglas Young "Notes on the Text of Pindar," *Greek, Roman, and Byz. Studies* 7 (1966): 17 suggests emending the text to read "heels" (πτέρναισιν) instead of wings (πτεροῖσιν) because otherwise the competition between Pelops and Oenomaus would be "so visibly unfair." But this is to apply the cultural values of our own society. The point is instead that in order to win the contests, Pelops acquires the powers of a divinity. The competition among Pherenicus' and the other horses is on a similarly unequal basis.

23. The text of lines 103-104 reads, literally, "I believe no friend in both respects is knowing of beautiful things and at the same time more masterful in power." Some sort of comparative seems to be required: "more knowing of beauty" (μᾶλλον instead of ἅμα?); see Douglas Young (n. 22 above) p. 20.

24. In commemorative inscriptions, the Olympic victor is characterized as "crowning" his home and city; see, e.g., inscriptions 7 and 12 in Joachim Ebert, *Griechische Epigramme auf Sieger an Gymnischen und Hippischen Agonen (Abhandlungen der Sächsischen Akademie der Wissenschaften zu Leipzig, Phil. hist. Klasse* 63. 2; Berlin, 1972) pp. 48, 49, 58.

25. Instead of the unconventional κᾶδος ("concern, worry") traditionally associated with the world of man, one manuscript of the ode has "glory" (κῦδος): "god devises and has this glory for your cares (concerning future success)," which makes a "smoother" sentence from our point of view; see Edwin D. Floyd, "Kydos in Pindar, *Olympian* 1, 107," *Hermes* 100 (1972): 485-487. But Pindar, as we have seen, is characteristically unconventional in his use of language.

26. The command "look no longer for some other star" and its echo in the final epode "search no longer beyond," both begin with the same word, which is the twenty-first word both after the poem's beginning and before its end. On this and other symmetrical correspondences in the ode, see Frances S. Newman, "Thematic Unity in the Early Epinician Odes of Pindar" (diss. Univ. of Illinois, 1972; Univ. Microf. # 72-19, 897) pp. 34-64, esp. p. 46, and David Young, *Three Odes* (Intr. n. 3) pp. 121-123. Perhaps these and still other sound patterns were further reinforced in music, e.g. ἔχει δ'ἀπάλαμον βίον ("he has a life he cannot control") at the beginning of strophe 3, and ἔλεν δ'Οἰνομάον βίαν ("he seized Oenomaus' power" at the beginning of strophe 4, and τύμβον ἀμφίπολον ("a tomb with many visitiors," 93) and μή τιν' ἀμφότερα ("no other . . . and," 104); see Stockert (ch. I n. 8) p. 59.

27. See Gertrude Stein, *Picasso* (Boston, 1967) p. 30: "a creator is not in advance of his generation, but he is the first of his contemporaries to be conscious of what is happening to his generation."

Chapter III

On the basis of what we have seen so far we would expect the openings of odes we have not read to be assertive, phrased in sudden metaphors that are restated and explained only gradually as the ode continues. The narrative that follows will concentrate on issues compactly stated in the opening lines, but in relatively straightforward language. The initial tension will return in the conclusion, with its general commands to victor and statements about the poet's professional obligation. We can also in a general way anticipate content: the description of victory will in some way include reference to defeat; there will be praise of victor at beginning and end, elaboration on some aspect of victory (or defeat) in a myth, and discussion of the poet's role in seeing that the victory is recognized.

But victory odes are so flexible in emphasis that they defy further definition. The length of time spent on any of these topics and the way in which they are treated can appear to transform an ode into an apology or an epic narrative or a hymn to human achievement. This Protean adaptability has led critics to classify odes in special genres, as poetic epistles, political diatribes, and the like. But so to categorize is to underestimate the importance that the ancients themselves attached to winning at the games. Victory is seen as proof of the excellence of all other achievements, rather than vice versa.

So *Pythian* 1, in the course of celebrating Hieron's victory in the chariot race at Delphi in 470, commemorates his founding of the town Aetna six years before; Bacchylides' *Ode* 3 balances praise of Hieron's chariot victory at Olympia in 468 with impressions of man's ultimate defeat; in *Pythian* 3 victory provides occasion for contemplation of the limitations of human potential. Emphasis in *Pythian* 1 on an enduring legacy, the establishment of a community, and in *Ode* 3 and *Pythian* 3 a concern with the imminence of death, set these odes apart from the optimistic *Olympian* 1 and the confidence inversely acknowledged in the admonitions of *Ode* 5. The conclusions of *Ode* 3 and of *Pythian* 3 contain no projections of future victory. Subject matter in a general way may thus reflect historical fact: Hieron died in 467.

The more abstract content of these odes is also matched by increasingly self-conscious repetition and antithesis in language, so that even the conventional concluding advice to the victor to rule generously and justly emerges in extended metaphor, "on an anvil without falsehood forge your tongue's bronze" (*Pythian* 1. 86), instead of "into everything a straight-tongued man bears his area forth" (*Pythian* 2. 86); "prosperity's most beautiful flowers you have shown to mortals" (*Ode*. 3. 92-94), instead of "Pherenicus brings you the leaf of good fortune" (*Ode* 5. 184-186); "man's prosperity does not come through a long length safe" (*Pythian* 3. 106), instead of "if (the god) does not leave soon" (*Olympian* 1. 107). Such abstraction is the mark of the mature artist. The cascading ornamentation of Debussy's earlier piano works disappears toward the end of his career, revealing in elemental form the structures that were always present, but less audible, to the listener. Bacchylides and Pindar in these later odes seem to express a not dissimilar awareness of the potential of their medium.

Pindar's *Pythian* 1

The introduction to *Pythian* 1 is by any standard extraordinary. Only at the end of the fifth stanza do we hear the formal reference to the victor and his victory that in other odes occurs in the opening strophe. The postponement builds suspense; we wait to see how the opening description of the lyre, eagle, and the monster Typhos will apply to the celebration of Hieron's victory.

The chorus of Aeschylus' *Agamemnon* similarly begin their song not by commenting, as we would expect, on the news of Agamemnon's return, but by reflecting on the war at Troy, the loss and suffering on both sides, before they speak of themselves and the summons from Clytemnestra that has drawn them from their homes. The effect of the chorus' "digression" is to remind us of the brutal past that resulted in the present victory at Troy.

So in *Pythian* 1, a description of order and chaos, the positive and negative effects of force, precedes the announcement of success, enhancing the significance of Hieron's achievement by including it in this larger context. As we would anticipate from the other odes we have read, each separate subject in these opening lines is related to the others, and themes are here established that will become the principal subjects of the ode.[1]

> Χρυσέα φόρμιγξ, Ἀπόλλωνος καὶ ἰοπ'λοκάμων
> σύνδικον Μοισᾶν κτέανον· τᾶς ἀκούει
>   μὲν βάσις ἀγ'λαΐας ἀρχά,
> πείθονται δ' ἀοιδοὶ σάμασιν

ἁγησιχόρων ὁπόταν προοιμίων
ἀμβολὰς τεύχῃς ἐλελιζομένα.
5   καὶ τὸν αἰχματὰν κεραυνὸν σβεννύεις
αἰενάου πυρός. εὕδει δ᾽ ἀνὰ σκά-
πτῳ Διὸς αἰετός, ὠκεῖ-
αν πτέρυγ᾽ ἀμφοτέρωθεν χαλάξαις,

(1-6, strophe 1)

Though the ode begins like a hymn, its subject (remarkably) is not the god of music, Apollo, to whom invocations are ordinarily made (e.g., Hom. Hymn 25), but the instrument that he plays, "gold lyre, right possession of Apollo and the dark-haired Muses; their stepping hears you, leader of brightness, and bards obey your signs of beginnings that lead the dance, whenever shaking you make turns upward." In Ode 5 Bacchylides also speaks of the physical beauty of song, the Muses' violet crowns and gold bands (ἰοστεφάνων, 3; χρυσάμπυκος, 13). But the designation of song in legalistic language, σύνδικον κτέανον, is new: σύνδικος elsewhere means an advocate in a lawsuit (δίκη).[2]

Since in Pythian 2, which like this ode begins as a hymn, each of Syracuse's attributes encapsulates an important theme to come, we can expect to hear in subsequent lines frequent references to wealth and law, along with description of the powers of song, as in the next lines, where hearing is coordinated with obeying (ἀκούει μέν . . . πείθονται δέ). That the lyre has been personified as an advocate for Apollo and the Muses prepares us for a reversal of ordinary roles: the lyre itself makes "turns upward," when bards usually "turn (literally, "throw") up their heads" (ἀναβάλλεσθαι) to sing, and the lyre itself rather than the dancers who strike the earth with their feet, is ἐλελιζομένα.

Then new detail adds to the dramatic tension of these first lines: "and the spearer lightning of ever-welling fire you quench, and on his staff Zeus' eagle sleeps, loosing his swift wings on both sides." The lyre controls rather than conquers; the quenched fire is, paradoxically, ever-welling; the eagle sleeps but his wings are still swift, like the wings of Bacchylides' flying eagle in Ode 5 (18-19). The careful detail "on both sides loosing" calls attention to the possibility of motion.

The idea of the eagle perched on his staff near Zeus' throne had special meaning for Hieron, who had coins struck with a picture of Zeus seated with his eagle to commemorate the founding of the town Aetna in 476, the year Pherenicus won the horse race at Olympia. But where Bacchylides in Ode 5 celebrates the power of Zeus' eagle in flight, Pindar in Pythian 1 and Hieron on his coin depict the eagle at rest, the ruler in peace, rather than the general at war.[3] The stanza ends in precarious balance, with the lyre both shaking and quenching, singers and dancers about to move, and the lightning and the eagle in the process of settling down.

Pindar's Pythian 1

> ἀρχὸς οἰωνῶν, κελαινῶπιν δ' ἐπί οἱ νεφέλαν
> ἀγκύλῳ κρατί, γ¹λεφάρων ἁδὺ κλάϊ-
> ϑ¹ρον, κατέχευας· ὁ δὲ κ¹νώσσων
> ὑγ¹ρὸν νῶτον αἰωρεῖ, ταῖς
> 10 ῥιπαῖσι κατασχόμενος. καὶ γὰρ βια-
> τὰς Ἄρης, τραχεῖαν ἄνευϑε λιπών
> ἐγχέων ἀκ¹μάν, ἰαίνει καρδίαν
> κώματι, κῆλα δὲ καὶ δαιμόνων θέλ-
> γει φρένας ἀμφί τε Λατοί-
> δα σοφίᾳ βαθυκόλπων τε Μοισᾶν.
> (7-12, antistrophe 1)

In the next stanza, description of the eagle continues: ". . . leader of birds, and a dark-faced cloud on his bent head, sweet barrier on eyelids, you poured down; and he dreams and sways his wet back held down by your hurlings." **ἀρχὸς οἰωνῶν**, in direct metrical echo of the opening **χρυσέα φόρμιγξ** heightens the tension between opposed forces. The term **ἀρχός** aligns the eagle with the dancers and the lightning. The dancer's movement is **ἀγλαΐας ἀρχά; ἀρχός** in Homer is a leader in battle; the lightning is **αἰχματάς**, like a Homeric soldier (5). Song "quenches" the lightning; for the eagle also song is a dark cloud that brings a downpour (**κατέχευας**) and forces him, like other birds in the rain, to fold his wings, bend his head, and close his eyes. **κλάϊθρον** implies that the eagle is contained, as if behind a door. The **ἀρχός οἰωνῶν**, swaying his back, has become like the dancer's movement, **ἀγλαΐας ἀρχά**, that hears and responds not to its own will but to the lyre's. **ῥιπαί** hold him in place—the term in Homer and in *Ode* 5 connotes the force of a storm—he cannot fly because his back is wet, **ὑγρόν**.[4]

Further illustrations of the lyre's power follow, in confirmation of what we have just heard: "and even forcer Ares, leaving aside the spear's harsh peak, warms his heart in sleep, and your arrows charm the gods' minds too in the art of the son of Leto and the deep-robed Muses." **λιπών**, like **χαλάξαις** (6), tells of motion suspended. In contrast to **τραχεῖαν ἀκμάν**, song **ἰαίνει καρδίαν**, a phrase that in Homer always connotes physical pleasure. Song was for the eagle too a "sweet (**ἁδύ**) barrier on his eyelids."

Dramatic alliteration, **καρδίαν κώματι** leads up to **κῆλα**. The lyre's metamorphosis from sender of rain cloud to bow may strike us as surprising, but the ancient audience would have seen an inherent similarity in rain and missiles thrown from above: Zeus throws winged lightning bolts and makes the rain drops fall. Bows and lyres were both made by the same process from bent wood and gut: Pindar's contemporary Heraclitus speaks of identical "backstretched joining of the bow and lyre" (B 51 DK). The lyre's "arrows," as we would expect, like its "rain" bring pleasure. To "charm" is one of song's traditional roles: Hesiod's bards make men "turn aside" from their sorrows. "In the art of the son of Leto and the deep-robed Muses" mirrors "Apollo and the violet-crowned Muses' wealth" in the ode's opening lines. The echo, falling at stanza end, suggests that the description of the lyre's powers has reached a conclusion.

These two opening stanzas, with characteristic density, have stated many amazing things at once. We know from other odes we have read of song's traditional association with increase (e.g., the violet crowns and deep robes of *Ode* 5. 3, 9) and of its ability to charm men from their cares (e.g., *Ode* 5. 7). But the emphasis in these lines on song as physical force, possessing powers equal to Zeus' own lightning and eagle, takes us from the more reflective world of epic, with its celebration of the past, directly to the violence and competition of the games themselves. Struggle precedes success: the spearer-lightning, the eagle with swift wings, Ares and the harsh peak of spears. Celebration of victory brings comfort and forgetfulness to the competitors, and elicits from others attention and respect. What more appropriate beginning for a victory ode for a king renowned for military success?

> ὅσσα δὲ μὴ πεφίληκε Ζεύς, ἀτύζονται βοάν
> Πιερίδων ἀΐοντα, γᾶν τε καὶ πόν-
> τον κατ' ἀμαιμάκετον,
> 15 ὅς τ' ἐν αἰνᾷ Ταρτάρῳ κεῖται, θεῶν πολέμιος,
> Τυφὼς ἑκατοντακάρανος· τόν ποτε
> Κιλίκιον θρέψεν πολυώνυμον ἄντρον· νῦν γε μάν
> ταί θ' ὑπὲρ Κύμας ἁλιερκέες ὄχθαι
> Σικελία τ' αὐτοῦ πιέζει
> στέρνα λαχ'νάεντα· κίων δ' οὐρανία συνέχει,
> 20 νιφόεσσ' Αἴτνα, πάνετες χιόνος ὀξείας τιθήνα·
>
> (13-20, epode 1)

The strophe and antistrophe describe the lyre's effect on Zeus' lightning and eagle, and on his fellow gods. The epode now tells what song does to his enemies: "those Zeus loves not, are terrified when they hear the Pierides' cry, on earth and vast sea, and he who lies in dread Tartarus, enemy of gods, hundred-headed Typhos." To the eagle's eyelids the lyre is a "sweet barrier" (8); it causes Ares to "warm his heart" (11) in pleasant sleep; it "charms the hearts" (12) of the gods. But towards enemies the Muses' song becomes a **βοά**; **ἀτύζονται** in epic denotes panic, fleeing for one's life.

"Along earth and vast sea" takes us from the comfortable domesticity of the wet eagle on his staff into the world beyond with all its dangers. Typhos "lies in dread Tartarus"; **κεῖται** connotes not the sweet sleep of the eagle, but defeat on the battlefield, the hero lying in the dust, the inscription "here I lie" (**κεῖμαι**) on tombs. **θεῶν πολέμιος** makes explicit what "Pierides' war cry" implied, recalling the traditional myth of Zeus' battle against Typhos, the final step in securing his reign. The monstrous ἑκατοντακάρανος adds a further contrast to Zeus' eagle with his "bent head" (8), controlled and at peace with the music.

The next lines begin to tell the story of Typhos: "him once the Cilician raised, cave of many names." The word order emphasizes the geographical designation, "Cilician." πολυώνυμος reminds us that the cave plays a role in several different myths: the wounded Zeus himself was hidden by Typhos in the cave, and Homer relates that Typhos' final "bed" was among the Arimoi, also in Asia Minor (*Il.* 2. 783).[5] The next lines therefore could only come as a surprise: "sea-fenced cliffs of Cumae above and Sicily crush his hairy chest." The revision of the myth's geography pays a stunning compliment to Hieron, who defeated the Etruscans at Cumae in 476. Like Typhos, the Etruscans were believed to originate from Asia Minor. By stating that Typhos is held down in the west, beneath Hieron's homeland and the site of his military triumph, Pindar firmly aligns Hieron's military power on the side of Zeus and of the lyre. "Crush his hairy chest" stresses how Typhos' fate differs from the eagle's whose wet back is soothed by the falling rain that brings sweet sleep.

The distinction between friend and enemy becomes most explicit in the closing lines of the epode: "and heaven's column holds him close, white Aetna, nurse of bitter snow year round." The eagle is "held down" (κατασχόμενος) by the lyre's hurlings, but sways his wet back to the music (9-10). His response is willing and cooperative. But Typhos is "held close" (συνέχει) by Aetna, imprisoned. The mountain is "heaven's column," in contrast to the hollow cave in earth where he was born. νιφόεσσα (literally, "with falling snow") contrasts the mountain to the "dark-faced cloud" that brings sleep to the eagle (7), and the lyre's "hurlings" that temporarily hold him down: unlike the rainstorm, the snow on Aetna lasts "year round." The fallen snow (χιών) on Aetna is "bitter" (ὀξεῖα), but the black cloud pours down a "sweet (ἁδύ) barrier" for the eagle's eyelids (8). τιθήνα, the emphatic last word of the triad, matches Typhos' end to his beginning, when he was raised (θρέψεν) by the Cilician cave. Aetna nourishes for him instead eternal bitter snow.

This description of a cold, snowy Aetna is startling, because it omits all reference to what we would expect, her famous fires, and the frequent volcanic eruptions that occurred during Hieron's reign. Hesiod speaks also of the winds which come from Typhos and fall on sea and land, destroying men and crops (*Theogony* 869-880). How and whether Pindar will deal with the traditional stories of the residual powers of Typhos in Tartarus is held in suspense, as the first triad ends.

τᾶς ἐρεύγονται μὲν ἀπ'λάτου πυρὸς ἁγ'νόταται

ἐκ μυχῶν παγαί· ποταμοὶ δ' ἀμέραισιν
μὲν προχέοντι ῥόον καπ'νοῦ
αἴθων'· ἀλλ' ἐν ὄρφναισιν πέτρας
φοίνισσα κυλινδομένα φλὸξ ἐς βαθεῖ-
αν φέρει πόντου πλάκα σὺν πατάγῳ.
25 κεῖνο δ' Ἀφαίστοιο κρουνοὺς ἑρπετόν
δεινοτάτους ἀναπέμπει· τέρας μὲν
θαυμάσιον προσιδέσθαι,
θαῦμα δὲ καὶ παρεόντων ἀκοῦσαι,
(21-26, strophe 2)

The second strophe, remarkably, continues to describe Aetna. Ordinarily we would have expected to hear by now directly of Hieron's Pythian victory; instead we discover, as the stanza progresses, that the volcano's fires derive from the monster Typhos, not Hephaestus' force, in still another significant revision of traditional myth: "from her belch unapproachable fire's purest springs, out of her depths. And rivers in the days pour forth a stream of smoke blazing. But in nights red spinning flame brings rocks into the deep sea's flats with clattering."

The initial ἐρεύγονται contrasts dramatically with the lyre's orderly rhythm and harmonious sound. ἄπλατος, epithet of monsters (e.g., Echidna in *Ode* 5. 62), suggests an isolation explicitly absent in the opening stanza, where singers and dancers together listen and obey the lyre's sounds. πυρὸς παγαί states the antithesis between fire and song even more vividly. Describing fire as if it were water makes us think of the lyre's soothing rain quenching the lightning's "ever-welling fire" (αἰενάου πυρός, 6). μυχῶν makes the opposition of song and fire still more explicit: song, order, and harmony come from the sky; fire, disorder, and noise "out of the depths" of the earth, like Typhos himself, raised in the Cilician cave.

The lyre "poured down" (κατέχευας) a rain of song that was sweet and soothing (8-9), now rivers "pour" (προχέοντι) instead a "stream of smoke blazing." Reiterated p-sounds, ἀπλάτου πυρός ... παγαί ποταμοί ... προχέοντι ... καπνοῦ lead up to the next lines ἐν ὄρφναισιν πέτρας φοίνισσα ... φλὸξ ... φέρει ... πλάκα ... πατάγῳ. The lyre was "shaking" as it built turns upward (4); now flame is "spinning," inviting comparison between forces of order and disorder, the lyre's harmonious "dance-ruler" proems and the fire river's noisy clattering rocks, Aetna's white snow, and the blood-red (φοίνισσα) flame. The deliberate reference to "nights," in balance to "rivers in days" implies that Typhos, unlike the eagle and Ares, can never enjoy repose.

The next lines suddenly take us back to Typhos: "that crawling thing sends up Hephaestus' wells most fearful." The word order directly links the monster and the fire in our minds, κεῖνο Ἀφαίστοιο κρουνούς, in a surprising reworking of Hesiod's traditional tale, that Typhos was the source of the moist destructive winds on land and sea (*Theogony* 869-880). κρουνοὺς ἀναπέμπει continues the amazing characterization of fire as water from the earth (πυρὸς παγαί). ἑρπετόν again expresses the difference between Typhos crushed beneath Aetna and the eagle swaying on his staff. The eagle sleeps, having loosed his "swift wings," but Typhos keeps to earth, like a snake. δεινοτάτους recalls the terror Zeus' enemies feel when they hear the cry of the Muses (13); ἀναπέμπει is the mirror image of the lyre's pouring down rain on the sleeping eagle (8).

The strophe ends with an emphasis on sight and sound that also characterized the opening strophe of the ode. Again, as in the description of Aetna's fire, there is emphatic alliteration, τέρας ... θαυμάσιον προσιδέσθαι θαῦμα ... παρεόντων, "a marvel wondrous to look upon, wonder for people there to hear." The dancer's movement also "hears" (ἀκούει, 2) the lyre. This direct reminiscence of the opening lines, along with the balanced θαυμάσιον προσιδέσθαι/θαῦμα ἀκοῦσαι seem to indicate that the narrative of Typhos' confinement is complete.

> οἷον Αἴτνας ἐν μελαμφύλλοις δέδεται κορυφαῖς
> καὶ πέδῳ, στρωμνὰ δὲ χαράσσοισ' ἅπαν νῶ-
>   τον ποτικεκ⟨λι⟩μένον κεντεῖ.
> εἴη, Ζεῦ, τὶν εἴη ἁνδάνειν,
> 30 ὃς τοῦτ' ἐφέπεις ὄρος, εὐκάρποιο γαί-
>   ας μέτωπον, τοῦ μὲν ἐπωνυμίαν
> κλεινὸς οἰκιστὴρ ἐκύδανεν πόλιν
> γείτονα, Πυθιάδος δ' ἐν δρόμῳ κά-
>   ρυξ ἀνέειπέ νιν ἀγγέλ-
> λων Ἱέρωνος ὑπὲρ καλλινίκου
>   (27-33, antistrophe 2)

The second antistrophe, like the strophe that precedes it, continues to defy our expectations. "Wondrous to look upon, wonder to hear for people there" seemed like a summary of what had gone before, implying that the poet was about to move, in the new stanza, to the ode's subject, Hieron's victory. But first our attention is turned back instead to Aetna, the land mass that holds Typhos down: "who is bound in Aetna's dark-leaved summits and plain, and his bed cuts into all his back and spurs him as he lies." The summits of the mountain are μελαμφύλλοι, dark like the κελαινῶψ cloud that brings sleep to the eagle (8-9). But Zeus' enemy Typhos can never rest; while the eagle sways his back and spurs him as he lies." The summits of the mountain are μελαμφύλλοι, dark like the κελαινῶψ cloud that brings sleep to the eagle (8-there is alliteration of k-sounds, ποτικεκλιμένον κεντεῖ, as in the first reference to Typhos in the ode, κεῖται ἑκατοντακάρανος (15-16).

κεντεῖ denotes taming of bestiality (cf. the proverbial advice in *Pythian* 2. 94-96, "kicking against the κέντρον is a slippery road"). Reference to control brings us naturally back to Zeus, with whom Typhos' story began (13): "may, Zeus, may it please you, who grasp this mountain, the fruitful earth's brow." ὃς τοῦτ' ἐφέπεις ὄρος uses an epic description of hunters "grasping the summits of mountains" (κορυφὰς ὀρέων ἐφέποντες, *Od*. 9. 121) in search of game to recall the myth of Zeus' final chase and defeat of Typhos. Specific reference to the mountain as the "earth's brow" compares Aetna to the eagle with his bent head (8), and to "hundred-headed Typhos" (16). All things are controlled by Zeus, but whether in pleasure or in pain depends upon their response to his rule. That the mountain he holds is εὔκαρπος confirms that Sicily is on the side of Zeus.

From this prayer to Zeus and the description of Zeus' special precinct Aetna, the poet comes at last to Aetna's ruler Hieron: "whose (Aetna's) like-named city a famed colonizer has made glorious his neighbor" again postpones the expected reference to victory, instead describing Hieron by allusions, as if in riddles. The sentence reiterates the structure of the clause preceding, suggesting some affinity between the colonizer who glorifies the city/neighbor and Zeus who holds the mountain/brow of land. "Colonizer" (οἰκιστήρ) is not the first reference to construction in the ode: the lyre "builds" (τεύχῃς) turns upward (4); sleep is "barrier" (κλάϊθρον) to the eagle's eyelids (8); Aetna, "heaven's column" (κίων), holds Typhos down (19).

Finally in the stanza's closing line the victory scene is recreated: "in the Pythian race a herald spoke proclaiming her for Hieron Victor," with the title καλλίνικος falling emphatically at line end. Elaborate subordination of clauses, as in the proems to *Pythian* 2 and *Olympian* 1, makes Hieron's victory stand as illustration of the enduring statements about Zeus' rule which precede it.

> ἅρμασι. ναυσιφορήτοις δ' ἀνδράσι π‹ρῶτα χάρις
> ἐς πλόον ἀρχομένοις πομπαῖον ἐλθεῖν
> οὖρον· ἐοικότα γάρ
> 35 καὶ τελευτᾷ φερτέρου νόστου τυχεῖν. ὁ δὲ λόγος
> ταύταις ἐπὶ συντυχίαις δόξαν φέρει
> λοιπὸν ἔσσεσθαι στεφάνοισί ν‹ιν› ἵπποις τε κ‹λυτάν
> καὶ σὺν εὐφώνοις θαλίαις ὀνυμαστάν.
> Λύκιε καὶ Δάλοι' ἀνάσσων
> Φοῖβε Παρνασσοῦ τε κράναν Κασταλίαν φιλέων,
> 40 ἐθελήσαις ταῦτα νόῳ τιθέμεν εὔανδρόν τε χώραν.
>
> (33-40, epode 2)

The first word of the epode, ἅρμασι, "in his chariot," is set in emphatic isolation from its proper sentence, reminding us of the primacy of chariot racing over other contests, and directing our thoughts specifically to the world of men. The theme of travel is reiterated in the next word, the new ναυσιφορήτοις, "brought on ships," which matches "chariots" in grammatical structure. Only as the song continues can we realize that ναυσιφορήτοις refers to men (ἀνδράσι), and the topic has become a proverb about sea voyages "for men brought on ships first joy when they lead into sailing is for a sending wind to come; then it's likely that in the end by luck they'll win return to bring them home."

The long introduction to the praise of the victor prepares us for the sudden shift of topic from chariots to ships by setting the single instance of victory into the larger context of Zeus' ordering of the world. Zeus' enemies "on land and vast sea" were terrified when they heard the Muses' cry (13-14). Again there is emphasis on beginning, ἀρχομένοις: the dancers' movement starts the song, ἀγλαΐας ἀρχά (2); the eagle is ἀρχὸς οἰωνῶν (7). A storm of song, with a dark-faced cloud (8) and "hurlings" of rain (10) brought order and peace; now a πομπαῖος wind brings luck to men on the sea. The proverb, with its balanced ναυσιφορήτοις/φερτέρου, states in general terms what we could infer from the negative illustration of Typhos: he was raised in the Cilician cave, where he imprisoned Zeus; his story ends under Aetna, where he lies buried beneath the earth.

The next lines make the connection to Aetna's victory explicit: "the saying for this good luck of yours brings the opinion that she'll be in the future renowned for her crowns and horses and named in celebrations with singing."[7] Echoes from the preceding line τυχεῖν/συντυχίαις, φερτέρου/φέρει link the prediction about Aetna to the general proverb. Repetition also establishes further the contrast with Typhos, whose flame "brings" (φέρει) rocks into the sea with clattering (24), whose cave is πολυώνυμον, whereas the "saying" of the sea voyage φέρει that Aetna (ἐπωνυμίαν in 30) will be κλυτὰν καὶ ὀνυμαστάν in εὐφώνοις θαλίαις, the harmonious sound that denoted Zeus' order in the ode's introduction.

A prayer reiterates in hymn form the poet's prediction that Aetna's first victory is harbinger of many more: "Lycian and lord of Delos, Phoebus, who loves Parnassus' spring Castalia, may you in your mind wish this and make her land rich in men." The ode began with reference to Apollo and the Muses' possession, the gold lyre; now Apollo is asked to guarantee a more general prosperity, that Aetna be εὔανδρος, as her mountain is εὔκαρπος (30). κράναν φιλέων sets Apollo in clear antithesis to Typhos, whom Zeus "loves not" (μὴ πεφίληκε, 13), and whose flame sends forth wells of fire (κρουνούς, 25).

The second triad began with Aetna's fires and moves from there to Zeus, to Hieron's victory, to men on ships, and finally to Apollo. The range of topics is dizzying: after the description of Aetna's fires, with its exciting onomatopoeia, and the prayer to Zeus, the fact of victory itself seems dwarfed. The proverb of the sea voyage and the prayer to Apollo divert our attention once again from the specific incident of success to enduring truths. Putting Hieron's victory into this framework does not minimize his achievement, but on the contrary, makes it seem analogous to Zeus'. Victory is won, disorder is controlled, song in celebration brings pleasure and relief to both divine and human victors.

The relationship among different subjects is stated overtly in a complex series of subordinate clauses, beginning with the second strophe's opening "from her belch" (21) and continued in the antistrophe "who is bound" (27), "who grasp" (30), "whose city" (32). But more covert connectives, the repetition of words and ideas, and the format of sentences helped the ancient audience realize without explicit reminder how each new theme relates to what has gone before: both sea voyage and celebration are beginnings, both Aetna and Castalia have springs. Details that at first seem merely decorative turn out to suggest a series of relevant comparisons: the eagle's bent head to Typhos' hundred heads to Aetna brow of the earth; the spears' harsh peak abandoned in song to the cutting and spurring of Typhos' bed.

Comparison of the brief description of victory in this ode with the more detailed accounts given in the two odes for the horse race victory in 476 is enlightening. In both Pindar's *Olympian* 1 and Bacchylides' *Ode* 5 the description of Pherenicus' running and the myths keep the focus on individual achievement. *Pythian* 1 seems instead to stress the participation of all involved: the city Aetna is proclaimed, two gods are invoked; lightning, eagle, Ares, gods, Zeus' enemies, and Typhos all hear the lyre's sound. The different emphasis in *Pythian* 1, composed six years later, may reflect the atmosphere of a more settled regime. Hieron's power has been firmly established, the great struggles of his first years in power are over, the battle of Himera in 480, the battle of Cumae in 476. But control is not synonymous with stability: Typhos, though crushed beneath Aetna, still sends forth streams of rocks and smoke. The threat of violence and destruction continues even under Zeus; we can expect no less for Hieron.

> ἐκ θεῶν γὰρ μαχαναὶ πᾶσαι βροτέαις ἀρεταῖς,
> καὶ σοφοὶ καὶ χερσὶ βιαταὶ περίγ'λωσ-
>   σοί τ' ἔφυν. ἄνδρα δ' ἐγὼ κεῖνον
> αἰνῆσαι μενοινῶν ἔλπομαι
> μὴ χαλκοπάραον ἄκονθ' ὡσείτ' ἀγῶ-
>   νος βαλεῖν ἔξω παλάμᾳ δονέων,
> 45 μακ'ρὰ δὲ ῥίψαις ἀμεύσασθ' ἀντίους.
> εἰ γὰρ ὁ πᾶς χρόνος ὄλβον μὲν οὕτω
> καὶ κτεάνων δόσιν εὐθύ-
>   νοι, καμάτων δ' ἐπίλασιν παράσχοι·

(41-46, strophe 3)

The opening lines of the new strophe confirm that god must initiate all human accomplishment: "from gods are all means to mortal achievement, and men grow wise and forceful in arms and powerful in tongue." The statement again links song to power: Apollo and the Muses' σοφία charms the gods' hearts (12); Ares himself is βιατάς (10). The significance of the new περίγλωσσοι is revealed in the next lines: "that man I hope to praise striving not to throw my bronze-cheeked javelin (as it were) outside the contest whirling in my hand, but to hurl far and pass by my opponents."

In *Olympian* 1 Pindar similarly moves from a generalization about the meaning of victory to Hieron in particular "the good that lasts day after day comes highest to every mortal. And that man (κεῖνον) I must crown in a horseman's song" (99-102). The next word χαλκοπάρᾳον, epithet of helmets in Homer, implies that Pindar will now praise Hieron's prowess in battle. But suddenly we hear that the epithet describes a javelin, and that the sentence concerns the poet. ὡσεἴτ' warns us that the analogy is unconventional: the poet himself has become a competing athlete.[8] The losing shot, ἀγῶνος ἔξω δονέων, like Typhos' "spinning flame" (κυλινδομένα, 23-24), contrasts with the constructive τεύχης ἐλελιζομένα of the lyre in the first strophe (also in the fourth line). But the winning shot, ῥίψαις, retains the directed force of the lyre's "hurlings" (ῥιπαῖσι, 10), permitting the poet to ἀμεύσασθ' ἀντίους as the lyre has power over even the spearer lightning (5) and the swift eagle (6), forcer Ares (10-12), and Zeus' enemies (13-14).

The closing lines of the stanza continue to describe the straight course of a winning shot: "if all time would thus steer his prosperity straight and his giving of wealth and would also hold forth forgetting of weariness." The lyre in the ode's opening, κτέανον of Apollo and the Muses (2), made the eagle dream and let Ares warm his heart in sleep, as time now brings κτεάνων δόσιν and καμάτων ἐπίλασιν. Time "holds forth" (παράσχοι); the eagle is held (κατασχόμενος) by the lyre's hurlings (10); Aetna holds Typhos fast (συνέχει, 19). But the stanza ends with the sentence incomplete, and the optative mood compounds uncertainty: we expect a conclusion, "it could . . . ," at least one remove from reality.

> ἦ κεν ἀμνάσειεν, οἵαις ἐν πολέμοισι μάχαις
> τλάμονι ψυχᾷ παρέμειν', ἁνίχ' εὑρί-
> σκοντο θεῶν παλάμαις τιμάν
> οἵαν οὔτις Ἑλλάνων δρέπει
> 50 πλούτου στεφάνωμ' ἀγέρωχον. νῦν γε μὰν
> τὰν Φιλοκτήταο δίκαν ἐφέπων
> ἐστρατεύθη· σὺν δ' ἀνάγκᾳ νιν φίλον
> καί τις ἐὼν μεγαλάνωρ ἔσανεν.
> φαντὶ δὲ Λαμνόθεν ἕλκει

τειρόμενον μεταβάσοντας ἐλθεῖν
(47-52, antistrophe 3)

"Yes, he would remember," concludes the conditional statement begun in the strophe, "with what battles in war he stood firm with enduring soul, when they found with the gods' hands honor such as no Greek harvests, a respected crown of richness." The terminology used for Hieron's military success also describes victory in games: Hieron wins wars through the gods' παλάμαις; the poet whirls a javelin παλάμᾳ in song (44); Hieron's honor is a στεφάνωμα like the crowns (στεφάνοισί, 37) for which Aetna will be famous in the future. Hieron "harvests" (δρέπει) his wealth; Aetna is the "fruitful land's brow" (30).

But the condition "if all time would . . . he would remember" remains uncertain of fulfillment. Illustration is provided by the mixture of pain and success in Hieron's present fortune: "now grasping Philoctetes' right he is general of his army. Through necessity as friend even a great man fawned on him. They say that from Lemnos exhausted by his wound, they went after him and came." Reference to the hero with his incurable wound tells us that time has not yet held forth to Hieron "forgetting of weariness" (46). Dramatically, Hieron "grasps" Philoctetes' δίκαν the way Zeus "grasps" (ἐφέπεις) the mountain Aetna, in his controlling of Typhos (30), turning the conventional term δίκαν, "in the manner of," into an act of choice. The gold lyre is also "right" (σύνδικος, 2). In the exercise of leadership the forces of violence and destruction can be contained but not removed.[9] ἐστρατεύθη clearly indicates his pre-eminence.

τις μεγαλάνωρ ἔσανεν states the essentials of the story: Odysseus was forced to beg the man he had driven into exile to return, so the Greeks could win the long war against Troy. μεταβάσοντας ἐλθεῖν encapsulates the action of another sea voyage. The proverb about good beginnings is told of men hoping for an auspicious return (33-35); for the Greek leaders, too, the voyage to bring back Philoctetes will lead to victory.

ἥροας ἀντιθέους Ποίαντος υἱὸν τοξόταν·
ὃς Πριάμοιο πόλιν πέρσεν, τελεύτα-
σέν τε πόνους Δαναοῖς,
55 ἀσθενεῖ μὲν χρωτὶ βαίνων, ἀλλὰ μοιρίδιον ἦν.
οὕτω δ' Ἱέρωνι θεὸς ὀρθωτὴρ πέλοι
τὸν προσέρποντα χ'ρόνον, ὧν ἔραται και-
ρὸν διδούς.
Μοῖσα, καὶ πὰρ Δεινομένει κελαδῆσαι
πίθεό μοι ποινὰν τεθρίππων·
χάρμα δ' οὐκ ἀλλότ'ριον νικαφορία πατέρος.

60   ἄγ' ἔπειτ' Αἴτνας βασιλεῖ φίλιον ἐξεύρωμεν ὕμνον·
(53-60, epode 3)

The opening line of the epode surprisingly ranks the archer Philoctetes with the fighters in hand-to-hand combat: "(they went after him), heroes like gods, Poias' son the archer." But the lyre itself is a bow, controlling violence with its hurlings (10) and its arrows (12). As Pindar tells the story, the victory over Troy, which Homer and the epic poets attribute to the work of many men, belongs to Philoctetes alone, "who sacked Priam's city and ended the Danaans' labors, with weak flesh he went, but it was destined." P-alliteration, **Πριάμοιο πόλιν πέρσεν**, matches the violent sound of Aetna's rocks falling into the sea **πόντου πλάκα ... πατάγῳ** (24). **τελεύτασεν** makes Philoctetes' achievement conform to the proverb of the men starting the sea voyage with a favorable wind: "then it's likely that in the end (τελευτᾷ) they'll win return to bring them home" (34-35).

The many references to body surfaces throughout the ode prepare us for the curiously unspecified designation of Philoctetes' wound, **ἀσθενεῖ χρωτί**. Aetna crushes Typhos' "hairy chest" (19); "it cuts into all his back and spurs him as he lies" (28); the eagle sways his "wet back" in the storm of song (9). These descriptive details have made us aware of feeling, sensitive to the fact of pain. But Philoctetes is not like Typhos; he retains the power to move (**βαίνων**), and to accomplish.

The next lines relate Philoctetes' story directly to the present time: "thus for Hieron may god become straight guider of time coming on and of what he wants in straight measure giver." God as **ὀρθωτήρ** can do what time could not, "steer his prosperity straight" (εὐθύνοι, 46).

In other odes, return to the general themes with which narration of the myth began introduces a second praise. Here again this ode defies expectation, praising first not Hieron but his son: "Muse also at Deinomenes' house, persuade me to sing of chariot's reward: no other's joy is his father's bringing of victory. Come then for Aetna's king let's find a song of friendship." The Muse is asked to persuade the poet (**πίθεο**) as the singers in the first strophe obey (**πείθονται**) the lyre (3). Song is **ποινά**, a price paid for deprivation (as in *Pyth* 2. 14); the lyre is the "wealth" of Apollo and the Muses (2). The achievement of Hieron **καλλίνικος** (32) is now **νικαφορία**; "bringing" has been emphatically associated with success (**ναυσιφορήτοις, φερτέρου, φέρει**, 33, 35, 36).

Hieron and his brothers found (**εὑρίσκοντο**) honor beyond all other Greeks' (48-49); now the poet hopes to find (**ἐξεύρωμεν**, "invent") a song of friendship. The new beginning, at the end of the third strophe, is phrased in the language of the old, suggesting that the second praise will follow the outlines of the first.

τῷ πόλιν κείναν θεοδ'μάτῳ σὺν ἐλευθερίᾳ

Ὑλλίδος στάθ'μας Ἱέρων ἐν νόμοις ἔ-
κτισσε· θέλοντι δὲ Παμφύλου
καὶ μὰν Ἡρακλειδᾶν ἔκγονοι
ὄχθαις ὕπο Ταϋγέτου ναίοντες αἰ-
εὶ μένειν τεθμοῖσιν ἐν Αἰγιμιοῦ
65 Δωριεῖς. ἔσχον δ' Ἀμύκ'λας ὄλβιοι
Πινδόθεν ὀρνύμενοι, λευκοπώλων
Τυνδαριδᾶν βαθύδοξοι
γείτονες, ὧν κλέος ἄνθησεν αἰχμᾶς.
(61-66, strophe 4)

The song of praise for Deinomenes quickly turns back into a song of praise for Hieron, through the kind of intricate evolution of subordinates that introduced the first reference to Hieron's victory ("*whose* like-named city a famed colonizer has made glorious, his neighbor, *for whom* the herald spoke proclaiming," 30-32): "*for whom* (Deinomenes) that city with freedom tamed by god within the right ways of Hyllus' standards, Hieron founded." As in the opening of the third triad, man and god work together for achievement. Along with "Hyllus' standard," reference to Pamphylus and the Heraclids quickly outlines the history of the Dorian invasion of the Peloponnesus, and their settlement in Sparta: "and they wish, Pamphylus', and yes, the Heraclids' offspring, who lived under Taygetus' banks, always to stand firm in Aegimius' laws as Dorians."

That the Dorians abide by laws (**στάθμας, νόμοις, τεθμοῖσιν**) in freedom and "wish" to live beneath Taygetus' contrasts with Typhos' involuntarily "bound in Aetna's dark leaved summits" (27-28). They choose to "stand firm" (**μένειν**), as Hieron **παρέμεινε** in battle with enduring soul (48).

The Dorians' achievements are described in terms that earlier denoted triumph and order: "and they held Amyclae, prosperous, setting forth from Pindus, the white-horsed Tyndarids' neighbors of deep renown, whose spear's fame flowered." ἔσχον emphatically reiterates how the lyre's hurlings hold the eagle (**κατασχόμενος**, 10), and Aetna holds Typhos (**συνέχει**, 19). Reference to the battle of Amyclae, in which Pindar's ancestors, the Aegidae, fought, and to Mt. Pindus in Thessaly, from which the poet's name derives, establishes a bond between poet and victor.[10] Hieron is celebrated for **ὄλβος** (46), the Aegidae are **ὄλβιοι**; **λευκοπώλος** pays brief tribute to an important Spartan cult, which has special meaning for the Dorians in Syracuse, who are also known for their horses (37); Pindar has just asked the Muse to help him sing a **ποινὰν τεθρίππων** (59).[11]

Aetna is Hieron's **γείτων** (31-32), the Aegidae are **γείτονες**; the new **βαθύδοξοι** denotes a fame first associated in the ode with Aetna (**κλυτάν**,

Pindar's Pythian 1

37) and the happy end of the sea voyage (δόξαν, 36). Aetna is the "fruitful land's brow" (30); Hieron harvested a crown of wealth (49-50); now the fame of the Dorians' spear flowered (ἄνθησεν). αἰχμᾶς aligns their power with Zeus' **αἰχματὰς κεραυνός** (5), controlled by the lyre's sound.

> Ζεῦ τέλει', αἰεὶ δὲ τοιαύταν Ἀμένα παρ' ὕδωρ
> αἶσαν ἀστοῖς καὶ βασιλεῦσιν διακρί-
> νειν ἔτυμον λόγον ἀνθρώπων.
> σύν τοι τίν κεν ἁγητὴρ ἀνήρ,
> 70 υἱῷ τ' ἐπιτελλόμενος, δᾶμον γεραί-
> ρων τράποι σύμφωνον ἐς ἡσυχίαν.
> λίσσομαι νεῦσον, Κρονίων, ἥμερον
> ὄφρα κατ' οἶκον ὁ Φοίνιξ ὁ Τυρσα-
> νῶν τ' ἀλαλατὸς ἔχῃ, ναυ-
> σίστονον ὕβριν ἰδὼν τὰν πρὸ Κύμας,
>
> (67-72, antistrophe 4)

A prayer returns us to the present: "Zeus accomplisher, always by the Amenus' water determine such a fate as this for her citizens and kings, the true speech of men." The poet does not stop yet to consider the effects of envy, the false **λόγος** that kept Pelops from getting the glory he deserved (Ol. 1. 28b). Instead he concentrates on the interrelationship of leadership and harmony, "with you (Zeus) a ruling man in accomplishment with his son and honoring his people might turn to harmonious repose." **σύμφωνος ἡσυχία** characterizes Zeus' order in the ode's opening stanzas: we have already heard how Aetna will be named in **εὐφώνοις** celebrations (38).

But Typhos still sends up his fires, so Hieron's repose is also threatened: "I ask your consent, Cronion, that gentle at home, the Phoenician and the Tyrrhenian war cry hold their ship-groaning violence, since they saw at Cumae." Again maintaining order involves enclosure, **ἥμερον κατ' οἶκον**. Song is a **κλᾴθρον** to the eagle's eyelids (8); Aetna's **κίων** holds Typhos close (19). The name **Φοίνιξ** also describes Typhos' spinning flame (**φοίνισσα**, 24). The Phoenicians' and Tyrrhenians' aggression is expressed in terms of noise, **ἀλαλατός** and **ναυσίστονος ὕβρις**; the Muses' **βοά** stuns Zeus' enemies (13) and Typhos' fires **ἐρεύγονται** (21).[12]

The stanza ends abruptly **ὕβριν ἰδὼν τὰν πρὸ Κύμας**, with final emphasis on the site of Typhos' imprisonment (18-19). This dramatic brief account has linked Hieron's victory at Cumae inextricably to Zeus' conquest and control of Typhos.

> οἷα Συρακοσίων ἀρχῷ δαμασθέντες πάθον,
> ὠκυπόρων ἀπὸ ναῶν ὅ σφιν ἐν πόν-
> τῳ βάλεθ' ἁλικίαν,

75 Ἑλλάδ' ἐξέλκων βαρείας δουλίας. ἀρέομαι
πὰρ μὲν Σαλαμῖνος Ἀθαναίων χάριν
μισθόν, ἐν Σπάρτᾳ δ' ⟨ἀπὸ⟩ τᾶν πρὸ Κιθαιρῶ-
νος μαχᾶν,
ταῖσι Μήδειοι κάμον ἀγκυλότοξοι,
παρ⟨ὰ⟩ δὲ τὰν εὔυδ'ρον ἀκτὰν
Ἱμέρα παίδεσσιν ὕμνον Δεινομένεος τελέσαις,
80 τὸν ἐδέξαντ' ἀμφ' ἀρετᾷ, πολεμίων ἀνδρῶν καμόντων.
(73-80, epode 4)

Further description of the battle confirms the analogy between Hieron and Zeus: "(since they saw at Cumae) what they suffered tamed by the Syracusans' leader, who from their swift-journeying ships threw their youth in the sea, dragging Hellas away from heavy slavery." Hieron is ἀρχός of Syracusans, as Zeus' eagle is ἀρχός of birds (7), the dancers' movement is ἀρχά of brightness (2). Taming, as in *Pythian* 2, represents constructive order and civilization: Typhos under Aetna is a "crawling thing" (25); the great man, humbled, "fawned" on Philoctetes (52).

The surprising "dragging" (ἐξέλκων) also described Philoctetes, ἕλκει τειρόμενον (53), coming in his pain to end the Greeks' labors. Slavery is "heavy"; the mountain crushes Typhos' chest and holds him close (18-19). The youth are thrown into the sea from their ships, as Typhos' rocks are brought up from the mountain (24).

A swift comparison ranks the battle at Cumae with other great Greek victories: "I will win at Salamis the Athenians' joyful thanks as pay, in Sparta, from the battles before Cithaeron, in which the Medes with bent bows were worn down, and by Himeras' well-watered shore, by accomplishing a song of praise for Deinomenes' sons, which they took for achievement, after the enemies were worn down." Song, as in the introduction, is wealth (2); τελέσαις again denotes success (τελεύτασεν, 54; τέλειε, 67; ἐπιτελλόμενος, 70). The lyre's sound makes the eagle sleep "with bent head" (ἀγκύλῳ κρατί, 8); now the Medes in defeat have acquired the epithet of the Trojan allies, the Paiones ἀγκυλότοξοι, in contrast to the victorious τοξότας Philoctetes (53). Defeat is weariness, with emphatic repetition, κάμον/καμόντων. Victory can let Hieron forget his weariness (καμάτων, 46), but the mountain bed will never let Typhos rest (28).

καιρὸν εἰ φθέγξαιο, πολλῶν πείρατα συντανύσαις
ἐν βραχεῖ, μείων ἕπεται μῶμος ἀνθρώ-
πων· ἀπὸ γὰρ κόρος ἀμβλύνει
αἰανὴς ταχείας ἐλπίδας,
ἀστῶν δ' ἀκοὰ κρύφιον θυμὸν βαρύ-

νει μάλιστ' ἐσλοῖσιν ἐπ' ἀλλοτρίοις.
85 ἀλλ' ὅμως, κρέσσον γὰρ οἰκτιρμοῦ φθόνος,
μὴ παρίει καλά. νώμα δικαίῳ
πηδαλίῳ στρατόν· ἀψευ-
δεῖ δὲ πρὸς ἄκ|μονι χάλκευε γλῶσσαν.

(81-86, strophe 5)

Pindar begins the new triad by telling us why in the last triad he has chosen to describe past success only in brief mention: "if you speak of right measure, stretching close the bounds of many in a short space, smaller blame from men follows." Again the poet's art is described in the language of games: first he spoke of himself as an athlete hurling his javelin with accuracy beyond his opponents'. Now he speaks of the measurement of achievement, the referee's marking with a javelin of distances (πείρατα) in a contest.[13] The language is deliberately ambiguous: ἐν βραχεῖ can denote extent of both time and space; πολλῶν can refer either to events or to men.

The process of "stretching close the boundaries of many" was illustrated for us in the swift account of the triumphs of the Dorian invasion, and in the rapid comparison of Salamis, Plataea, and Himera, where no victory was made to seem more important than the others. The singular achievement, like Pherenicus' running undefiled by dust from other horses (*Ode* 5. 43-44) elicits resentment. Accordingly, to be safe, praise must take the form of comparison with past events of equal importance or be expressed in antithesis, through stories of failure—Typhos supressed beneath Aetna, Tantalus under his stone, Ixion on his wheel.

Reference to envy returns us to the present: "for everlasting satisfaction blunts swift hopes, and what citizens hear makes their hidden hearts heavy, especially about others' good." The mountain "cuts into" Typhos' back (χαράσσοισ', 28); so satisfaction "blunts hopes" (ἀμβλύνει ἐλπίδας) that, like the eagle's wings, are "swift" (6), and can potentially lead to positive accomplishment: "I hope (ἔλπομαι) to praise (Hieron) striving not to throw my bronze-cheeked javelin outside the contest . . . but to hurl far and pass by opponents" (43-44). To the extent that it can arouse hopes, envy has a positive function: Hesiod in the *Works and Days* speaks of the two strifes among men, the good who elicits healthy competition, the bad who leads them to injustice and greed (11-41).

In *Pythian* 1, destructive envy is characterized in terms of Typhos' violence, as **ἀκοά**, what men hear; Zeus' enemies flee when they hear the Muses (13-14); Typhos' fires are a "wonder to hear" (ἀκοῦσαι, 26). This **ἀκοά** "weighs on the hidden heart" (**κρύφιον θυμὸν βαρύνει**); Typhos is crushed beneath Aetna (19); his fires come from invisible depths (22). "About another's good" (ἐσλοῖσιν ἐπ' ἀλλοτρίοις) marks a contrast with Deinomenes, for whom his father's victory is "no other's joy" (χάρμα οὐκ ἀλλότριον, 59).

But the rest of the stanza returns to the positive uses of success: "but all the same, envy's a stronger thing than pity; do not let the beautiful go. Steer your army with a righteous rudder. On an anvil without falsehood forge your tongue's bronze." This advice recapitulates the lesson of the story of Philoctetes, himself general of his army (ἐστρατεύθη, 51). Again a sea voyage will lead to success (33-35); the ship's rudder is δίκαιος as the gold lyre is σύνδικος (2); Hieron, who founded Aetna Ὑλλίδος στάθμας ἐν νόμοις ("in the right ways of Hyllus' standard," 62) must νωμᾶν; like the ideal king Hesiod describes in the *Theogony*, he must be both administrator of justice and persuasive speaker (*Theogony* 88-93).

Pindar restates the traditional advice dramatically in the special language of the ode: Hieron must forge his tongue like a weapon (χάλκευε); Aetna cuts and spurs Typhos' back, as a smith forges metal (28); the lyre hurls arrows that bring restful sleep and charm the gods' hearts in song (11-12); the poet hurks a bronze-cheeked (χαλκοπάραον) javelin on a true course to praise Hieron (43-44); by contrast, everlasting satisfaction blunts swift hopes.[14]

> εἴ τι καὶ φλαῦρον παραιθύσσει, μέγα τοι φέρεται
> πὰρ σέθεν. πολλῶν ταμίας ἐσσί· πολλοὶ
>   μάρτυρες ἀμφοτέροις πιστοί.
> εὐανθεῖ δ' ἐν ὀργᾷ παρμένων,
> 90 εἴπερ τι φιλεῖς ἀκοὰν ἁδεῖαν αἰ-
>   εὶ κλύειν, μὴ κάμνε λίαν δαπάναις·
> ἐξίει δ' ὥσπερ κυβερνάτας ἀνὴρ
> ἱστίον ἀνεμόεν {πετάσαις}. μὴ δολωθῇς,
>   ὦ φίλε, κέρδεσιν ἐντραπέ-
>   λοις· ὀπιθόμβροτον αὔχημα δόξας
>   (87-92, antistrophe 5)

In the antistrophe the cryptic commands that conclude the strophe are gradually explained: "if anything—even something little—is blazing, it's brought out great from you. You are the dispenser of many; many witnesses are faithful to both." The sudden metaphor, "is blazing . . . is brought forth" (παραιθύσσει . . . φέρεται) reminds us that power can destroy as well as save. Typhos sends forth a stream of smoke blazing, his "red spinning flame brings (φέρει) rocks into the sea" (23-24), in a passage that, like these lines and the description of Philoctetes' sack of Troy (54), resounds with p-alliteration. The insignificant can become important, the great man (μεγαλάνωρ τις) fawned on Philoctetes, with his weak flesh, who was necessary for victory (52-55).

But Zeus' Homeric title, "dispenser" (ταμίας) reaffirms that Hieron's intentions are good; the poet, too, is an orderer of an unspecified "many" (πολλῶν, 81). Reference to "many witnesses faithful to both," i.e., to great and small achievements, again specifies the point of view of the audience. In the introduction dancers hear and singers watch the lyre (1-4); Aetna's eruption is a wonder to see and hear for those who are there (26). The careful balance of ἀμφοτέροις is expressed also in the description of the powerful eagle at rest, "loosing his swift wings on both sides" (ἀμφοτέρωθεν, 6).

Hieron's power must, of course, be used for continued achievement: "stand firm in flowering mood, if you always like to hear said what is sweet, don't be worn too much by expenditures. Like a helmsman let go your sail in the wind. Don't be tricked, O friend, by gains that turn back in. Increase of renown that follows death . . . " The advice to be generous, "stand firm" (παρμένων), "do not be worn" (μὴ κάμνε) is phrased in the language that described Hieron's perseverance in war (παρέμειν', 48), and the Heraclidae who wished to stand firm as Dorians (μένειν, 64,), whose "spear's fame flowered" (ἄνθησεν, 66), as Hieron's mood must now be εὐανθής. Hieron's enemies, by contrast, are "worn down" (κάμον, καμόντων, 78, 80) in defeat.

Fame is characterized as sweet hearing (ἀκοά), like the lyre's sound, itself the antithesis of the ἀκοά of envy that makes the citizens' hearts heavy (84), and the violent sound of Typhos' eruptions (26). Success is, as we can by now expect, clear sailing (33-34, 86); selfish gain accordingly is here characterized as ἐντράπελος, "in-turning." The stanza ends in mid-sentence, with a general statement about future renown (δόξα).[15] Hieron's ancestors the Dorians are now βαθύδοξοι (66); how can Hieron achieve the same enduring distinction?

οἷον ἀποιχομένων ἀνδρῶν δίαιταν μανύει
καὶ λογίοις καὶ ἀοιδοῖς. οὐ φθίνει Κροί-
σου φιλόφρων ἀρετά.
95 τὸν δὲ ταύρῳ χαλκέῳ καυτῆρα νηλέα νόον
ἐχθρὰ Φάλαριν κατέχει παντᾷ φάτις,
οὐδέ νιν φόρμιγγες ὑπωρόφιαι κοινανίαν
μαλθακὰν παίδων ὀάροισι δέκονται.
τὸ δὲ παθεῖν εὖ πρῶτον ἀέθλων·
εὖ δ' ἀκούειν δευτέρα μοῖρ'· ἀμφοτέροισι δ' ἀνήρ
100 ὃς ἂν ἐγκύρσῃ καὶ ἕλῃ, στέφανον ὕψιστον δέδεκται.
(93-100, epode 5)

The opening line of the epode restates the traditional relation between poetry and fame: "increase of renown that follows death alone reveals the life of men gone by through speakers and singers." We could not have expected otherwise in an ode that celebrates so explicitly the powers of song, with its opening description of bards (ἀοιδοί) obeying "the signs of dance ruler proems" (3-4). "Reveals" (μανύει) has the authority of prophecy; the anvil on which Hieron's tongue is forged is "without falsehood" (ἀψευδής), like Apollo's oracle at Delphi (86).

Specific illustrations follow: "Croesus' kind-thinking achievement doesn't wither, but the burner in the bronze bull, unpitying mind, Phalaris, hating talk holds down everywhere. For him no lyres in halls take in soft interchange in the voices of boys." The new φιλόφρων describes Croesus in the terms Pindar uses to address Hieron (φίλε, 92) and Deinomenes (φίλιον, 60); his fame "doesn't wither," as Sicily is "fruitful" (30), the Dorians' fame "flowered" (66), and Hieron's mood is "flowering" (89).

But Phalaris, with his antithetical "unpitying mind," like Typhos with his red spinning flame (24), is a "burner" (καυτήρ). Hating talk holds him down (κατέχει), as Aetna holds Typhos close (συνέχει, 19), and the eagle is held down (κατασχόμενος) by the lyre's "hurlings" (10). But where the sleeping eagle can move in time to the music, Phalaris is held down "everywhere," like Typhos crushed by Cumae and Sicily. A description of the song Phalaris never hears marks the polarity between the hating talk (φάτις) he receives and the fame of Croesus: for him there are no lyres or the "business exchange" (κοινανία) of voices that the lyre, the wealth of Apollo and the Muses, can bring (2).[16]

The poem concludes with a statement of the general significance of victory: "to do well is first of prizes; to hear well is a second share. The man who gets both and seizes on them, takes in the highest crown." *Olympian* 1 ended similarly with reflections on success: "the last summit is scaled by kings. Search no longer beyond" (113-114). But the way each statement is phrased reflects the character of its ode: *Olympian* 1 speaks in terms of vision ("search no longer beyond"), *Pythian* 1 tells instead of "doing well' (παθεῖν εὖ), as opposed to Hieron's enemies who "suffered." (πάθον) at Cumae (73), and of "hearing well" (εὖ ἀκούειν), in an ode filled with sound, where fame itself is called ἀκοά (84, 90).

Verbal echo helps us think of the "man" (ἀνήρ) who both does well and hears well as Hieron, helmsman of his people (κυβερνάτας ἀνήρ, 91) and "leader (ἀγητὴρ ἀνήρ, 69). A balancing "both" earlier described his achievements (ἀμφοτέροις, 88) and the eagle on his coins (ἀμφοτέρωθεν, 6). He has already found a "crown" (στεφάνωμα) of richness such as no other Greek harvests (49-50); his city Aetna will be famed for "crowns" (στεφάνοισι, 37). "Highest" (ὕψιστον) explicitly marks his fate as the antithesis of Typhos', buried under Aetna.

But the last stanza, for all its similarity in language, provides no mirror image for any other passage in the ode. The complex orchestration of the introduction evolves for Croesus simply into the sound of lyres and the soft voices of boys. There is in the odes no exact correspondence in repetition and antithesis, any more than there is measured balance in length of exposition. As in the case of men and horses in *Pythian* 2, the forces of violence can momentarily bear close resemblance to each other:

Zeus' lightning and Typhos both have fires (6, 21); the eagle and Typhos and Phalaris are each held down (10, 19, 96). Both victors and vanquished are worn by victory: we hear of Typhos restless in his bed beneath Aetna (28), of Hieron's weariness in war (46), of Philoctetes exhausted by his wound (52), of Hieron's enemies and the defeated Persians "worn down" (78, 80).

Variation holds our attention and continually reveals new possibilities. The extraordinary length of the ode's introduction obviates the need for a long story to exemplify the interrelation of song and leadership. Instead the myth that ordinarily follows the first praise of the victory provides only a brief illustration of the effect of the leadership and cooperation expressed in detail in the proem. The second praise follows immediately, with detailed listings of qualities already exemplified by the lyre and by Typhos.

The detailed descriptions of battles make the ode seem to celebrate Hieron's military and political achievements almost more than his chariot victory at the Pythian games. Then remarkably also, the diction of the last stanza is allusive and condensed where in other odes it has been expansive and explicit: "if you speak right measure, stretching close the bounds of many in a short space," "on an anvil without falsehood forge your tongue's bronze," "hating talk holds down Phalaris everywhere"—each of these statements expresses several ideas at once, contracting syntax, straining the imagination, like phrases ordinarily found in proems, "priest ram of Aphrodite" (*Pythian* 2. 17), "best is water" (*Olympian* 1. 1), the eagle's "light-haired mane" (*Ode* 5. 28-29).

The skill with which Pindar can deviate from the norm seems to indicate that he was consciously aware that each statement of praise in an ode must reflect on every other. Euripides in much the same way calls attention to and breaks standard dramatic and metrical conventions. Such experimentation, paradoxically, appears simultaneously to invigorate and to destroy: both Pindar and Euripides were the last great composers in their respective genres.

Bacchylides' *Ode 3*

Pindar's predictions in *Pythian* 1 of Hieron's future success were fulfilled at the next Olympiad: in 468 Hieron won the chariot victory that Pindar had spoken in 476 of hoping to celebrate (*Ol.* 1. 109-111). But the only ode that has come down to us commemorating this victory is by Bacchylides. After *Pythian* 1, with its confident emphasis on future growth and fame, Bacchylides' new ode, with its story of the end of Croesus' kingdom and its emphasis on man's confrontations of death, seems strangely retrospective, as if the peak of Hieron's glory were past, and the end of his life were imminent. The opening stanzas are distinctive in their omission of direct praise for the victor. In *Ode* 5, composed eight years before, the first subject of attention was Hieron: "well-destined general . . . you know the brightness . . . make your heart cease from cares . . . look here in your mind" (1-8). *Ode* 3 instead begins as a hymn to Syracuse's patron deities and to Hieron's winning horses.

> Ἀριστο[κ]άρπου Σικελίας κρέουσαν
> Δ[ά]ματρα ἰοστέφανόν τε Κούραν
> ὕμνει, γλυκύδωρε Κλεοῖ, θοάς τ' Ὀ-
> λυμ]πιοδ'ρόμους Ἱέρωνος ἵππ[ο]υς.
> (1-4, strophe 1)

"Of best-harvest Sicily's queen Demeter and the violet crowned Maiden sing, Cleo sweet-giver, and of the swift Olympia-runner mares of Hieron." The initial ἀριστόκαρπος transforms Demeter's Homeric epithet ἀγλαόκαρπος ("shining-harvest") into a statement of general excellence, like the initial "best (ἄριστον) is water" in *Olympian* 1. Like the new εὔμοιρος which introduces *Ode* 5, ἀριστόκαρπος states a theme that will be elaborated as the ode continues, that god is the source of wealth and achievement.

After *Ode* 5, with its direct address to Hieron, we might have expected that "king" would follow "of best-harvest Sicily," instead we hear "queen Demeter and the violet crowned Maiden," as if the ode were a hymn to the goddesses of Sicily's grain, with ἰοστέφανος connoting the spring that leads to Demeter's harvest. Then suddenly it appears that the hymn includes also Hieron's mares that won the chariot race. The new Ὀλυμπιόδρομος, like the athlete's designation δολιχόδρομος ("long-distance-runner") specifies the occasion, introducing the first praise.[17] In *Ode* 5, Pherenicus was, more timelessly, ἀελλοδρόμας ("storm-wind-runner," 39).

> 5 σεύον]το γὰρ σὺν ὑπερόχωι τε Νίκαι
> σὺν Ἀγ']λαΐαι τε παρ' εὐρυδίναν
> Ἀλφεόν, τόθι] Δεινομένεος ἔθηκαν
> ὄλβιον τ[έκος στεφάνω]ν κυρῆσαι·
> (5-8, antistrophe 1)

". . . with high Victory . . . and Brightness, by the wide-whirling . . . they made Deinomenes' prosperous . . . win." Here again, instead of hearing direct praise of Hieron himself, of how he "grasps his righteous staff in Sicily of many apples" (*Ol.* 1. 12-13), we learn more about the horses and their victory. As in the strophe, the focus is on the participation of two patron goddesses, Victory and Aglaia. The horses run beside the "wide-whirling" Alpheus; Hieron is mentioned only at the end, as passive beneficiary of all this action.

Finally in the epode comes the expected praise, but again in an unconventional manner:

θρόησε δὲ λ[αὸς ∪__.
10 ἆ τρισευδαίμ[ων ἀνήρ,
ὃς παρὰ Ζηνὸς λαχὼν
πλείσταρχον Ἑλλάνων γέρας
οἶδε πυργωθέντα πλοῦτον μὴ μελαμ-
φαρέϊ κ[|]ρύπτειν σκότωι.

(9-14, epode 1)

"and cried out . . . ah thrice-fortunate . . . who got from Zeus honor leading-most of Hellenes; he knows his towered wealth, not to hide it in black-robed darkness." The speaker does not seem to be the poet, who would "sing," but some third person who "cries out" (θρόησε) at the games, in response to Hieron's victory. His speech is patterned on the Homeric formula "thrice blessed (τρὶς μάκαροι) they who . . ," that describes some past achievement.[18] But in Ode 3 "blessed," epithet of the gods, has become the less exalted εὐδαίμων, which in Ode 5 described human experience, "no, not anyone on earth was in all things fortunate (εὐδαίμων)" (53-55).

Hieron's good fortune derives not from victories in games or war but from honor given by Zeus, assessed quantitatively in the new πλείσταρχος ("leading-most"). Hieron responds with matching generosity, by knowing not to "hide" his wealth. Alliteration of p- and t- sounds emphasizes the dramatic language of the epode's conclusion, πυργωθέντα πλοῦτον μὴ μελαμφαρέϊ κρύπτειν σκότῳ. Hieron's wealth is "towered," like a fortified city; danger comes not from enemies or envious men but from "black-robed darkness," antithesis of Sicily's goddess violet-crowned Kore (2) and of high Victory and Aglaia, the Brightness who accompanies Hieron's winning horses (5-6).[19]

15 βρύει μὲν ἱερὰ βουθύτοις ἑορταῖς,
βρύουσι φιλοξενίας ἀγυιαί·
λάμπει δ' ὑπὸ μαρμαρυγαῖς ὁ χρυσός,
ὑψιδαιδάλτων τριπόδων σταθέντων

(15-18, strophe 2)

The first lines of the new triad take us within the walls of Hieron's "towered wealth:" "the shrines swell with feasts of cattle sacrificed; the streets swell from hospitality to friends." βρύει, which is used of buds on trees or of life growing within the womb, is emphatically repeated. The sacrifice of cattle denotes wealth and piety; φιλοξενία a cosmopolitan hospitality like Hieron's.[20] The expectation is that these lines describe Syracuse, in a traditional statement of friendship of poet for patron, as in Ode 5 where Bacchylides comes as ξένος to Hieron's "famed city" (11-12).

But the next lines tell us that we are at Delphi, where Hieron and his brother Gelon, in commemoration of their victory at Himera, set up gold tripods that were the richest gifts sent to the shrine since the days of the fabulous kings of Lydia, Gyges and Croesus: "the gold shines beneath flashes as the high-ornate tripods stand."[21] The tripods are described by the new adjective ὑψιδαιδάλτων; in the first epode Hieron's wealth is "towered" (13). In contrast to *Olympian* 1, where "gold like blazing fire shines (διαπρέπει) in the night" (1-2), the gold of the tripods in *Ode* 3 shines more dimly "beneath flashes," acknowledging the imminence of "black-robed darkness" (14).

πάροιθε ναοῦ, τόθι μέγι[στ]ον ἄλσος
20 Φοίβου παρὰ Κασταλίας [ὀ]εέθ'ροις
Δελφοὶ διέπουσι. θεὸν θ[εό]ν τις
ἀγ'λαϊζέθὼ γὰρ ἄριστος [ὄ]λβων·
(19-22, antistrophe 2)

The next stanza continues to describe Delphi: "before the god's dwelling, there is the greatest grove of Phoebus beside Castalia's streams; this the Delphians pursue." After *Ode* 5 and *Olympian* 1, with their detailed descriptions of Pherenicus' winning race, beside the Alpheus (38, 20) the concentration in *Ode* 3 on the maintaining of Apollo's shrine beside Castalia's streams appears the more remarkable. A concluding generalization states explicitly why attention is diverted from the victor: "to god, to god give brightness, for he is the best of prosperities." Ritualistic repetition, θεὸν θεόν, recapitulates the tribute paid in the opening stanzas to Demeter, Kore, Victory, and Aglaia (2, 5-6) who rule Sicily and accompany Hieron's winning chariot.[22]

ἐπεί ποτε καὶ δαμασίπ[π]ου
Λυδίας ἀρχαγέταν,
25 εὖτε τὰν πεπ'[ρωμέναν
Ζηνὸς τελέ[σσαντος κρί]σιν
Σάρδιες Περσᾶ[ν ἁλίσκοντο στρ]ατῶι,
Κροῖσον ὁ χ'ρυσά[ορος
(23-28, epode 2)

As in *Ode* 5 (50-56), the generalization that summarizes the first praise introduces the myth, with ποτε immediately signalling transition to the past: "since once also the leader of horse taming Lydia when the fated . . . Zeus brought to an end . . . Sardis by the Persian . . . army, Croesus . . . Gold-sword." The eptihets δαμασίππος and ἀρχαγέτας immediately suggest an analogy between Croesus and Hieron, with his πλείσταρχον honor (12) and his Olympian-runner mares (ἵππους, 4).[23] Completion of the sentence is postponed: we hear first that Zeus, who gave Hieron his "honor ruling-most" brings to an end a fated judgment (?), and that Sardis has been taken by the Persian army.

At the epode's end comes Croesus' name, and the first hint of how the story will exemplify the generalization about god being the best of prosperities: "Gold-sword" (χρυσάορος) is Apollo's Homeric title, as defender of Troy; Hieron sent gold to his shrine at Delphi (17). This brief "digression," so characteristic of the archaic style, in fact constitutes an important statement of theme. The insertion between Croesus' title ἀρχαγέτας and his own name of reference to his fate and to the Persians' capture of Sardis characterizes him as ruler of a city in time of war, confronting his own death. Bacchylides' description of Hieron's victory celebration placed unusual emphasis on the civic aspects of victory, feasting, the streets, the Delphians with their temple and sacred grove. Hieron's wealth is "towered" (13), fortified like a city, and the threat to it is a darkness dressed in the black robes of death (14).

φύλαξ᾽ Ἀπόλλων. [ὁ δ᾽ ἐς] ἄελπτον ἆμαρ
30 μ[ο]λὼν πολυδ[άκ'ρυο]ν οὐκ ἔμελλε
μίμνειν ἔτι δ[ουλοσύ]ιαν, πυρὰν δὲ
χαλκ[ο]τειχέος π[ροπάροι]θεν αὐ[λᾶς

(29-32, strophe 3)

"Apollo guarded" completes the sentence suspended in the epode, reaffirming the generalization which introduced Croesus' story, "god is the best of prosperities" (22). φύλαξ᾽ again suggests the context of war, the need for protection first implied in Hieron's "towered wealth" (13). This initial statement about Apollo guarding Croesus, like Pindar's summarizing "Pelops for whom the Earth-holder great-in-strength lusted" in *Olympian* 1. 24-25, serves as a proem to the more detailed narrative that follows: "when he came to the day beyond hope, he was not ready to wait for slavery with its many tears, and in a pyre before his bronze-walled palace . . . "

We have already heard of Zeus' "fated" judgment that caused Sardis to be taken (25); now the event is described from Croesus' point of view, "when he came to the day beyond hope." μολών reverses the customary notion: instead of "before dawn comes" (μόλῃ ἠώς, *Il.* 24. 781) or of "time coming on" (τὸν προσέρποντα χρόνον, *Pyth.* 1. 57), Croesus himself goes to meet the day, assuming the initiative. He "is not ready to wait for slavery" (μολὼν οὐκ ἔμελλε μίμνειν, with emphatic alliteration).

Applying the Homeric epithet of war, πολυδάκρυος, to slavery, the outcome of war for Croesus, intensifies the sense of defeat. His pyre is set before a palace with bronze walls, the mark of quasi-divine status and tremendous wealth. Alcinous' palace has bronze walls (*Od.* 7. 86) in a land untouched by war, where men are like the gods, and share meals with them, and crops grow year round. In Cyrene bronze plaques lined the wall of Apollo's temple—no private dwelling has them.[24] Again the stanza ends with a sentence incomplete, leading us to expect, on the Homeric pattern, "burned" or "made" his pyre.

> νάησατ᾽, ἔνθα σὺ[ν ἀλόχωι] τε κεδ᾽[ναῖ
> σὺν εὐπλοκάμοι[ς τ᾽] ἐπέβαιν᾽ ἄλα[στον
> 35 θ]υ[γ]ατ᾽ράσι δυρομέναις· χέρας δ᾽ [ἐς
> αἰ]πὺν αἰθέρα σ[φ]ετέρας ἀείρας
>
> (33-36, antistrophe 3)

"... he built, and there with ... his good [wife] ... he went up and with his fair-haired daughters grieving without forgetting. And he raised their hands into the steep air." Apollo at Delphi has a "dwelling" (**ναός**, 19) with gold; the first word of the new antistrophe is not "burned" or even "made" (**ἐποίησεν**), but "built" (**νάησατ᾽**, literally, "heaped up for himself"), further delineating the contrast between Croesus' fate and Hieron's. Hieron in the proem had "towered wealth" (13); now Croesus goes up on a heap of wood before his bronze-walled palace, to die.

Again the narrative places special emphasis on Croesus' initiative. He mounts the pyre himself, with his wife and daughters; no one forces him to go. Homeric echoes add to the sense of defeat: **εὐπλοκάμος** is the special epithet of Trojan women; **ἄλαστον δυρομέναις** is the terminology used to describe Eumaeus' fears for Telemachus' death (*Od.* 14. 174). In contrast to their "grieving," Croesus again takes positive action. He raises not only his own, but his family's hands ("their," **σφετέρας**) into the "steep air." The forbidding **αἰπύν** stresses Croesus' remoteness from the heights earlier associated with success, "high Victory" in the race (5), Hieron's "towered wealth" (13), and the "high-ornate tripods" (18) sent by Hieron and his brothers to the god at Delphi.

> γέ]γ[ω]νεν· ,,ὑπέρ[βι]ε δαῖμον,
> πο]ῦ θεῶν ἐστι[ν] χάρις;
> πο]ῦ δὲ Λατοίδ[ας] ἄναξ;
> 40 ἔρρουσ]ιν Ἀλυά[τ]τα δόμοι
> _∪_×_∪_×] μυρίων
> _∪_×_∪_]ν.
>
> (37-42, epode 3)

His daughters weep, but Croesus cries out in articulate speech, questioning the gods: "and he cried, 'fortune of high force, where is the god's joyful thanks? where the lord, Leto's son? .. the home of Alyattes ... of ten thousand ....'" The first words of this epode, **γέγωνεν ὑπέρ-**

βιε δαῖμον echo the opening of the first epode, θρόησε ἆ τρισευδαίμων (". . . cried out, 'ah thrice fortunate,'" 9-10). ὑπέρβιος is a term reserved in Homer for men who exceed the bounds of ordinary conduct: god, like man, should repay kindness; Croesus had sent gifts to Apollo's shrine at Delphi. The rest of the stanza seems to describe the capture of Sardis, with special reference to the home (δόμοι) of Croesus' father Alyattes. The detail is carefully selected: we have already heard that his son is building a pyre before his bronze-walled palace (31-33).

×‿⏑⏑×‿⏑⏑‿⏑]ν ἄστυ,
ἐρεύθεται αἵματι χρυσο]δίνας
45 Πακτωλός, ἀ[ε]ικελίως γυνα[ῖ]κες
ἐξ ἐϋκτίτων μεγάρων ἄγονται·
(43-46, strophe 4)

At the beginning of the new triad Croesus speaks of the "-whirling Pactolus" (-δίνας), in grim contrast to the "wide-whirling" Alpheus (εὐρυδίνας, 6), where Hieron won his victory. Then we hear again particulary of the fate of women in the defeated city: "shamefully women are led from the well-built halls." Each word recalls a meaningful context from Homer: ἀεικελίως denotes the suitors' abuses to the women in Odysseus' household (Od. 16. 109); ἐϋκτιτος is a standard epithet of cities and houses; μέγαρον is a specifically Homeric term that had dropped out of ordinary usage by the fifth century.

The scene, with women "being led" (ἄγονται) follows the outline of the passage in *Iliad* 9 where Meleager's wife Cleopatra "begged him grieving, and listed for him all the sorrows that come to men whose city is taken: they kill the men"; fire turns the city to dust; "other men lead (ἄγουσι) off the children and the deep-bound women" (591-594). Why Croesus has brought the women with him on the pyre requires no further explanation. The Greek audience could think of similar suicides in recent history: the Carthaginian general Hamilcar threw himself into a sacrificial fire when his army was defeated by Hieron and his brothers at Himera in 480. In 476, Boges, the Persian governor of a town in Thrace, refused to surrender to the Athenians, and burned his family and the city's gold and himself on a pyre.[25]

τὰ πρόσθεν [ἐχ]θρὰ φίλα· θανεῖν γλύκιστον."
τοσ᾽ εἶπε, καὶ ἁβ'[ρο]βάταν κ[έλε]υσεν
ἅπτειν ξύλινον δόμον. ἔκ'[λα]γον δὲ
50 παρθένοι, φίλας τ᾽ ἀνὰ ματρὶ χεῖρας
(47-50, antistrophe 4)

The opening line of the antistrophe states with paradoxical brevity the reasons for Croesus' decision: "what was hateful is dear; dying is sweetest." The superlative γλύκιστον at the end of the line is emphatic; the beneficent deities of the ode, Demeter, Zeus, and Apollo, have been described with superlatives (1, 12, 22); the Muse Cleo is γλυκύδωρος (3). Again Croesus takes the initiative, ordering a Persian "fine stepper" (ἁβροβάτας), whose name connotes the luxury Croesus has abandoned, "to set fire to his wooden home." The dramatic δόμον, instead of "pyre," makes explicit the contrast between his present fate and his earlier life in the "bronze-walled palace" (32) which was his father Alyattes' "home" (δόμοι, 40), and the "well-built halls" from which the women are being led (46).[26]

The last lines of the stanza again describe his daughter's weeping: "and the maidens screamed, and their dear hands up to their mother . . ." Vocal expression accompanies every significant event in the poem: the daughters grieve (35) and Croesus cries out from the pyre (37), someone cries out that Hieron is "thrice fortunate" (9). παρθένοι gives new emphasis to the daughter's vulnerability; their hands are lifted up to their mother, as Croesus raised their hands to the gods when he spoke (36). The concentration on daughters and mother has special poignancy in an ode that began with an invocation to Demeter and Kore.[27]

> ἔβαλλον· ὁ γὰρ προφανὴς θνα-
> τοῖσιν ἔχθιστος φόνων·
> ἀλλ' ἐπεὶ δεινο[ῦ π]υρὸς
> λαμπρὸν διάϊ[σσεν μέ]ν̣ος,
> 55 Ζεὺς ἐπιστάσας [μελαγκευ]θὲς νέφος
> σβέννυεν ξανθὰ[ν φλόγα.
> (51-56, epode 4)

The first word of the epode ἔβαλλον, instead of "raised," as Croesus does earlier (36), expresses a new urgency. The girls' weeping has replaced Croesus' spoken prayer, with its logical questioning of repayment of debts. Then abruptly a general statement breaks the narrative, explaining the daughter's behavior: "for most hateful is the slaughter mortals see before them." We might have expected this idea to be stated in more personal terms, from the girls' point of view, who could, like Alcestis in Euripides' drama, see death standing before them, and describe his face and clothing (252-257, 259-263). But the generalization, phrased impersonally: (θνατοῖσιν ἔχθιστος) corresponds to Croesus' paradoxical "what was hateful (ἐχθρά) is dear; dying (θανεῖν) is sweetest" (47). Death is προφανής; in the ode's introduction attention was turned to Hieron's towered wealth (13) and the gold of the tripods standing before the temple (18).

The contrast between Croesus' reactions and his daughters' adds tension to the narrative; excitement is increased by the language Bacchylides uses to describe the fire: "but when the dread fire's shining force rushed through." πυρὸς μένος describes Hector at his most powerful, after he has killed Patroclus (*Il.* 17. 565), and later, the flames of Hector's own pyre (24. 792). The fire's force is λαμπρός, like the gold of Hieron's tripods that "shines" (λάμπει) beneath flashes (17).[28] Hieron's mares are swift (3), the Alpheus and Pactolus are "whirling" (6, 44); now the fire rushes through (διάϊσσεν). There is a dramatic contrast between this rapid motion and the stability of the rescue brought by god: "Zeus stood over them (ἐπιστάσας) . . . a cloud and quench the yellow flame." The tripods "stand" (σταθέντων) before the god's dwelling at Delphi (18). Darkness was a threat to Hieron's wealth (14), but to Croesus, a rain cloud and its accompanying darkness, as in *Pythian* 1, bring peace and order. The flame, by contrast is ξανθός, in color like the shining gold (17) of the tripods and the bronze walls of Croesus' palace (32), as if in illustration of the reversal of fortune described in Croesus' speech: "what is hateful is dear" (47).

> ἄπιστον οὐδέν, ὅ τι θ[εῶν μέ]ριμνα
> τεύχει· τότε Δαλογενὴ[ς Ἀπό]λλων
> φέρων ἐς Ὑπερβορέο[υς γ]έροντα
> 60 σὺν τανισφύροις κατ[έν]ασσε κούραις
> (57-60, strophe 5)

Again a general statement breaks the narrative, confirming the assertion that introduced the myth, "god is the best of prosperities" (21-22). In *Olympian* 1 Pindar attributed the power of making the unbelievable believable (ἄπιστον πιστόν) to the Joy of song (31), in *Ode* 3 credit goes to the gods. Zeus stood the cloud over the pyre, but it is Apollo, in repayment for Croesus' gifts, who carries Croesus and his daughters to safety: "nothing's beyond belief that . . . planning makes. Then Delos-born Apollo brought the old man to the Hyperboreans to dwell with his slim-ankled girls." The new epithet Δαλογενής reminds us that Apollo too was rescued miraculously at his birth.[29] The unusual **νάησατ'** described Croesus' construction of his pyre (33); now the god with the gold tripods before his **ναός** (19) makes Croesus and his daughters dwell (**κατένασσε**) in the land of the Hyperboreans. Hesiod describes how Zeus gave to some of the heroes of the Theban and Trojan wars "a life apart from men and a living place . . . and made them dwell (**κατένασσε**) at the bounds of the earth . . . in the islands of the blessed, beside the deep-whirling Oceanus" (*Works and Days* 167-171). The epic reminiscence confirms that the land of the Hyperboreans is for Croesus and his daughters like the islands of the blest for the Heroes of Troy and of Thebes. The phrase **τανίσφυροι κοῦραι**, which Hesiod uses to describe Oceanus' daughters (*Theogony* 364) reinforces the impression that Croesus has moved into another existence, nearer to the life of the gods.[30]

> δι' εὐσέβειαν, ὅτι μέ[γιστα] θνατῶν
> ἐς ἀγαθέαν ⟨ἀν⟩έπεμψε Π[υθ]ώ.
> ὅσο[ι] ⟨γε⟩ μὲν Ἑλλάδ' ἔχουσιν, [ο]ὔτι[ς,
> ὦ μεγαίνητε Ἱέρων, θελήσει
>
> (61-64, antistrophe 5)

The antistrophe returns us to the beginning of Croesus' story. His rescue came as reward for piety, "since he had sent the greatest gifts of mortals to holy Pytho." "Greatest" (**μέγιστον**) also described Phoebus' grove at Delphi. **θνατῶν** marks the essential distinction already emphasized in Croesus' story (**θανεῖν γλύκιστον**, 47; **θνατοῖσιν ἔχθιστος**, 51-52). Reference to Hellas signals a return to Hieron, who has "from Zeus honor leading most of Hellenes" (11-12), and the start of a second praise: "of all who hold Hellas, no one, O great-praised Hieron, will wish." Croesus' gifts are **μέγιστα**; the new **μεγαίνητος** now describes Hieron. At stanza end the sentence is left tantalizingly incomplete, postponing the long awaited comparison between Croesus and Hieron.

> 65 φάμ]εν σέο πλείονα χρυσὸν
> Λοξί]αι πέμψαι βροτῶν.
> εὖ λέ‚γειν πάρεστιν, ὅσ-
> τις μ]ὴ φθόνωι πιαίνεται,
> .....]λη φίλιππον ἄνδρ' ἀ[ρ]ήϊον
> 70 ....]ίον σκᾶπτρ[ο]ν Διό[ς]
>
> (65-70, epode 5)

As in the first epode, where a witness cried out "O thrice blessed," praise is expressed in terms of speech: "no one, O great-praised Hieron, will wish to say that he has sent more gold than you to Loxias." In the introduction the witness described Hieron as recipient of honor "leading most" (**πλείσταρχος**, 12), and giver of gold to Apollo (**χρυσός**, 17); here again he sends **πλείονα χρυσόν** than all Greeks. **βροτῶν** reinforces the association between Hieron and Croesus who of "mortals" (**θνατῶν**) of his day sent the greatest gifts to Delphi (61-62). The next lines continue to stress the importance of the spoken word: "it's easy to speak good, when one does not fatten oneself on envy." In the introduction, shrines swelling with feasts of cattle sacrificed (15) marked Hieron's success; those who begrudge success are accordingly characterized as gluttons, like Archilochus in *Pythian* 2. 55-56 (**πιαινόμενον**). After this requisite statement of the sincerity of his intent, the poet can again recite Hieron's achievements: his horses, here, with the new adjective **φίλιππος**, his wars, in the Homeric phrase **ἀρήϊος**; his justice, with reference to the "staff of Zeus" depicted on his coins and in *Pythian* 1. 6.[31]

> ἰοπ'λό]κων τε μέρο[ς ἔχοντ]α Μουσᾶν·
> ....]μαλέαι ποτ[ὲ......].'ιων
> ....]νος ἐφάμερον α[......]·
> ....]α σκοπεῖς· βραχ[ύς ἐστιν αἰών·
> (71-74, strophe 6)

Praise of Hieron continues in the first line of the new triad, with reference to the "share in the Muses" that has been celebrated consistently in other odes (e.g., *Ode* 5. 3-4). Here, as at the end of *Olympian* 1 ("I believe there is no other friend who knows beauty more," 103-104) mentioning the Muses introduces the advice that customarily concludes the ode. In *Olympian* 1 Pindar is concerned primarily with future achievement, by both poet and victor. In *Ode* 3, as far as we can determine from what is left of the papyrus, the subject is recognition of mortality: "of a day . . . you look (**σκοπεῖς**) . . . short," as opposed to "the last summit is scaled by kings; search (**πάπταινε**) no longer beyond" (*Ol.* 1. 113-114).

> 75 πτε₁ρ]όεσσα δ' ἐλπὶς ὑπ[∪∪_ν]όημα₁
> ἐφαμ]ερίων· ὁ δ' ἄναξ [Ἀπόλλων
> ....].'λος εἶπε Φέρη[τος υἷι·
> ,,θνατὸν εὖντα χρὴ διδύμους ἀέξειν
> (75-78, antistrophe 6)

The topic is hope—Prometheus gave man "blind hopes" to keep him from foreseeing when he will die (*Prometheus Bound* 250). Further advice is attributed to Apollo himself, from what he said to Admetus when he spent a year on earth as Admetus' slave, in punishment for trying to bring his son Asclepius back to life: "if one is mortal one must grow twin . . ." Apollo's remarks were celebrated in a special set of songs sung at drinking parties, the "Speeches to Admetus" ('**Ἀδμήτου λόγοι**).[32] But in Bacchylides' ode the way this traditional advice is phrased has special relevance for Hieron: the first word is "mortal" (**θνατόν**); Croesus' story concerned dying (**θανεῖν**, 47; **θνατοῖσιν**, 51-52); Hieron must "grow" (**ἀέξειν**, which in Homer refers to raising children or crops or cherishing some emotion); Hieron's wealth makes shrines and streets "swell" (15-16). Again the stanza ends in mid-sentence: what sort of twins should his hope for the future concern?

> γνώμας, ὅτι τ' αὔριον ὄψεαι
> 80 μοῦνον ἁλίου φάος,
> χὤτι πεντήκοντ' ἔτεα
> ζωὰν βαθύπ'λουτον τελεῖς.
> ὅσια δρῶν εὔφραινε θυμόν· τοῦτο γὰρ

κερδέων ὑπέρτατον."
(79-84, epode 6)

The epode reveals that Apollo's advice is to grow "thoughts" (γνώμαι) rather than what conventional patterns of language would lead us to expect, "grief" or one's "work" on a farm. The twin thoughts express what we have already heard in Croesus' story (*a*) that, as Croesus expects for himself, "you'll see only tomorrow's light," and (*b*) that, as his daughters wish, "you'll complete for fifty years a life of deep wealth." After the dramatic statement that Hieron "knows his towered wealth, not to hide it in black-robed darkness" (13-14), and the description of his gold "shining beneath flashes" (17), the traditional ἁλίου φάος and the new βαθύπλουτος have immediate significance. Apollo's concluding advice recapitulates the general truth that Croesus' story is meant to illustrate "by doing what's holy make your heart happy; for this is the highest of gains." The ode's introduction concluded with a description of the Delphians "pursuing Apollo's greatest grove" (18-21), and the statement "to god, to god give glory, for he is best of wealth" (21-22). The value previously assigned to victory (ὑπέροχος, 5) and to wealth (πυργωθείς 13; ὑψιδαιδάλτος, 18) in fact belongs to piety, since "doing what is holy" can give continued life.

85 φρονέοντι συνετὰ γαρύω· βαθὺς μέν
αἰθὴρ ἀμίαντος· ὕδωρ δὲ πόντου
οὐ σάπεται· εὐφροσύνα δ' ὁ χρυσός·
ἀνδρὶ δ' οὐ θέμις, πολιὸν π[αρ]έντα
(85-88, strophe 7)

The seventh triad explains how piety can bring life and joy to Hieron. The poet's "I speak" (γαρύω) marks a transition away from Apollo's advice to Admetus back directly to Hieron himself: "since you are wise I speak what can be understood." All general statements in the ode are expressed in formal speeches: the first praise is spoken by a witness of Hieron's achievement, "(he) cried out, 'ah thrice fortunate'" (9-10); Croesus speaks on the pyre about the reasons for his suicide (37-47); the second praise is also set in terms of what is said, "of all who hold Hellas, no one, O great-praised Hieron, will wish to say . . . " (63-65); we hear what Apollo *said* to Admetus, not of what he *did* during his stay on earth (76-84). But where Apollo's advice to Admetus concerned contentment (εὔφραινε, 83), the poet's formal statement of advice concerns understanding (φρονέοντι, συνετά). Hieron is the wise king who "knows (οἶδε) his towered wealth" (13). The lines derive special impact from their recollection of a passage in Pindar's *Olympian* 2, an ode composed for Hieron's brother-in-law Theron of Acragas, who won the chariot race in 476, the same year that Hieron won the horse race with Pherenicus:

> πολλά μοι ὑπ'
> ἀγκῶνος ὠκέα βέλη
> ἔνδον ἐντὶ φαρέτρας
> 85 φωνάεντα συνετοῖσιν· ἐς δὲ τὸ πᾶν ἑρμανέων
> χατίζει. σοφὸς ὁ πολλὰ εἰδὼς φυᾷ·
> μαθόντες δὲ λάβ'ροι
> παγγλωσσίᾳ κόρακες ὣς ἄκραντα γαρυέτων
> Διὸς πρὸς ὄρνιχα θεῖον·
>
> (83-88)

As in *Olympian* 1. 111-112 and *Pythian* 1. 12, words are arrows, shot from the poet's bow; like a warrior-athlete, he must perform with accuracy: "there are beneath my arm many swift arrows in my quiver that sing with what can be understood, and in everything they yearn for interpreters." Like the victor also, he must possess natural talent: "wise is he who knows many things by nature." Learning unsupported by innate ability will result in speech that cannot be understood "and those who learn, noisily, in every tongue, like crows let them speak what cannot be fulfilled against Zeus' holy bird." The comparison of the eagle to crows unable to accomplish their objective, like the simile of the eagle and the "shrill-voiced birds" in *Ode* 5. 22-23, pays tribute at once to poet and victor. In his brief recollection in *Ode* 3 (φρονέοντι συνετὰ γαρύω) of *Olympian* 2; Bacchylides has removed the contrast between those who are "wise by nature" and those "who have learned" and between the eagle and the crows; gone with the comparison is the sense of competition and the possibility of defeat. The focus is no longer on the poet's or the victor's supremacy, but rather on the content of what is said and heard.

The next lines continue to set what Pindar said into new perspective: "the deep air cannot be defiled. And the sea's water does not rot, and gold is heart's happiness." The reference to the opening of *Olympian* 1 is unmistakable. But in Bacchylides' catalogue the emphasis falls not on the light of water, gold, fire, and sun, but instead on physical decay. Air is not "empty" (ἐρημᾶς, *Ol.* 1. 6) but ἀμίαντος, "without blood-pollution." Instead of the unqualified declaration ἄριστον ὕδωρ, we hear that the sea's water "does not rot" (οὐ σάπεται). Gold does not "shine like blazing fire in the night" but is characterized rather from a practical point of view as εὐφροσύνη; Apollo's advice to Admetus was εὔφραινε θυμόν (83).[33]

What has already been said in *Ode* 3 about air, water, and gold adds further dimension: Croesus made his family's hands reach up into the "steep air" (αἰπὺν αἰθέρα, 36); Hieron's victory was won by the river Alpheus (6-7); the Delphians care for Apollo's grove beside Castalia's streams (20-21); the Pactolus river, by contrast, as the context implies, is polluted by death in Sardis' defeat (44-45). Only the sea's water can resist such "defilement." Bacchylides has turned Pindar's exciting, confident statement about the immortality of the games and the meaning of victory into a reminder of human mortality. Like all the other speeches in the poem, his words that "can be understood" (συνετά) concern death: the witness speaks of the black-robed darkness that threatens Hieron's wealth (13-14); Croesus says "dying is sweetest" (47); Apollo's advice concerns one's attitude toward the timing of life's end (79-84).

The last line of the strophe develops still further the list of constant truths: "and for a man it's not right to put aside gray . . ." The reference to mortality in the preceding lines have prepared us to include man's conduct—along with air, water, and gold—in a list of absolutes. θέμις, god's law, reiterates the contrast made throughout the ode between divine and human capability. Comparison to *Olympian* 1 adds poignancy, "gray" (πολιός), color of the stormy sea and of old age, has replaced the bright radiance of the sun.

> γῆρας, θάλ[εια]ν αὖτις ἀγκομίσσαι
> 90 ἥβαν. ἀρετᾶ[ς γε μ]ὲν οὐ μινύθει
> βροτῶν ἅμα σ[ώμ]ατι φέγγος, ἀλλὰ
> Μοῦσά νιν τρ[έφει.] Ἱέρων, σὺ δ' ὄλβον
> (89-92, antistrophe 7)

The list of constants is brought to a climax: "old age and bring back again full youth." ἀγκομίσσαι and παρέντα (88) treat γῆρας and ἥβαν as if they were personified; the myth contrasted the old man Croesus to his young daughters. θάλειος, Homeric epithet of banquets, now describes youth, suggesting at once its pleasure and impermanence; Hieron's victory made the shrines and streets burgeon (15-16). Bacchylides offers no "star radiant through the empty air hotter in day than the sun" (*Ol*. 1. 6), but instead what is within our reach, like the "leaf of good fortune" that Pherenicus brings to Hieron in *Ode* 5. 186: "for achievement's light does not grow weak with men's bodies, but the Muse nurses it." Witnesses can see the towered wealth that is not hidden in black-robed darkness (13-14); the gold of the tripods shines beneath flashes (17). The god may not bring Hieron to the Hyperboreans, but his achievement can live on through song. τρέφει stresses again men's dependence on divinity; in *Olympian* 1, Hieron's fame shines and Pelops' fame "looks far out" (23-24, 93-94) without reference to divine support. The stanza ends in mid-sentence, "Hieron, your prosperity's." The myth began with the statement "(god) is best of prosperities" (ὄλβων also at stanza end, 22):

we may expect renewed confirmation in the epode.

> κάλλιστ' ἐπεδ[είξ]αο θνατοῖς
> ἄνθεα· π¹ράξα[ντι] δ' εὖ
> 95 οὐ φέρει κόσμ[ον σι]ω-
> πά· σὺν δ' ἀλαθ[είαι] καλῶν
> καὶ μελιγ¹λώσσου τις ὑμνήσει χάριν
> Κηΐας ἀηδόνος.
>
> (93-98, epode 7)

Recapitulation indicates that the ode is drawing to a close. "(Prosperity's) most beautiful flowers you have shown to mortals," restates in positive terms the witness' assertion that Hieron "knows not to hide towered wealth in black-robed darkness" (13-14). God is ἄριστος ὄλβων; Hieron shows ὄλβου κάλλιστ' ἄνθεα; his wealth, like the εὐδαιμονίας πέταλον brought him by Pherenicus in *Ode* 5. 186 is beautiful but transient. The myth and Apollo's and the poet's advice concern man as θνατός: Croesus says that θανεῖν is sweetest (47); the foreseen death is most hateful θνατοῖσιν (also at the second line of an epode, 51); Apollo advises "if one is mortal" (θνατόν, 78). κόσμος, emblem of victory, is brought by speech: "for a man who does well, silence brings no ornament." The first praise of Hieron was a quotation from a witness of his achievement (9-14); everyone will say that he has sent the most gold to Apollo (63-66). The song the poet brings the victor will likewise be celebrated by other poets: "with true memory of the beautiful someone will sing praise of the joy also of the honey-tongued Cean nightingale." Hieron and Bacchylides will not, like Croesus, go to the land of the Hyperboreans, but Hieron's achievement and Bacchylides' joy will live on in song.

Echoes of what we have heard before keep us from sensing in these final lines any notes of triumph. μελιγλώσσου ἀηδόνος characterized Bacchylides at once as both a sweet and sad singer: in Homer the nightingale "sings beautifully (καλόν) when spring first comes in the thick leaves of the trees, turning her voice lamenting her child Itylus," whom she killed (*Odyssey* 19. 518-523).[34] By speaking of himself as the "singer" bird (ἀηδών), rather than as an eagle, as in *Ode* 5. 16-30, Bacchylides reminds us once again that his song concerns the passing of the seasons and death. Nothing in the ode could have led us to expect that he would conclude with "may you through this time walk high, and may I stay so long with winners of victory, and be seen first in poetry among Greeks everywhere" (*Olympian* 1. 115-116).

An ode that concentrates on death and defeat may seem a curious way to celebrate a victory, particularly the victory in the chariot race at Olympia that Hieron had worked toward for so long. Hieron must have known, from *Ode* 5, with its long narrative of Meleager's struggles and cruel death, what sort of an ode he could expect from Bacchylides. Why would a song that seemingly undermines the whole notion of success appeal to him?

We need look no further than contemporary drama to find the answer. The wealthy and powerful are struck down at the height of their success, like Xerxes in *The Persians*, or Agamemnon. No Zeus or Apollo comes to save them. Success elicits envy, from gods as well as men. Accordingly the most comfortable way to celebrate achievement is to emphasize its transience and frailty. *Ode* 3 recalls *Olympian* 1 explicitly in order to deny the value that Pindar places on success. Victory at Olympia is no longer the radiant sun, but has instead been diminished to a "light" the Muse "nurses" (91-92) in a world where "black-robed darkness" (13) threatens to hide the evidence of man's accomplishment. Pindar in *Pythian* 1 says Croesus is remembered for "his achievement, his friendly thought" (94). In *Ode* 3 we see Croesus on his funeral pyre, commanding his own death. He is rescued not for his achievement nor for his generosity to men but because of his piety, since he had sent more gifts than any man to Loxias. The importance of Hieron's role in winning the victory is minimized: his horses and his patron deities, not he himself, garner the opening praise. By denying recognition of success, *Ode* 3 acts as insurance against the catastrophic failures that inevitably seem to follow acknowledgement of great achievement.

In his insistence in *Ode* 3 on the transience of human accomplishment, Bacchylides expresses, as he does also in *Ode* 5, the outlook and apprehensions of his contemporaries. His appeal as a poet derives in no small measure from his being so well attuned to the tastes and concerns of his times. He employs the dramatists' technique of having events reported rather than enacted: in *Ode* 5, the poet strikes the ground and swears (42), Meleager tells the story of his life, the poet quotes Hesiod's saying about praise (191-193); in *Ode* 3 a witness cries out in praise of Hieron, Croesus speaks on the pyre, the girls scream at approaching death, Apollo talks to Admetus, and the poet speaks to Hieron, in the stately Dorian meter of the epodes, in contrast to the more excited Lydian meter of the narrative in the strophes.[35] Antitheses are sharply drawn: the Alpheus is matched by the Pactolus (6-7, 44-45); the hateful becomes dear (47); Hieron's towered wealth is set against Croesus' "wooden home" (13, 49), and gold, shining beneath flashes (17) is mirrored in the shining flames of the pyre (53-56). Direct repetition lends special emphasis: βρύει/βρύουσι (15-16); θεὸν θεόν (21); ποῦ . . . ποῦ (38-39). Less obvious to us, but none the less characteristic of his time, is the degree to which Bacchylides relies for effect on recognition of reminiscence. As Heraclitus seems to expect his audience to know Xenophanes' poetry and the sayings of Pythagoras that he criticizes so bitterly,

Bacchylides likewise counts on his audience to hear and enjoy the way he revises the proem to Pindar's *Olympian* 1 in the second praise of *Ode* 3, his own "Olympian 2" for Hieron. Imitation of this sort was a mark of inventiveness and virtuosity. Attic drinking songs each begin with the same phrases; the audience took pleasure in seeing how each new speaker would make his version end.

Bacchylides' adherence to traditional style would inevitably have made his work more readily comprehensible than Pindar's. His tendency to reiterate, rather than to develop, themes also helps the listener grasp his central message without prolonged reflection. The statement "he knows his towered wealth, not to hide it in black-robed darkness" (13-14) is quickly restated in the gold of the tripods (17), then finds direct antithesis in the yellow flame of Croesus' pyre (53-56), and brief recapitulation in the "light of achievement" (90-91).[36] In *Pythian* 1, by contrast, where the proem is more complex than in *Ode* 3, analogies and antitheses are less easily charted. Singers and dancers hear and watch the lyre (2-4); witnesses see and hear Aetna's eruptions (26), but sound also becomes a dark cloud (7) that is counterposed to Aetna's white snows (20) and then by blazing streams of smoke (22) and the sleeping eagle (6) is contrasted first to the restless Typhos (28), and later to the exhaustion of both the victorious Hieron (46) and his defeated enemies (78, 80). The lyre's sound also becomes rain (5) that in turn is like arrows shot from a bow (10): the poet casts his javelins on target (44-45), archer Philoctetes wins the war for the Greeks (53), the Medes have bent bows (78), the victor's tongue is forged like a javelin or an arrow tip upon an anvil (86).

Pindar's ability to amalgamate disparate ideas reveals itself most dramatically in intensely compacted phrases like "everlasting satisfaction dulls swift hopes" (82-83), which has several meanings, none of which make sense out of context. But even Bacchylides' compressed introductory statements are not incomprehensible initially or when seen in isolation. "He knows his towered wealth, not to hide it in black-robed darkness" relies on familiar analogies; the description of a lyre's arrows quenching darkness, or of a tongue forged in bronze require us to rethink old configurations of myth and language. Bacchylides, more reassuringly, reminds us of what we already know. Traditionalism makes his poems appear more detached and impartial; Pindar's poetry seems more expressive of personal commitment, because in his consistent efforts to combine and compare he involves his own aspirations and achievements closely with the victor's. There is no analogue in *Ode* 3 to "that man I hope to praise striving not to throw my bronze-cheeked javelin outside the contest" (*Pyth.* 1. 43-45), or to "so for me the Muse nurses (τρέφει) her strongest weapon with courage" (*Ol.* 1. 111-112), where the Muse "nurses achievement's light" (90-91). Bacchylides instead remains impersonally excellent, like the Homeric bard, describing his role in archetypal terms as ξένος (*Ode* 5. 11) or ἀηδών (*Ode* 3. 98), identifying himself only by nationality (*Ode* 5. 10-11, 3. 98). The poet's portrayals of themselves provide accurate brief characterizations of their styles: Pindar's is straining and combative, Bacchylides' reflective and accepting.

Pindar's *Pythian* 3

But Pindar could compose an ode for Hieron in more conventional language and in the traditional archaic manner, stressing human weakness, by telling myths of failure, and by explicitly demonstrating their relevance to Hieron's present success. The ode called *Pythian* 3 in our collection impressed Thoreau as "one of the most memorable," and he translated long sections of it, more than from any other ode, as if in testimony to the clarity of its message. This apparent simplicity makes it anomalous; it seems less like a victory ode than a "poetic letter" or elegy of some sort, remote from the fact of victory, concerned with the larger issues of human mortality. Its format also is unconventional, with a long narrative introduction before the first praise, like *Pythian* 1. Again, Pindar appears to be attempting to circumvent limitations of established norms, and to say more than the occasion of victory would ordinarily demand. This time his experimentation results in what appears, at least on the surface, to be a new poetic genre.

> Ἤθελον Χίρωνά κε Φιλλυρίδαν,
> εἰ χρεὼν τοῦθ᾽ ἁμετέρας ἀπὸ γλώσσας
>   κοινὸν εὔξασθαι ἔπος,
> ζώειν τὸν ἀποιχόμενον,
> Οὐρανίδα γόνον εὐρυμέδοντα Κρόνου,
>   βάσσαισί τ᾽ ἄρχειν Παλίου φῆρ᾽ ἀγ'ρότερον
> 5   νόον ἔχοντ᾽ ἀνδρῶν φίλον· οἷος ἐὼν θρέψεν ποτέ
> τέκτονα νωδυνίας
>   ἥμερον γυιαρκέος Ἀσκλαπιόν,
> ἥροα παντοδαπᾶν ἀλκτῆρα νούσων.
>
>   (1-7, strophe 1)

The first sentence, a wish that cannot be fulfilled, establishes the principal theme of the ode: the definition of what is possible:[37] "I would wish that Chiron, Phillyra's son, if I must pray from my tongue this word that we share, were living, who is gone, wide-ruler son of Heaven's son Cronus, and that he were leader in Pelion's valley, a wild beast who had a mind friendly to men." The initial designation of the Centaur Chiron by his mother's name denotes the human side of his nature. **κοινὸν ἔπος** establishes that whatever will be said about Chiron applies to both poet and patron.[38] The narrative centers on death: ζώειν τὸν ἀποιχόμενον completes the opening condition. There is emphasis also on parentage; Cronos, Cheiron's father, in addition to his mother Phillyra, is named. Geography is precise; "in Pelion's valley." Cheiron's νόος φίλος is contrasted to his physical make-up, φῆρ ἀγρότερον. The reference to his "friendly mind" leads to a more precise definition of theme; "such as he was, he raised once a carpenter of limb-guarding painlessness, hero Asclepius, hero-rescuer from all kinds of diseases." Our experience with other odes should prepare us to anticipate that the strange phrase τέκτονα νωδυνίας would later be elaborated in the myth and is meant to associate medicine with other skills and achievements. The specific references to parentage, geography, and healing in the strophe, as we might by now expect, constitute a statement of themes, and set the direction of the narrative to follow.

> τὸν μὲν εὐίππου Φλεγύα θυγάτηρ
> πρὶν τελέσσαι ματροπόλῳ σὺν Ἐλειθυί-
> ᾳ, δαμεῖσα χ᾽ρυσέοις
> 10 τόξοισιν ὕπ᾽ Ἀρτέμιδος
> εἰς Ἀΐδα δόμον ἐν θαλάμῳ κατέβα,
> τέχ᾽ναις Ἀπόλλωνος. χόλος δ᾽ οὐκ ἀλίθιος
> γίνεται παίδων Διός. ἁ δ᾽ ἀποφλαυρίξαισά νιν
> ἀμπλακίαισι φρενῶν,
> ἄλλον αἴνησεν γάμον κρύβδαν πατρός,
> πρόσθεν ἀκερσεκόμᾳ μιχθεῖσα Φοίβῳ,
>
> (8-14, antistrophe 1)

As in *Pythian* 1, the introduction to the ode expands into a narrative, instead of moving in the conventional manner, to praise of the victor. The narrative at first concerns not Asclepius himself, but his mother Coronis: Chiron was first introduced to us as "Phillyra's son" (1): "him (Asclepius) once horseman Phlegyas' daughter, before she could accomplish with the attendant of mothers, Eleithuia, tamed with the gold bow by Artemis, she went down to Hades' home, in her bedroom, through the skill of Apollo." Coronis' story is told in the archaic style, with conclusion first, as in *Pythian* 2; "Ixion says this to mortals as he is whirled everywhere on his winged wheel" (21-22). The way in which the story is told emphasizes the gods' powers: Eleithuia is needed for birth, Artemis causes her death by disease, Apollo somehow devises it with unspecified τέχναις. The significance of skill was established in the strophe with the designation of Apollo's son Asclepius as "carpenter of limb-guarding painlessness" (6). The concluding lines of the antistrophe tell why Coronis died: "No wasted anger comes of Zeus' children. She made small of him (Apollo); in the errors of her heart she praised another marriage, hidden from her father; earlier she had been mixed with Phoebus with unshorn hair." The disparity between mortal and god is brought out by diction: ἄλλον γάμον is opposed to the Homeric ἀκερσεκόμᾳ **Φοίβῳ**, with the god's name falling emphatically at line end.

> 15 καὶ φέροισα σπέρμα θεοῦ καθαρόν
> οὐκ ἔμειν' ἐλθεῖν τράπεζαν νυμφίαν,
> οὐδὲ παμφώνων ἰαχὰν ὑμεναίων, ἅλικες
> οἷα παρθένοι φιλέοισιν ἑταῖραι
> ἑσπερίαις ὑποκουρίζεσθ' ἀοιδαῖς· ἀλλά τοι
> 20 ἤρατο τῶν ἀπεόντων· οἷα καὶ πολλοὶ πάθον.
> ἔστι δὲ φῦλον ἐν ἀνθρώποισι ματαιότατον,
> ὅστις αἰσχύνων ἐπιχώρια παπταίνει τὰ πόρσω,
> μεταμώνια θηρεύων ἀκράντοις ἐλπίσιν.
> (15-23, epode 1)

The next stanza describes her error in more detail: "and she bore the pure seed of the god: she did not wait to come to the bride's table, nor to the cry of all-sounding wedding (songs) which girls her age, her companions, sing young in friendly evening songs." Surprisingly, the impurity that results from her "other marriage, hidden from her father" (13) gets less attention than her unwillingness to wait for marriage approved in the traditional fashion: the wedding table, the ritual song, the singing which girls her age normally enjoy—**ἅλικες παρθένοι ἑταῖραι ὑποκουρίζεσθαι**. The next lines restate the problem in more general terms. "But you see, she lusted for what was far away, and this many have done. There is a tribe among men, most foolish: someone who is ashamed of what is in his hand and reaches for what is far beyond, and hunts what is in the wind with hopes that cannot be fulfilled." The basic thought in these lines is traditional; Pindar in *Pythian* 2 comments on Ixion's story that "one must always see according to oneself the measure of everything" (34), that is, know one's limitations as a mortal. In *Pythian* 3 the idea is expressed not in terms of vision, but in terms of the near and the far; the songs at home as compared to "hunting what is in the wind." The stanza ends emphatically with **ἀκράντοις ἐλπίσιν**. The ode began with a wish for Chiron's life (1-3) impossible of fulfillment.

> ἔσχε τοι ταύταν μεγάλαν ἀνάταν
> 25 καλλιπέπ'λου λῆμα Κορωνίδος· ἐλθόν-
> τος γὰρ εὐνάσθη ξένου
> λέκτροισιν ἀπ' Ἀρκαδίας.
> οὐδ' ἔλαθε σκοπόν· ἐν δ' ἄρα μηλοδόκῳ
> Πυθῶνι τόσσαις ἄιεν ναοῦ βασιλεύς
> Λοξίας, κοινᾶνι παρ' εὐθυτάτῳ γνώμαν πιθών,
> πάντα ἰσάντι νόῳ·
> ψευδέων δ' οὐχ ἅπτεται, κλέπτει τέ μιν
> 30 οὐ θεὸς οὐ βροτὸς ἔργοις οὔτε βουλαῖς.
> (24-30, strophe 2)

The new triad reviews in detail the paradoxical statement with which the story began, about how Coronis died of disease before Asclepius was born: "She had this great delusion, the will of Coronis, fair-gowned. When a stranger came from far Arcadia she slept with him in her bed." What was first called "the errors of her heart (13) is now specifically ἀυάταν, the "delusion" that also brought Ixion (*Pyth.* 2. 28) and Tantalus (*Ol.* 1. 57) punishments. That the subject of the sentence turns out to be λῆμα Κορωνίδος rather than Coronis herself, reminds us of the importance of intention established in the opening lines of the description of Chiron's "friendly mind" (5). How the statement about the folly of lusting for what is far away applies specifically to Coronis now becomes clear: she slept with a stranger who came from Arcadia.[39] The seemingly redundant εὐνάσθη λέκτροισιν is a sinister reminder that she died ἐν θαλάμῳ. As in the cases of Ixion and Tantalus, her punishment fits her crime.

The audience now waits to hear how Apollo learned of Coronis' infidelity, and how he killed her. The traditional story was that a crow (κορωνίς) sees the girl Coronis and her lover Ischys, and tells Apollo, who punished the crow for bringing the bad news by turning him from white to black. But Pindar, characteristically, never mentions the crow. In a departure from tradition that matches his alteration of Pelops' myth, he makes Apollo omniscient, so that wrong-doing, ignorance and deception remain the exclusive characteristics of mortal men. "But she did not escape her watcher. He happened to be in sheep-taking Pytho when he heard, Loxias the temple's king, and he persuaded his knowing with his straightest sharer, his mind that sees all." When Pindar revised the story of Pelops, he told us explicitly why and where he made the change: "For me there is no way to say one of the blessed is a glutton. I stand aside" (*Ol.* 1. 52). But here there is no warning; in fact till the end of the sentence, one might assume that Apollo was holding a conversation with a trusted friend, κοινᾶνι παρ' εὐθυτάτῳ γνώμαν πιθών, like his sacred bird, the raven: the poet shares with his patron a κοινὸν ἔπος (2) in the ode's introduction. But then dramatically comes πάντα ἰσάντι νόῳ, reinforced in the closing lines of the stanza by "He does not touch lies, no one deceives him, not god nor man in deeds or plans." The good Chiron has a φίλον νόον (5), but Coronis has only a λῆμα (25), since she is one of the tribe of men who hunts what is in the wind (23).

> καὶ τότε γ'νοὺς Ἴσχυος Εἰλατίδα
> ξεινίαν κοίταν ἄθεμίν τε δόλον, πέμ-
> ψεν κασιγ'νήταν μένει
> θυίοισαν ἀμαιμακέτῳ
> ἐς Λακέρειαν, ἐπεὶ παρὰ Βοιβιάδος
> κρημνοῖσιν ᾤκει παρθένος· δαίμων δ' ἕτερος

35 ἐς κακὸν τρέψαις ἐδαμάσσατό νιν, καὶ γειτόνων
πολλοὶ ἐπαῦρον, ἁμᾶ
δ' ἔφθαρεν· πολλὰν δ' {ἐν} ὄρει πῦρ ἐξ ἑνός
σπέρματος ἐνθορὸν ἀίστωσεν ὕλαν.
(31-36, antistrophe 2)

 Now the narrative again returns to the established plot, but with the emphasis again on geography: Coronis must die in her home where she belongs. "And then (Apollo) knew Ischys, Eilatus' son, the stranger's bed and the unlawful treachery, and he sent his sister with vast power raging to Lakereia, since beside the banks of Borbas the girl made her home." That Artemis is θυίοισα suggests that her revenge, like a bacchant's, will be both irrestible and indiscriminate. We hear in the next lines that many innocent people die along with her. "Another fate turned to evil and tamed her, and many neighbors were taken, and with her were destroyed. For on a mountain, fire impregnated from a single seed makes much wood unseen." The very act Coronis thought would bring pleasure leads to unexpected destruction; δαίμων ἕτερος ἐς κακὸν τρέψαις, as in the case of Ixion for whom εὐναὶ παράτροποι ἐς κακότατα ἀθρόαν ἔβαλον, "the bed turned-round threw him into crowded evil" (*Pyth.* 2. 35-36). The disease is not described, only its effects, and then by analogy to a spark that starts a forest fire. But the fire itself is described in sexual terminology: it is ἐνθορὸν σπέρματος, "impregnated from a single seed"; Coronis carried "the pure seed (σπέρμα) of the god (15). ἀίστωσεν, "made unseen" contrasts the fate of the trees and the people they represent to god's omniscience, πάντα ἰσάντι νόῳ (29).

ἀλλ' ἐπεὶ τείχει θέσαν ἐν ξυλίνῳ
σύγγονοι κούραν, σέλας δ' ἀμφέδ'ραμεν
40 λάβ'ρον Ἁφαίστου, τότ' ἔειπεν Ἀπόλλων· 'Οὐκέτι
τλάσομαι ψυχᾷ γένος ἁμὸν ὀλέσσαι
οἰκτροτάτῳ θανάτῳ ματρὸς βαρείᾳ σὺν πάθᾳ.'
ὣς φάτο· βάματι δ' ἐν πρώτῳ κιχὼν παῖδ' ἐκ νεκροῦ
ἅρπασε· καιομένα δ' αὐτῷ διέφαινε πυρά.
45 καί ῥά νιν Μάγ'νητι φέρων πόρε Κενταύρῳ διδάξαι
πολυπήμονας ἀνθρώποισιν ἰᾶσθαι νόσους.
(38-46, epode 2)

 The fire that concluded the antistrophe becomes in the epode a funeral pyre. "But when they placed the maiden in a wooden wall, her relatives, and the brilliance of Hephaestus ran hungry about her, then Apollo said, 'No, I will not endure in my heart to destroy my offspring in his mother's most pitiful death, in her heavy suffering.'" The scene of sudden rescue and the phrase τείχει ξυλίνῳ, the description of the bright flames (σέλας λάβρον 'Αφαίστου) resemble Bacchylides' account of Croesus' burning ξύλινον δόμον (Ode 3. 49) and the πυρὸς λαμπρὸν μένος around him (53-54). Here too the presence of death is emphasized, by the juxtaposition of Asclepius' οἰκτροτάτῳ θανάτῳ and Coronis' βαρείᾳ πάθᾳ in a single line. In Ode 3, after Bacchylides describes how the maidens wept and threw their arms around their mother, he comments ὁ γὰρ προφανὴς θνατοῖσιν ἔχθιστος φόνων (51-52). But in Pindar's account the emphasis is on compassion rather than on reward. Apollo pities his son and Coronis; the importance of kinship is stressed also in the juxtaposition σύγγονοι κούραν describing the relatives placing Coronis on the pyre (39). Apollo in Ode 3 brought Croesus to the Hyperboreans; Pindar's account describes the rescue of Asclepius in terms of near and far: "and he came in his first step and seized his son from the corpse. The burning pyre shone through to him, and he brought him to Magnesia and gave him to the Centaur to teach him to heal the many pains of men's diseases." The god Apollo can traverse in a single step the distances that keep men separate from each other, just as he can see from Delphi what Coronis is doing in Thessaly (27-29); to him there is no far-away to hunt with hopes unfulfilled (22-23). Fire makes forests unseen (ἀΐστωσεν, 37); but the burning pyre provides light for Apollo. The last lines of the stanza return us to the starting point of the story; "such as he was he raised once a carpenter of limb-guarding painlessness, gentle Asclepius, hero-rescuer from all kinds of diseases" (5-7). The last word of the second epode is νόσους; the first strophe ends with νούσων (7).

>   τοὺς μὲν ὦν, ὅσσοι μόλον αὐτοφύτων
>   ἑλκέων ξυνάονες, ἢ πολιῷ χαλκῷ μέλη τετ'ρωμένοι
>   ἢ χερμάδι τηλεβόλῳ,
> 50 ἢ θερινῷ πυρὶ περθόμενοι δέμας ἢ
>   χειμῶνι, λύσαις ἄλλον ἀλλοίων ἀχέων
>   ἔξαγεν, τοὺς μὲν μαλακαῖς ἐπαοιδαῖς ἀμφέπων,
>   τοὺς δὲ προσανέα πί-
>   νοντας, ἢ γυίοις περάπτων πάντοθεν
>   φάρμακα, τοὺς δὲ τομαῖς ἔστασεν ὀρθούς·
>
>   (47-53, strophe 3)

The third strophe provides more specific illustration of the general description of Asclepius at the end of the preceding epode; πολυπήμονας ἀνθρώποισιν ἰᾶσθαι νόσους (46), and the initial characterization of Asclepius as τέκτονα νωδυνίας γυιαρκέος and ἥροα παντοδαπᾶν ἀλκτῆρα νούσων (5-7). As in other odes, ideas which first appeared in compressed compound adjectives such as γυιαρκής (6) and πολυπημών (46), or in metaphorical terms like τέκτων or the Homeric ἀλκτήρ (6, 7) are "opened out" into full sentences: "some men who came as comrades to wounds grown in them, either with their limbs hurt by grey bronze or by far-thrown stone, or with their bodies ravaged by hot fire or winter storm, (these) he freed, one after the other and led them out; some he grasped with gentle incantations, and others drank potions, or he touched drugs to their limbs all over, and stood others straight with incisions." The detail indicates the extent of his skill; reminiscences of Coronis' story make his art seem more potent: men stricken with fevers are **θερινῷ πυρὶ περθόμενοι**; Coronis' disease killed others as well, as **πῦρ** from one seed destroys a whole forest (36-37); Asclepius himself was rescued miraculously from the flames of his mother's **πυρά** (44). Men "came as comrades to wounds grown in them" (**αὐτοφύτων ἑλκέων ξυνάονες**, 47-48); the god Apollo instead has his mind as close companion (**κοινᾶνι**, 28).

        ἀλλὰ κέρδει καὶ σοφία δέδεται.
55 ἔτ'ραπεν καὶ κεῖνον ἀγάνορι μισθῷ
        χρυσὸς ἐν χερσὶν φανείς
        ἄνδρ' ἐκ θανάτου κομίσαι
        ἤδη ἁλωκότα· χερσὶ δ' ἄρα Κ'ρονίων
        ῥίψαις δι' ἀμφοῖν ἀμπνοὰν στέρνων κάθελεν
        ὠκέως, αἴθων δὲ κεραυνὸς ἐνέσκιμψεν μόρον.
        χρὴ τὰ ἐοικότα πὰρ
        δαιμόνων μαστευέμεν θναταῖς φρασίν
60 γνόντα τὸ πὰρ ποδός, οἵας εἰμὲν αἴσας.
                      (54-60, antistrophe 3)

But in the antistrophe the ideal world described in the strophe comes abruptly to an end. "But even art is bound by gain." The language is again general, suggesting wide application, to arts other than medicine; Pindar's word for poetry is **σοφία** (*Pyth.* 2. 56, *Ol.* 1. 9, *Pyth.* 1. 12). The particular case of Asclepius is now detailed: "Gold turned even him with great man's pay, shining in his hands, to bring back a man from death already taken." **ἔτραπεν** comes, emphatically, first in the sentence. "Turning" already has sinister connotations: "another fate turned (**τρέψαις**) to evil and tamed" Coronis (34-35); Apollo, by contrast, has his mind as "straightest" (**εὐθυτάτῳ**, 28) counsellor. The gold **φανείς** in Asclepius' hands as Coronis' pyre **διέφαινε** for Apollo (44). But man cannot repeat god's miracle. Asclepius dies the fiery death from which his father had saved him: "and with his hands both, Cronus' son threw and took the breath from his breast swiftly, and a blazing lightning bolt hurled his fate on him." Apollo snatched (**ἅρπασε**) the baby Asclepius from the fire (44); now Zeus' lightning seizes (**κάθελεν**) the breath from Asclepius' body. Asclepius had saved men by touching drugs to their limbs (52-53); now Zeus **χερσὶ ῥίψαις δι' ἀμφοῖν** seizes the breath from

Asclepius' breast in grim reminder of the distinction between divine and human capability. A general statement returns us to the start of Asclepius' story and the impossible wish expressed at the ode's opening: "we must seek what is fitting from the gods with our mortal hearts, knowing what is before our feet, of what destiny we are." γνόντα τὸ πὰρ ποδός restates the traditional maxim γνῶθι σαυτόν into the idiom of distance. Fools, like Coronis, are ashamed of "what is in their land" (τὰ ἐπιχώρια) and look for τὰ πόρσω (22) but "what is far off" is accessible only to a god.

> μή, φίλα ψυχά, βίον ἀθάνατον
> σπεῦδε, τὰν δ᾽ ἔμπρακτον ἄντλει μαχανάν.
> εἰ δὲ σώφρων ἄντρον ἔναι᾽ ἔτι Χίρων, καί τί οἱ
> φίλτρον ⟨ἐν⟩ θυμῷ μελιγάρυες ὕμνοι
> 65 ἁμέτεροι τίθεν, ἰατῆρά τοί κέν νιν πίθον
> καί νυν ἐσλοῖσι παρασχεῖν ἀνδράσιν θερμᾶν νόσων
> ἤ τινα Λατοΐδα κεκλημένον ἢ πατέρος.
> καί κεν ἐν ναυσὶν μόλον Ἰονίαν τάμνων θάλασσαν
> Ἀρέθοισαν ἐπὶ κράναν παρ᾽ Αἰτναῖον ξένον,

(61-69, epode 3)

The third epode begins with a restatement of the limitations of mortality, but this time with special application to the present: "do not, dear life, rush for existence immortal, but drain the means that can be done." Man's life now appears to be a voyage; one should not rush, like the fools who hunt what is in the wind (23), for the immortal life that lies beyond our reach, but do what lies within our means, emptying the bilge so that the boat does not sink. The language is general enough to apply to both poet and patron. But the next lines indicate that the poet is primarily concerned with his own role. "If wise Chiron still lived in his cave and on his heart our songs, honey-talking, could place some charm, I would have persuaded him now also to provide good men with a healer from hot diseases, either someone called the son of Leto's son, or the father's." The impossible wish with which the ode began is restated, with special application to the poet's own art. The designation of song as **φίλτρον** makes it resemble Asclepius' potions (προσανέα, 52) and drugs (**φάρμακα**, 53) with their limitations. Again we hear of **νόσων**, as in 46 and 7, this time "hot" (**θερμᾶν**), like the **θερινῷ πυρί** that connoted fever in the description of Asclepius' cures (50). The detailing of genealogy, "son of Leto's son" (Asclepius); "son of the Father" (Apollo, son of Zeus, who is called simply "Father" also at line 98 and in *Olympian* 1. 57) reminds us of the importance of parentage. Such ability to cure belongs to the sons of gods. The closing lines of the stanza apply the unfulfillable condition directly to Pindar and Hieron: "and I would have come in a ship and cut the Ionian sea to Arethusa's spring to my Aetnaean friend." Pindar has turned the conventional statement about the foreign poet's ξενία for his patron (e.g. *Ode* 5. 10-12, *Pyth.* 2. 3-4) into yet another expression of human limitations. Again, as in the epode's opening lines there is an impossible voyage, again as in the story of Coronis, geographical detail emphasizes distance. Hieron is not called φίλος (as in *Pyth.* 1. 92), but ξένος, "friend-from-abroad"; Coronis slept with ξένος from Arcadia (25).

> ὃς Συρακόσσαισι νέμει βασιλεύς,
> πραΰς ἀστοῖς, οὐ φθονέων ἀγαθοῖς, ξεί-
>   νοις δὲ θαυμαστὸς πατήρ.
> τῷ μὲν διδύμας χάριτας
> εἰ κατέβαν ὑγίειαν ἄγων χρυσέαν
>   κῶμόν τ' ἀέθ'λων Πυθίων αἴγλαν στεφάνοις,
>   τοὺς ἀριστεύων Φερένικος ἕλεν Κίρρᾳ ποτέ,
> 75 ἀστέρος οὐρανίου
>   φαμὶ τηλαυγέστερον κείνῳ φάος
> ἐξικόμαν κε βαθὺν πόντον περάσαις.
>
> (70-76, strophe 4)

The first praise—so long postponed—now begins indirectly, as it does also in *Pythian* 1 (30), with a relative clause; "who steers the Syracusans as king, kind to his citizens, not envious to good men, and a wondrous father to friends (from abroad)." The usual elements of tribute are all here; kingly power, generosity, ξενία. πραΰς ἀστοῖς adds a dimension to Hieron's character not mentioned in the more authoritarian praise of the other odes: Asclepius was man's "gentle" (ἥμερος) hero-rescuer. But instead of the conventional reference to the specifics of victory, the poet describes a wish that could not be fulfilled: "to him if I had gone down and brought twin Joys, golden health and a celebration of Pythian prizes, the brightness with crowns which Pherenicus as best took once at Cirrha, I say a light shining further than a heavenly star to him I would have come when I crossed the deep sea." In the preceding stanza the poet stated that if his song could bring a healer he would have come across the sea with him to Sicily (63-69); the wish is reiterated now with new detail. We expect first that he will speak of the traditional Charites that accompany victory, as Bacchylides describes himself in *Ode* 5, "now with the Charites deep-bound he has woven a song of praise from the holy island, a friend to your famed city he sends it" (9-12). But then we hear that the first *charis* he has in mind is "Golden health," and the second the victory celebration itself, the αἴγλα (not the traditional *Charis* Ἀγλαΐα) with crowns that Pherenicus won once at Delphi; ποτέ which also designates the indefinite past time of Asclepius' upbringing

(5), implies that the victories are long past. Pherenicus won the horse race on the coastal plain at Cirrha below Delphi in 482 and 478. The earlier statement that his song could not bring a healer to Sicily makes it clear that he could have brought only one of the twin *charites*, the celebration. The *charis* golden health is beyond his skill. Had he been able to bring both he would have come as ἀστέρος οὐρανίου τηλαυγέστερον φάος: the terminology suggests both the Homeric saving light of rescue in battle and the φαεννὸν ἄστρον in *Olympian* 1 that signified the ultimate achievement, victory at Olympia (6).

> ἀλλ' ἐπεύξασθαι μὲν ἐγὼν ἐθέλω
> Ματρί, τὰν κοῦραι παρ' ἐμὸν πρόθυρον σὺν
> Πανὶ μέλπονται θαμά
> σεμνὰν θεὸν ἐννύχιαι.
> 80 εἰ δὲ λόγων συνέμεν κορυφάν, Ἱέρων,
> ὀρθὰν ἐπίστᾳ, μανθάνων οἶσθα π^ιροτέρων
> ἓν παρ' ἐσλὸν πήματα σύνδυο δαίονται βροτοῖς
> ἀθάνατοι. τὰ μὲν ὦν
> · οὐ δύνανται νήπιοι κόσμῳ φέρειν,
> ἀλλ' ἀγαθοί, τὰ καλὰ τ^ιρέψαντες ἔξω.
>
> (77-83, antistrophe 4)

The impossible wish is followed by a declaration of possible action; the poet earlier advised: "do not, dear life, rush for existence immortal, but drain the means that can be done." The ἔμπρακτον μαχανάν involves, as we might expect, an action close to home and not the futile chase of a voyage whose destination cannot be reached: "but I want to pray to the Mother, whom girls near my door with Pan sing often at night, holy goddess." The poet is aware of the limits of his art; he will pray to the goddess near his door. ματήρ is the title of Demeter, patron goddess of Sicily (*Ode* 3. 1-2); the implication is that Pindar is with Hieron in Syracuse.[40] After the story of the κούρα Coronis (39), who would not wait to hear girls (παρθένοι) her age sing (ὑποκουρίζεσθαι) the ritual wedding song (18-19), the description here of the girls (κοῦραι) singing and dancing before the poet's door connotes right conduct and piety.

Direct address to Hieron marks the beginning of the myth that traditionally follows the first prayer; "if you see how to understand the straight summit of sayings, you know you are learning from what is before. For one good, the immortals give mortals shares of two pains. Those (i.e., both good and bad) fools cannot bear in ornament. But good men can, turning the beautiful outside." προτέρων could mean "words," "events" or "men" before, and or all at once. The story of Coronis and Asclepius is a guide for conduct: the gods dispense more evil than good to men in *Iliad* 24. 515-533. But Pindar refers to πήματα "pains" rather than the traditional material **κακά**: Asclepius healed men's **πολυπήμονας νόσους** (46). Asclepius cured men by "grasping them with incantations" and by "touching drugs to their limbs everywhere" and by surgery (**τομαῖς** 51-53). Pindar's cure for pain likewise deals with the exterior; "turning the beautiful outside." Turning (**τρέψαντες**) again connotes change: Coronis' fate turned (**τρέψαις**) to evil (34-35). Gold turned (**ἔτραπεν**) Asclepius to bring a man back from the dead (55). Reference to fools also recalls the story of Coronis who is one of the **ματαιότατον φῦλον** who look for what is beyond (21).

> τὶν δὲ μοῖρ᾽ εὐδαιμονίας ἕπεται.
> 85 λαγέταν γάρ τοι τύραννον δέρκεται,
> εἴ τιν᾽ ἀνθρώπων, ὁ μέγας πότμος. αἰὼν δ᾽ ἀσφαλής·
> οὐκ ἔγεντ᾽ οὔτ᾽ Αἰακίδᾳ παρὰ Πηλεῖ
> οὔτε παρ᾽ ἀντιθέῳ Κάδ᾽μῳ· λέγονται {γε} μὰν βροτῶν
> ὄλβον ὑπέρτατον οἳ σχεῖν, οἵτε καὶ χρυσαμπύκων
> 90 μελπομενᾶν ἐν ὄρει Μοισᾶν καὶ ἐν ἑπταπύλοις
> ἄϊον Θήβαις, ὁπόθ᾽ Ἁρμονίαν γᾶμεν βοῶπιν,
> ὁ δὲ Νηρέος εὐβούλου Θέτιν παῖδα κ᾽λυτάν,
>
> (84-92, epode 4)

The advice about the proportion of pain to good is now applied to Hieron's own life, but again in a general way, so that his is compared not only to his contemporaries but also to the great rulers of the past: "you destiny of good fortune follows, great fate looks on you as ruler and leader, if on any man." In *Ode* 5 Bacchylides compares Hieron only to his contemporaries: "well-destined general . . . you know the brightness of the Muses, if any of men on earth today knows it rightly" (1-6). Pindar's broader perspective makes it possible to move immediately from praise of Hieron to illustrations from myth: "a safe lifetime was not born with Aeacus' son Peleus or with god-like Cadmus. They say that of mortals they had highest prosperity, who heard the gold-banded Muses singing on the mountain and in seven-gated Thebes, when he married ox-eyed Harmonia, and the other [married] wise Nereus' famous daughter Thetis." In *Iliad* 24 Achilles also illustrates for Priam his description of Zeus' dispensing good and evil from his jars with two stories: Priam's own life and the life of Achilles' father Peleus, contrasting their former happiness to their present sorrow, their children dead or about to die (534-548). Pindar's emphasis, following his opening statement about turning the beautiful outside, concerns the good things first: prosperity and hearing the Muses singing at their marriage. In the context of the ode the Muses' song has special meaning. Coronis did not wait to hear "the cry of all-sounding wedding songs" which girls her age like to sing in the evening (17). The poet, concentrating on what is possible, will pray to the Mother, whom girls near his door, "with Pan often sing (μέλπονται) at night" (78); Cadmus and Peleus heard the Muses singing (μελπομενᾶν) at their weddings at their respective homes on Mt. Pelion and in Thebes.

> καὶ θεοὶ δαίσαντο παρ' ἀμφοτέροις,
> καὶ Κρόνου παῖδας βασιλῆας ἴδον χρυ-
>   σέαις ἐν ἕδ'ραις, ἕδ'να τε
> 95 δέξαντο· Διὸς δὲ χάριν
> ἐκ προτέρων μεταμειψάμενοι καμάτων
> ἔστασαν ὀρθὰν καρδίαν. ἐν δ' αὖτε χρόνῳ
> τὸν μὲν ὀξείαισι θύγατ'ρες ἐρήμωσαν πάθαις
> εὐφροσύνας μέρος αἱ
>   τρεῖς· ἀτὰρ λευκωλένῳ γε Ζεὺς πατήρ
> ἤλυθεν ἐς λέχος ἱμερτὸν Θυώνα.
>   (93-99, strophe 5)

The list of the "beautiful" in the lives of Cadmus and Peleus is continued in the new triad, "and the gods shared meals with both, and they saw Cronus' sons the kings on golden thrones and received wedding gifts." In the stories of Tantalus and Ixion, the poet also tells of a time when gods were men's neighbors. But where Tantalus and Ixion tried to become like the gods, Peleus and Cadmus accept their mortal status. The description of their attitude dramatically restates how Asclepius the healer "stood some men straight with incision" (ἔστασεν ὀρθούς, 53): "for Zeus' sake they changed from troubles before and stood their hearts straight" (ἔστασαν ὀρθὰν καρδίαν). If we cannot find a healer, at least it is possible to soothe the pain in one's heart. More specific illustrations follow: "in time again Cadmus' daughters made desolate with sharp suffering his share of happiness, the three of them, but father Zeus came to the lovely bed of white-armed Thyone." In the initial summary of the two heroes' lives the beautiful events were listed in detail, with the pains only referred to as **καμάτων** (96). In the account of Cadmus' life the violent fates of his three daughters are characterized briefly as **ὀξείαισι πάθαις**, but Zeus' union with Semele is described in some detail, with Hera's epithet λευκώλενος connoting, as βοῶπις for Harmonia (91), her divine status as Thyone. It is as if we were to tell the story of Coronis' "heavy suffering" (42) not by an account of her relatives placing her on the pyre, but with a description of her union with Apollo.

> 100 τοῦ δὲ παῖς, ὅνπερ μόνον ἀθανάτᾳ
> τίκτεν ἐν Φθίᾳ Θέτις, ἐν πολέμῳ τό-
>   ξοις ἀπὸ ψυχὰν λιπών
> ὦρσεν πυρὶ καιόμενος

ἐκ Δαναῶν γόον. εἰ δὲ νόῳ τις ἔχει
    θνατῶν ἀλαθείας ὁδόν, χρὴ πρὸς μακάρων
    τυγχάνοντ' εὖ πασχέμεν. ἄλλοτε δ' ἀλλοῖαι πνοαί
105 ὑψιπετᾶν ἀνέμων.
    ὄλβος {δ'} οὐκ ἐς μακ⌊ρὸν ἀνδρῶν ἔρχεται
    σάος, πολὺς εὖτ' ἂν ἐπιβ⌊ρίσαις ἕπηται.
                               (100-106, antistrophe 5)

Now we hear immediately of Peleus' sorrow and recovery: "and Peleus' son, whom his only child, immortal Thetis bore in Phthia, in war through the bow he left life behind, and burning in the fire woke lamentation from the Greeks." Coronis also dies "through the bow" (**τόξοισιν**, 10) and is placed on a "burning pyre" (**καιομένα πυρά**, 44). A blazing thunderbolt hurled death on Asclepius (58). But Achilles dying **ἐν πολέμῳ τόξοις** and **πυρὶ καιόμενος** wakes lamentation not just from his family but from the Greeks. A summarizing statement concludes the illustrations from myth: "if any mortal holds in his mind truth's road, he must bear well what he gets from the gods." Analogy is drawn to a sea voyage, as at the beginning of the first praise ("do not, dear life, strive for immortal existence, but drain the means that can be done" (61-62). "One breeze after another comes from high-flying winds. Man's prosperity does not come through a long length safe, when it follows large and falls heavy." The high-flying winds (**ὑψιπετᾶν ἀνέμων**) connote what lies beyond man's control: the fool hunts what is in the wind (**μεταμώνια**) with hopes unfulfilled (23). Prosperity is like a sudden squall, bringing too much at once for man to bail from his boat.

    σμικ⌊ρὸς ἐν σμικ⌊ροῖς, μέγας ἐν μεγάλοις
    ἔσσομαι, τὸν δ' ἀμφέποντ' αἰεὶ φρασίν
    δαίμον' ἀσκήσω κατ' ἐμὰν θεραπεύων μαχανάν.
110 εἰ δέ μοι πλοῦτον θεὸς ἁβ⌊ρὸν ὀρέξαι,
    ἐλπίδ' ἔχω κλέος εὑρέσθαι κεν ὑψηλὸν πρόσω.
    Νέστορα καὶ Λύκιον Σαρπηδόν', ἀνθρώπων φάτις,
    ἐξ ἐπέων κελαδεννῶν, τέκτονες οἷα σοφοί
    ἅρμοσαν, γινώσκομεν· ἁ δ' ἀρετὰ κλειναῖς ἀοιδαῖς
115 χρονία τελέθει· παύροις δὲ πράξασθ' εὐμαρές.
                                  (107-115, epode 5)

The final epode concentrates, as in other odes, on the poet and his relation to the victor. But here instead of setting forth direct guidelines for future conduct to Hieron, as in *Pythian* 1, the poet speaks about himself in terms so general that they could apply to Hieron, like the admonition earlier in the ode, **χρὴ τὰ ἐοικότα πὰρ δαιμόνων μαστευέμεν θναταῖς φρασίν**, "we must seek what is fitting from the gods with our mortal hearts" (59), where "we" seems to include poet, patron, and audience.⁴¹ The poet's size in life will be determined by his environment, "I shall be small among small, great among great." He will observe the lesson of the stories of Peleus and Cadmus; "I shall honor the fortune that follows my heart and keep it according to my means." Earlier "fate's good fortune" followed Hieron (μοῖρ' εὐδαιμονίας ἕπεται, 84). ἀσκήσω θεραπεύων suggests a nourishing or raising close to home; Peleus and Cadmus, like the healer Asclepius curing with incisions (65), "stood their hearts straight" after troubles (96). What he keeps is not σοφία but the more limited μαχανά; the message of Asclepius' story is τὰν ἔμπρακτον ἄντλει μαχανάν (62). The language of the myths of Asclepius and Coronis also shapes the last lines of the ode: "if god should reach me fine wealth, I would hope to find high fame far beyond." Coronis, like other fools, "searches for what is far beyond (τὰ πόρσω) and hunts what is in the wind with hopes unfulfilled" (22-23). Only if a god grants (as he did to Cadmus and Peleus) can man have the κλέος ὑψηλόν that, like immortaity itself, is otherwise πρόσω. The fate of poet and patron are joined in the closing lines: "Nestor and Sarpedon, the talk of men, we know from sounding words, which the wise carpenters have joined. Achievement grows a long time in famed songs; it is easy for few to do." The description of Asclepius in the opening lines as τέκτων νωδυνίας (6), which was elaborated in the description of his healing art (47-53), now takes on its widest meaning. Poets are also τέκτονες of song, and their art, like Asclepius' carpentry, provides an extension of life, by enabling other men to "know" of achievement. γινώσκομεν bears the positive connotations of Apollo's wisdom (γνούς, 31 and γνώμαν, 28) and the advice γνόντα τὸ πὰρ ποδός (60). ἀρετά grows a long time (χρονία) in song, while ὄλβος πολὺς ἐπιβρίσαις cannot remain safe (or "healthy," σάος, 105-106). The deliberately general last sentence παύροις δὲ πράξασθ' εὐμαρές, like the general advice "drain the means that can be done" (ἔμπρακτον, 62), applies to both singers and the men whose achievement makes their song possible, serving elegantly as both the conventional final compliment to the victor (as in *Pythian* 1) and the conventional final statement of the poet's artistic excellence (as in *Olympian* 1).

Pythian 3 is easier to understand on first hearing than Pindar's other odes, because direct parallels and antitheses link the sections of the ode together, as in Bacchylides' *Ode* 3: fire brings death successively to Coronis and her neighbors, Asclepius, and Achilles; fevers are "fiery" (50). Traversing distance connotes danger for Coronis, poet, and patron. Only what is near home and at hand is safe or possible; the last word of the ode, εὐμαρές, derives from an archaic word for hand. The ode's diction is less compressed; its sentences longer. Instead of staccato imperatives (as in the last triad of *Pythian* 1) or questions (as in the last triad of *Pythian* 2), there are repeated conditions, or statements that follow logically from one another. Metaphors seem to be employed only one at a time. There is in *Pythian* 3 little of the unpredictable manipulation of language that makes Pindar's other odes for Hieron so exciting.

But the ode displays the same characteristic ability to make innovative association, and to see the covert similarities in different myths and apply them to present events. Hesiod speaks of poetry's ability to divert men from their sorrows; Pindar develops this traditional idea (restated also in *Ode* 5. 6-16) into an analogy between poetry and healing. Asclepius' crime of greed is made to resemble his mother's crime of lust, without any explicit statement about his likeness to her, with the result that their wrongdoings seem like a condition of mortality more than the inherited defects of one particular family: Coronis is one of a "most foolish tribe among men" (21). Poets and victors can make the same mistakes.

Pindar's deviation in *Pythian* 3 and *Pythian* 1 from the standard format of the victory ode also gives us insight into the way he evolves the complex diction of his praise and transitional phrases. In *Pythian* 3 brightness has negative connotations and fixity connotes right behavior, whereas in *Olympian* 1, brightness signifies excellence, and remaining in one place failure. Clearly, Pindar does not have a set system of "symbols" from which he draws in the composition of his poems. The meaning that fire and the near and far acquire in *Pythian* 3 seems to derive from the long opening narrative, just as in *Pythian* 1, the significance of rest and and noise seems to be set in the description of Typhos under Aetna. Since the basic sequence and events of inherited narrative cannot be altered it seems likely that the myth in each case has been the first determinant of the pattern of language in the ode. The way in which praise of the victor is expressed or the poet's powers are described, even when it precedes the myth, seems in fact defined by it. In *Ode* 3 the brief description of the gold that shines "beneath flashes" (17) is modelled proleptically from the pyre before Croesus' bronze-walled home (31-32, 54).

But *Pythian* 3, despite its more temperate diction, is innovative in one other respect, a quality so obvious that we tend not to notice it, but which may in fact constitute the poet's most influential legacy. The reason we can comprehend *Pythian* 3 without extensive exegesis is that in contrast to the other odes we have read, it is removed from specific place and time and the specific historical allusions we find so difficult. The two victories it mentions seem long past, Delphi appears as Apollo's shrine, the seat of his omniscience, rather than as the place where the Pythian races are run. There is no reference to the threat of citizens' envy; instead, as in *Ode* 3, the focus is on a subject we can readily appreciate, one's conduct in life as one confronts the realities of sickness and of death. So general has the ode become, that in the absence of external evidence, like a formal list of Pythian victors, it is impossible to give *Pythian* 3 a certain date.⁴² Perhaps this is what Pindar himself intended. The generic matters more than the individual; similarity to what has happened before gives actions both present and future meaning. It is not the single race but the winner's life that gives victory its ultimate meaning.⁴³ We can speculate that because this ode deals with death and health it was, like Bacchylides' *Ode* 3, composed toward the end of Hieron's life, but we cannot know for sure and perhaps it does not matter. Half a century later Thucydides was to write history in a not dissimilar fashion, stressing what should have occurred and what would occur again rather than relating specific details of every event exactly as and when it happened. In Pindar's desire to state the general meaning of events, the individual event for which the ode was commissioned is diminished in importance; the complex associations, with their generalizing tendency, that make odes like *Pythian* 1 and *Pythian* 3 more than routine encomia, themselves reveal the obsolescence of the form and occasion of the victory ode.

NOTES

1. On patterns of repetition and nuances of diction in *Pyth.* 1, see esp. Skulsky (Intr. n. 3). That her work appeared after a finished draft of this chapter had been written provides independent confirmation that these patterns exist.

2. On σύνδικος, see Skulsky (Intr. n. 3) p. 20.

3. For a picture of the Aetnaean coin see C.M. Kraay, *Greek Coins* (New York, 1966) Pl. 32 R. Zeus holds in his hand a lightning bolt, with a sharp metal point ("the spearer lightning," 6) and feathers to guide it, like an arrow, on its course. Perhaps Pindar had this coin in mind when he composed these lines; see R.W.B. Burton, Pindar's *Pythian Odes: Essays in Interpretation* (Oxford, 1962) pp. 95-96. The comparison to Zeus is high praise indeed; see Michael Simpson, "The Chariot and the Bow as Metaphors for Poetry in Pindar's Odes," *Trans. and Proc. of Amer. Philol. Assoc.* 100 (1969): 454-6.

4. The scholiasts interpreted κελαινῶπιν as "making the eyes black in sleep," κατέχευας as the "pouring on of sleep" and ὑγρόν as "easily poured in pleasure," i.e. charmed by the song. Their emphasis on the possible symbolic value of these words obscured the force of Pindar's metaphor of a rainstorm. Liddell-Scott-Jones suggest "simple," though there is no evidence that ὑγρός basically denotes anything but "wet" or "moist." Sandys' (Intr. n. 6) translation "buxom" shows the degree to which overinterpretation can cause meaning to be lost. Irwin, on the analogy of her interpretation of χλωρός (of birds) as "throbbing," suggests that ὑγρός connotes "the 'heaving' of the great bird's back in sleep" (ch. II n. 10) p. 73.

5. Hesiod says only that Zeus threw Typhoeus into Tartarus. The story of his burial under Aetna occurs first in *Pythian* 1 and Aeschylus' *Prometheus Bound* (365), in accounts with many points of close resemblance. The basic story of the combat of Zeus and the smoke (τυφ-) monster has many geographical variants; see Joseph Fontenrose, *Python* (Berkeley, 1959) pp. 70-76. Perhaps Pindar and Aeschylus were drawing on (or inventing) a Sicilian version of the myth. Both poets were brought to Sicily by Hieron in 476. Aeschylus' play *Aetnaean Women* celebrated the founding of the city Aetna, possibly as the third play of a trilogy beginning with *Prometheus Bound* and *Prometheus Loosed*; see Hugh Lloyd-Jones, *The Justice of Zeus* (Berkeley, 1971) pp. 100-103. In that case Pindar's account of Typhos in *Pythian* 1 (470) would be deliberately intended to recall Prometheus' description in the drama of Typhon's cruel suppression of Zeus.

6. The exact connotation of χαράσσοισ'... κεντεῖ is difficult to determine. χαράσσω, "cut, scratch, impress," connotes sharpening, by means of scratching, as in Hesiod of sickles (*Works and Days* 573) or of teeth (*Shield of Heracles* 235) or in the Homeric epithet καρχαρόδους, "sharp toothed," used to describe Cerberus in *Ode* 5. 60. Later χαράσσω was used specifically to denote the impression stamped on a coin (hence our word "character"). Unfortunately the one line in Aeschylus where χαράσσω is used is as hard to interpret as this line about Typhos' back in *Pythian* 1. In the *Persians* Darius asks the chorus "what labor is the city laboring? The ground moans, is struck (κέκοπται), is being cut (χαράσσεται)." (682-683). The basic idea is that because the sound of Persia's grief strikes and cuts the ground, Darius' ghost is disturbed and comes out from "beneath the earth" (624). See H.D. Broadhead, ed., *The Persae of Aeschylus* (Cambridge, Eng., 1960) pp. 173-174, 276. The unusual κέκοπται and χαράσσεται add special force to the description: κόπτω like χαράσσω can denote the "striking" of a coin from molten metal; the lamentation of the Persian elders has set its impression on the ground.

7. Skulsky (Intr. n. 3) pp. 14-17 translates δόξα as "renown" rather than "opinion." It is unnecessary to make the distinction in Greek, since good opinion is synonymous with renown. I have translated "opinion," since an actual expression of opinion follows "that she'll be in the future renowned for her crowns and horses" (an interpretative problem not discussed by Skulsky).

8. On the criteria for winning the javelin contest, see H.A. Harris, *Sport in Greece and Rome* (Ithaca, 1972) p. 36.

9. The scholiasts saw in the comparison of Hieron to Philoctetes reference to Hieron's suffering from kidney stones. They cite Aristotle, who said that Gelon, Hieron's brother, died of kidney trouble, and that Hieron himself was afflicted with it (*89ab* II pp. 17-18 Dr).

10. Pindar links Thessaly with Sparta also in the opening lines of *Pythian* 10; see Köhnken (Intr. n. 3) p. 155 n. 5 and n. 6. As a member of the clan of Aegidae who fought at Amyclae, Pindar can say in *Pythian* 5.72-3, "my desirable fame says it is from Sparta"; see my article, "The First Person in Pindar," (Intr. n. 9) pp. 229-232. The root *pind-* occurs only in the names *Pindos* (the mountain), *Pindar* (the poet), the late adjective *Pindareios* ("of Pindar"), and the name *Pindasos* (a dialectal variant of *Pindarus*, "from Pindos"), found in a late inscription

in Eresus on the island of Lesbos; see F. Bechtel, *Die historischen Personnennamen des griechischen bis zur Kaiserzeit* (Halle, 1917). Names deriving from geographical sites are relatively rare. For other nouns ending in *-aros,* see P. Chaintraine, *La Formation des noms en grec ancien* (Paris, 1927) p. 226.

11. Sacrifices were offered at the tomb of the hero Leucippus ("White horse") at Sparta by girls called Leucippides ("daughters of White horse"). Leucippus' own daughters Phoebe and Hilaera, also caled Leucippides, were worshipped in a sanctuary there (Pausanias 3. 13. 7, 3. 16. 1).

12. On echoes of the description of Typhos in antistrophe 4, see Greengard (Intr. n. 3) p. 164.

13. The process of laying out javelins close together as measuring rods may be illustrated in British Museum vase B 361a; see E. Norman Gardiner, *Greek Athletic Sports and Festivals* (London, 1910) p. 324 fig. 77, p. 338. The scholiasts interpret ταvύειv as "stretching and weaving" or "cutting and weaving" (157b, d II 26 Dr). But the basic meaing of ταvύω is to "lengthen out," as of bodies "laid out" in the dust (e.g., *Iliad* 18. 26); the adjective connotes "long" hence ταvίσφυρος, "long" or slender ankled, as in *Ode* 5. 59). πείρατα even in Homer has the generalized meaning of "bound," never the specific connotation of "rope end"; see Bergren (ch. II, n. 14) pp. 148-162.

14. It is also possible that "forge in bronze" would have suggested to the Greek audience Hephaestus forging Zeus' lightning bolts on Aetna. Aeschylus, in describing Typhos beneath Aetna in the *Prometheus Bound,* tells how "on her high peaks Hephaestus sits and strikes his anvil (μυδροκτυπεῖ) from where rivers of fire sometimes roar out and bite with hungry jaws the farm lands of Sicily with fair fruit" (366-369). The word Pindar uses here for anvil, ἄκμων, originally meant meteorite or thunderbolt: see Cedric H. Whitman, "Hera's Anvils," *Harvard Stud. in Class. Philol.* 74 (1970): 40-41. Since in primitive religion the thing acted upon acquires the characteristics of the actor, the anvil or rock struck has the same name as the striker; see Gregory Nagy, "Perkunas and Perunu," *Antiquitates Indogermanae* (Gedenkschrift H. Güntert: Innsbruck, 1974) 120, 123-124.

15. To interpret these lines as advice exclusively for Hieron or Deinomenes as, e.g., Burton (above n. 3) p. 108, or Adolph Köhnken, "Hieron und Deinomenes in Pindars erstem Pythischen Gedicht," *Hermes* 98 (1970): 1-13, is to misunderstand the generalizing nature of the victory ode. The victor's conduct is held up as an example for all to follow, his family, the poet, and the other witnesses of his achievement. Deinomenes in fact continued his father's practice of expressing thanks to the gods for his success. After Hieron's death he set up a monument in Olympia with the following inscription: "having once won, Olympian Zeus, your holy contest, one time with a chariot, twice with a single horse (i.e., in 476 and 472), Hieron gave these gifts to you in joyful thanks. His son Deinomenes set up this memorial to his father from Syracuse" (Pausanias 8. 42. 9). See Ebert (ch. II, n. 24) p. 69.

16. On the relation of this passage to the proem see also Greengard (Intr. n. 3) pp. 53, 55 and Köhnken, "Hieron und Deinomenes" (above n. 15) p. 13.

17. Unlike "stormrunner" (ἀελλοδρόμας) in *Ode* 5. 39 or "swift runner" (Arion

939.8P) or "mountain runner" (Simonides 519, Fr. 35b7) all of which evoke an epic context, "Olympia runner" (ὀλυμπιόδρομος), found only here, may be a technical term like "stadion runner" (σταδιόδρομος), "long (distance) runner" (δολιχόδρομος) or "double course runner" (διαυλόδρομος) from epigrams commemorating victories; see Ebert (ch. II n. 24) p. 68).

18. For the exclamatory pattern "ah blessed," see Archilochus 80. 5D and Theognis 101, "ah blessed and fortunate and prosperous." Jebb's note on this line incorrectly claims that Bacchylides' line is the only instance in Greek literature where "ah" is used in approbation; *Bacchylides* (Cambridge, 1905; repr. 1967) p. 254.

19. Penelope weaves a φᾶρος for Odysseus' father's burial in *Odyssey* 2. 97; 19. 142; 24. 132; Odysseus wears one when he is finally recognized for who he really is at the Phaeacian's banquet (8.84). On the significance of the φᾶρος in myth, see E.A. Butterworth, *Some Traces of the Pre-Olympian World in Greek Literature and Myth* (Berlin, 1966) pp. 84-122. σκότος is the darkness of death, especially in the formula "darkness covered his eyes," *Iliad* 4. 461, etc. Solon compares god-given wealth to a sound tree (13.9-10), but the idea of wealth as a tower is new: in Homer Ajax is a "fence" (ἕρκος) for the Achaeans (*Odyssey* 11. 556), and the seventh century elegist Callinus speaks of the brave man as a "tower" (πύργος) in the eyes of the citizens (1. 20).

20. The Greek distinguishes between the specific sacrifices, in the instrumental dative (βρύει βουθύτοις ἑορταῖς) and the general concept "hospitality" in the genitive (βρύουσι φιλοξενίας). Euripides observes the same distinction: "filling their hands with torches" (πλεροῦντες πεύκαισιν, *Heracles Mad* 372-272), but "I am full of evils" (γέμω κακῶν, 1245).

21. A picture and description of the base of one of the tripods set up by Gelon at Delphi, with its identifying inscription, may be found in J. Marcadé, *Receuil des signatures de sculpteurs grecs* I (Paris, 1953) p. 9 with Pl. 3. The scholia on *Pythian* 1. 152a preserve a dedicatory inscription about the heavy gold tripod, weighing more than fifty talents set up by Gelon, Hieron, and their brothers (=A.P. 6. 214) after their victory, one example of what Pindar in *Pythian* 1 called "a respected crown of richness" (5c). See also P.T. Brannan, S.J. "Bacchylides' Third Ode," *Classical Folia* 27 (1973): 193-195.

22. On the use of word echo in lines 20-22 to signify a conclusion, see Brannan (above n. 21) pp. 190-191. The repetition "god god" (θεὸν θεόν) may follow a ritual pattern. The conclusion to the story of Ixion in *Pythian* 2. 49-50 ends with similar repetition at the beginning of two consecutive lines "a god (θεός) comes up to every mark on his hopes, a god (θεός)" etc. A hymn by Pindar and Bacchylides' contemporary Diagoras begins "god god" (θεὸς θεός, 735.1P). But immediate repetition of this sort also has a rhetorical function; see, e.g., *Pythian* 2. 72-3 "beautiful is an ape among children always beautiful" (καλός . . . καλός), and below, n. 33.

23. On deliberate recollection in ἐπεί ποτε καὶ δαμασίππου of the ode's introduction, see Abbé Jean Dumortier, "De quelques associations d'images chez Bacchylide," (1922) in *Pindaros und Bakchylides,* ed. W.M. Calder and J. Stern (Intr. n. 4) p. 416; Emily D. Townsend, "Bacchylides and Lyric Style" (diss.

Bryn Mawr College, 1956) p. 69 and Brannan (above n. 21) p. 196. δαμάσιππος is another fashionable new word, used also of Athena by Bacchylides' contemporary Lamprocles (735.2P).

24. I am indebted to Prof. John G. Pedley of the Univ. of Michigan for the information about the bronze walls on the temple of Cyrene.

A bronze wall also surrounds Aeolus' house (*Odyssey* 10. 3-4). Homer's description of Aeolus' and Alcinous' homes may preserve the memory of bronze sheathed doors on Mycenaean palaces. Traces of bronze have been found in sockets on thresholds; see Lord William Taylour, *The Mycenaeans* (*Ancient Peoples and Places* 39: New York, 1964) p. 106. Bacchylides evidently had in mind descriptions of bronze walls in literature and/or Greek architecture that he had seen. There are no traces of bronze walls in the remains of Croesus' Sardis. His palace seems to have been made of mud and timber; see John Griffiths Pedley, *Sardis in the Age of Croesus* (Norman, Okla., 1968) pp. 117-118.

25. According to Charles P. Segal, Croesus is here "cast into the mold of a Homeric hero," though Segal acknowledges that there is perhaps an un-Homeric resignation in the grim conclusion to Croesus' speech; see "Croesus on the Pyre: Herodotus and Bacchylides," *Wiener Studien* n.f. 5 (1971): 40-41. The idea of self-immolation is probably oriental in origin; see Martin P. Nilsson, "Der Flammentod des Heracles auf dem Oite," (1022) in *Opuscula Selecta* (Lund, 1951) I 349, and Townsend (above, n. 23) pp. 58-59. Traces of oak ashes found in a mound known as the tomb of Alyattes at Sardis indicates that the kings of Sardis, like the Hittite kings, may have been cremated; see John Griffiths Pedley, ed., *Ancient Literary Sources on Sardis (Archaeological Exploration of Sardis Monograph* 2: Cambridge, Mass., 1972) p. 41. Myson's famous vase (ca. 500 B.C.) shows Croesus pouring oil onto his own pyre; see A.H. Smith, "Illustrations to Bacchylides," (1898) pp. 267-269 and fig. 1. But the influence of contemporary events on Bacchylides' characterization of Croesus should not be overlooked. For the story of Boges' suicide in Thrace in 476/475 and the Carthaginian Hamilcar's self-sacrifice in 480, see Herodotus 7. 107 and 167.

26. The force of δόμον in this context, ignored by Jebb (above, n. 18), was first pointed out by Dumortier (above, n. 23) p. 417. See also Jacob Stern, "Metrical and Verbal Patterns in the Poetry of Bacchylides" (diss. Columbia, 1965,. U.M. 47-16,048) pp. 48-49.

27. On similarities between the pyre scene and the myth of the rape of Persephone, see Stern (above, n. 26) pp. 144-146.

28. On the function of the reiteration of λαμπρός ("shining"), see Brannan (above, n. 21) pp. 203-204.

29. On the significance of the epithet "Delos-born," see Brannan (above, n. 21) p. 206.

30. Bacchylides may have chosen the land of the Hyperboreans for Croesus because that is where Apollo himself goes for the winter (Alcaeus 307, I. c). According to Pindar, "neither diseases or deadly old age are mixed with their holy race" (*Pythian* 10. 41-2). Herodotus tells the story of Abaris, a Hyperborean servant of Apollo (whom Pindar evidently associates with Croesus, fr. 270), who

lived without eating (Herodotus 4. 36. 1). On the Indo-European origins of the Hyperboreans, see Mary A. Grant, *Folktale and Hero-tale Motifs in the Odes of Pindar* (Lawrence, Kansas, 1967) p. 23.

31. On standard topics of praise in lines 69-71, see Bundy (Intr. n. 3) p. 25.

32. Bdelycleon sings a "saying for Admetus" to Philocleon in Aristophanes' *Wasps,* which was evidently the first line of a drinking song by Praxilla (Frag. 749-897P). Attic drinking songs commemorated Harmodius and Aristogeiton's tyrannicide (893, 896P). Cf. the general advice by Xenophanes (B 1 DK) and Theognis (211-212, 497-498, 499-502, 627-628) for proper conduct at drinking parties.

33. Bacchylides' lines have often been criticized as being unoriginal or inexpertly plagiarized; see, e.g., Leonard Woodbury, "Truth and the Song: Bacchylides 3. 96-98," *Phoenix* 23 (1969): 332. But as we have seen in *Ode* 5 and elsewhere, the Greeks considered creative adaptation to be a form of art; see my article, "Bacchylides' *Ode* 5" (Intr. n. 9) 46-48; Brannan, (above, n. 21) pp. 213-218 and R.L. Wind, "Bacchylides and Pindar: A Question of Imitation" *Class. Journ.* 67 (1971): 9-13. Critics have had particular difficulty in taking "gold is heart's happiness" as a serious expression of an acccpted value. But the poets of victory odes consistently express admiration for wealth and its expenditure; see esp. Leonard Woodbury, "Pindar and the Mercenary Muse: *Isthm.* 2. 1-13," *Trans. Amer. Philol. Soc.* 99 (1968): 540-547. Skulsky (Intr. n. 3) pp. 28-30 suggests that in *Pyth.* 1 Pindar may be imitating his own *Nemean* 1. But it can equally well be argued, since the date of *Nem.* 1 cannot be fixed with certainty, that similarities in diction in the two odes provide interesting evidence about Pindar's methods of composition, and of a continuing concern in his poetry with the conflict between the forces of peace and violence; cf. Eliot's reiterated discussions of the effects of memory on perception (ch. I, n. 10).

34. On the interpretation of the last line of this ode, see Woodbury, "Truth and the Song" (above, n. 33) pp. 331-335. On the conventional association of the nightingale with spring see Dumortier (above, n. 23) p. 417.

35. The function of the metrical distinction between strophe and epode in the myth was first observed by W. Headlam, "Greek Lyric Metre," *Journ. Hellenic Studies* 22 (1902): 214 n. 10.

36. In employing direct antithesis to give a sense of completeness and in using the same word repeatedly for emphasis, Bacchylides reflects contemporary stylistic trends both in drama and in what was later called "philosophy." See, e.g., for antithesis: Sophocles, *Ajax* 394-397; Heraclitus B 60, 62, 67 DK; and for anaphora: Heraclitus B 114 DK; Xenophanes B 24, 30, DK; Anaxagoras B 12 DK; and see also J.D. Denniston, *Greek Prose Style* (Oxford, 1952) pp. 3-4.

37. Failure to understand the force of the contrary to fact condition in these lines has led to serious misunderstanding of the poem; see Young, *Three Odes* (Intr. n. 3) pp. 28-30.

38. "Shared," "held in common," is the meaning of κοινός in Pindar's day. Young's translation "commonplace," based on the scholia, expresses a connota-

tion that the word acquired only in the fourth century; *Three Odes* (Intr. n. 3) pp. 30-31.

39. Pindar follows Hesiod (*Catalogue of Women*, fr. 60. 4 MW, quoted in the scholia to *Pyth.* 3. 52a, II 70-71) in describing Ischys as son of Elatus of Arcadia. But the mythographer Apollodorus (first century B.C.?) calls Ischys the brother of the Thessalian Caeneus. If Pindar knew both versions of the myth, he clearly picked the story which would best exemplify his theme of near versus far; see Young, *Three Odes* (Intr. n. 3) p. 35.

40. Young's analysis of the motif of the near and the far in this ode indicates that Pindar refers to the Mother's cult primarily because of its proximity; see *Three Odes* (Intr. n. 3) ch. II *passim* and appendix. See also my article, "The First Person in Pindar" (Intr. n. 9) p. 221.

41. On first personal statements in this ode as advice to Hieron see my article, "The First Person in Pindar" (Intr. n. 9) p. 224 and n. 107. The negative form of the advice does not indicate that Hieron is an unwilling listener (in spite of what I say in "The First Person," p. 224, where I rely on the scholiasts' account of a rift between Pindar and Hieron) but serves to stress that the poet and victor both must realize the limitations of their skill and their success.

42. In "Pindar's Poetical Epistles," (ch. I n. 33), David Young suggested that *Pythian* 3 is in fact the victory ode for the second of Pherenicus' victories at Delphi, on the grounds that "once" (ποτε, 74) is spoken from the point of view of future commemoration, like "having once (ποτε) won, Olympian Zeus, your holy contest . . . Hieron gave these gifts to you in joyful thanks . . ." on the inscription put up by Deinomenes at Olympia after Hieron's death (cited above, n. 15), where "once" is stated not so much from Deinomenes' point of view, to whom at least the chariot victory in 468 would have seemed recent, but from the outlook of those who will read the inscription many years later. Young cites the use of "once" on grave inscriptions 3, 8, 9, 36, 46, 76 in W. Peek, *Griechische Vers-Inschriften I: Grab-Epigramme* (Berlin, 1955), and Euripides, *Trojan Women* 1190. But there is a clear functional difference between a commemorative inscription put up for future reference and poems like victory odes or dramas, designed to communicate directly with specific individuals and audiences. If Pindar were attempting to reproduce the style and content of an inscription, we would expect him to say explicitly what he is doing, e.g., as Hecabe does in the passage from the *Trojan Women* cited by Young, "what will a poet write sometime (ποτε) about you (Astyanax) on your tomb? 'This child the Argives once (ποτε) killed because they were afraid of him.'" Andromache specifically refers to an inscription in the future. Pindar in *Pythian* 3 is talking about the past "If I had gone down and brought . . . I say I would have come."

43. On the social function of Pindar's odes, see esp. Rose (Intr. n. 2) 148-155, 175.

Chapter IV

Pythian 2: A Second Reading

After our first reading of *Pythian* 2, we deliberately left many questions unanswered. The assumption was that after looking at other odes we might begin to see ways to discover the ode's place and date, and to understand more fully the function of the ode's long concluding section, and of the emphasis throughout the ode on ingratitude and envy.

For what occasion was *Pythian* 2 composed? To judge by what happens in the other odes we have read, not for a victory at either Olympia or Delphi. In each of the other odes the athletic contest and the site of victory are identified in the first praise of the victor.[1] Bacchylides in *Ode* 5 describes how "blonde-haired Pherenicus beside the broad-whirling Alpheus, colt storm-runner, gold-armed Dawn saw victorious" (37-40). In *Olympian* 1 Pindar tells how Pherenicus "rushed beside the Alpheus and held his body unspurred in the race" (20-21). In *Pythian* 1 Pindar relates that "in the Pythiad race a herald spoke proclaiming her (Aetna) for Hieron victory in his chariot" (32). Bacchylides in *Ode* 3 speaks of "the swift Olympia-runner mares of Hieron . . . with high Victory . . . and Brightness . . . by the broad-whirling (Alpheus)" (5-7). Pindar in *Pythian* 3 refers to a "celebration of Pythian prizes, the brightness with crowns which Pherenicus, as best, took once at Cirrha" (73-74). In each case the site of the victory is described in some detail: the Alpheus in *Ode* 5. 38, *Olympian* 1. 10, 92, and *Ode* 3. 6-7: Phoebus "who loves Parnassus' spring Castalia" in *Pythian* 1. 39; Apollo's "temple" in "sheep-taking Pytho" in *Pythian* 3. 27; the town Pisa (18), the Alpheus (92), the Olympiad races (94), and the hill Cronion (111) in *Olympian* 1.

In the first praise of *Pythian* 2, only two places are mentioned in connection with Hieron's chariot victory: Thebes, Pindar's home, and Syracuse, Hieron's city. "Shining Thebes" (3) is mentioned briefly once, Syracuse in more detail: "Syracuse with your great city, precinct of Ares" (1); "Ortygia . . . shrine of Artemis of the river" who guided Hieron to victory (6-7). We hear again of Syracuse in the second praise of Hieron, as "ruler lord of many well-crowned streets and army," recalling how Hieron with his chariot "bound Ortygia high with crowns" (6). So Syracuse itself seems to be the most likely candidate for the site of Hieron's chariot victory. The scholia on *Olympian* 13 state that there were Isthmian games at Syracuse. Presumably these were modelled after the major games held in honor of Poseidon at the Isthmus near Corinth; Corinth established the Greek colony at Syracuse. In *Pythian* 2 Pindar describes how Hieron "yokes down the strength of horses and calls upon the trident mover god wide in force" (11-12).[2]

Other celebrations beside the four major festivals at Olympia, Delphi, Nemea, and the Isthmus, merit victory odes. Bacchylides' *Ode* 14 celebrates a chariot victory at the Petraia festival of Poseidon in Thessaly. Pindar wrote odes for Chromius of Aetna's chariot victory in the games of Apollo at Sicyon near Corinth (so-called *Nemean 9*); for Theaeus of Argos for the wrestling contest at the games of Hera in Argos (*"Nemean"* 10). *"Nemean"* 11 celebrates not an athletic victory but the inauguration of Aristagoras as chief magistrate of Tenedos. These three anomalous odes seem to have been included by ancient scholars at the end of the collection of *Nemean* odes for convenience. Their position may provide a clue to why the ode to Hieron that begins "O Syracuse with your great city" ended up between *Pythian* 1 and *Pythian* 3. The grouping is logical from a cataloguer's point of view: all the odes are for one victor, Hieron.[3]

But that the ode seems to have been written for a victory at Syracuse may be less important than the indication that it was not composed to celebrate a victory at one of the major games. That it celebrates a minor victory might offer some explanation of why so much of it concerns ingratitude and the problem of envying success. If the second praise and the concluding triad of the other odes we have read were intended only as advice to the poet himself, we might wish to regard the last stanzas of *Pythian* 2 primarily as expression of Pindar's reaction to Hieron's achievement. But our study of other odes, both by Pindar and Bacchylides, has shown that the final stanzas, however they are phrased, are directed also to the victor. The poet in the concluding triad may refer to himself and to his role, but always to set an example for the conduct of others, as well as for himself.

Bacchylides in *Ode* 5 describes himself as following advice that applies equally well to all witnesses of Hieron's achievement "for truth's sake one must praise, thrusting envy aside with both hands, if any mortal does well" (187-190). Pindar in *Olympian* 1, after describing song as a victory chariot (109-111), follows the advice he sets for Hieron: "may you through this time walk high, and may I stay so long with winners of victory, and be seen first in poetry among Greeks everywhere" (115-116). In *Pythian* 1 the final stanzas are stated as direct advice to Hieron;

in *Ode* 3 Bacchylides is concerned with the ability of song to bring immortality to the victor, and reinforces this idea in the final lines, by stating that his song about Hieron will bring immortality also to himself (96-98). Even at the end of *Pythian* 3, where the poet speaks of his being "small among small, great among great" (107-108), what he says, as we have seen, is intended for Hieron as much as for himself. His statement "the fortune that follows my heart I shall honor and keep according to my means" (108-109) echoes the more general advice he gave earlier in the ode "do not rush for existence immortal, but drain the means that can be done" (61-62). He uses himself as a positive example, just as he uses Asclepius and Coronis earlier in the ode as negative examples of conduct in the face of both failure and success.

If we look again at the puzzling last triad of *Pythian* 2, keeping in mind the last stanzas of the other odes we have read, we can see that what the poet says in the long concluding section applies not just to himself but to anyone who has enjoyed success and must face the prospect of eventual failure. The direct praise of Hieron's prowess in games and war ends in the third epode with the advice, "learn and become who you are" (γένοι' οἷος ἐσσὶ μαθών, 72). In positive terms this means that Hieron should recognize his limitations as a man, as the old adage has it, γνῶθι σαυτόν. Allusion to the story of the children and the ape (72b) provides negative illustration. Among children the ape is beautiful (καλός τοι πίθων παρὰ παισίν), as Heraclitus said, "the most beautiful ape is ugly compared to the human race," and "the wisest of men seems an ape compared to god" (82-83 DK).

> καλός. ὁ δὲ ῾Ραδάμανθυς εὖ πέπραγεν, ὅτι φρενῶν
> ἔλαχε καρπὸν ἀμώμητον, οὐδ' ἀπάταισι θυ-
>   μὸν τέρπεται ἔνδοθεν,
> 75 οἷα ψιθύρων παλάμαις ἕπετ' αἰεὶ βροτῷ.
> ἄμαχον κακὸν ἀμφοτέροις διαβολιᾶν ὑποφάτιες,
> ὀργαῖς ἀτενὲς ἀλωπέκων ἴκελοι.
> κέρδει δὲ τί μάλα τοῦτο κερδαλέον τελέθει;
> ἅτε γὰρ ἐννάλιον πόνον ἐχοίσας βαθύν
> 80 σκευᾶς ἑτέρας, ἀβάπτιστος εἰμι φελ-
>   λὸς ὣς ὑπὲρ ἕρκος ἅλμας.
>
> (73-80, strophe 4)

The story about Rhadamanthys in the beginning of the fourth strophe describes also a larger group saying something about an individual: "Rhadamanthys did well when he won from his mind worthy harvest, and did not delight his heart with delusions such as always follow a mortal through the hands of whisperers." ἀπάταισι and τέρπεται refer to central concerns of Ixion's story. The danger of self-delusion is ever-present, ἔπετ' αἰεί, threatening to hold a man (βροτῷ) with their παλάμαις, as Zeus trapped Ixion (40). The children too think that the ape is more beautiful than he really is, and they "always" (αἰεί) tell him so, καλός ... καλός (72b-73). We infer that the whisperers say similar things to Rhadamanthys: do they mislead him by telling him how great he is, so that he will forget, as Ixion did, that the true source of his happiness is the gods?

From the "delusions that always follow a man through the hands of whisperers," we turn to the "low speeches of slanders" (διαβολιᾶν ὑποφάτιες) that others hear, presumably also through the hands of these same whisperers. Pindar describes the process in detail in *Olympian* 1, "someone said straightway in secret, an envious neighbor, that into the water's peak, boiling with fire, with a knife they cut you limb by limb and at the table into portions of meat, they divided you and ate you" (47-51). In *Pythian* 2 the content of the low speeches is left to our imagination: the focus instead is on their motives. They are "an evil unconquerable" both for others and themselves, as Rhadamanthys said, "if a man should sow evil, he would reap evil gain" (fr. 286 MW). They are in their greed, "completely like the tempers of foxes," but the gain (κέρδος) they hope for will in the end not prove gainful (κερδαλέον), just as for Ixion, whose bed became "beautiful pain" (40). Poets, like whisperers and low speeches, can delude and blame. But the use of animal fables and the ancient saying of Rhadamanthys widens the scope of the discussion beyond victory at the games to conduct in all aspects of life.

In the final lines of the strophe the poet brings the description of the effects of envy back to himself: "for as when another set of ropes holds deep labor in the sea, I come undipped, like a cork up above the fence of the salt water." In *Olympian* 1 he also disassociates himself explicitly from the envious neighbor, "for me there is no way to say one of the blessed is a glutton. I stand aside" (52). But in *Pythian* 2 there is emphasis on the continuing danger of being included among the envious: the ropes to which the cork is attached hold a heavy burden; the cork floats "undipped up above the fence of the salt water," which could engulf it. So deceptions "always follow a man," and children "always" call the ape beautiful (72b). Earlier in the ode the poet stated that in singing Hieron's praise he would "embark on a well-flowering journey singing about your achievement" (62-63); his song was "sent on the Phoenician trade across the grey salt sea" (67-68). But now the poet has characterized himself not as a passenger, and his song not as a valued cargo, but as a cork, in a fisherman's world of "labor" (πόνον), close to the sea which threatens to divide him from Hieron. The use of this comparison trains our attention on the practical world of ordinary commercial transactions, so that we are prepared for a return in the next lines to commentary on the general effects of envy, again in the plain language of animal fables.

The description of the poet's conduct at the beginning of the last triad of *Pythian* 1 has a similarly generalizing function. Pindar there describes himself as a judge marking distances of achievements. His ability to sing "right measure" is compared to the actions of a larger group of other men whose "swift hopes" are dulled by the "everlasting satisfaction" of another's achievements, and also to the conduct of citizens whose "hidden hearts" are made heavy by what they hear about others' good (81-84). These lines first of all describe the poet's art, but in a larger sense they stand also as advice to Hieron, who as ruler shares the poet's concern with accuracy in speaking, and who accordingly must "forge his tongue's bronze on an anvil without falsehood" (86).

ἀδύνατα δ' ἔπος ἐκβαλεῖν κραταιὸν ἐν ἀγαθοῖς
δόλιον ἀστόν· ὅμως μὰν σαίνων ποτὶ πάντας ἅ-
  ταν πάγχυ διαπ'λέκει.
οὔ οἱ μετέχω θράσεος. φίλον εἴη φιλεῖν·
ποτὶ δ' ἐχθρὸν ἅτ' ἐχθρὸς ἐὼν λύκοιο
  δίκαν ὑποθεύσομαι,
85 ἄλλ' ἄλλοτε πατέων ὁδοῖς σκολιαῖς.
ἐν πάντα δὲ νόμον εὐθύγλωσσος ἀνὴρ προφέρει,
παρὰ τυραννίδι, χὠπόταν ὁ λάβ'ρος στρατός,
χὦταν πόλιν οἱ σοφοὶ τηρέωντι. χρὴ
  δὲ πρὸς θεὸν οὐκ ἐρίζειν,

(81-88, antistrophe 4)

Further negative and positive illustrations of attitude toward success are provided. The deceitful citizen "fawns on everyone and weaves his delusion complete." Insolence moved Ixion "into high-proud delusion" (28-29). The deceitful citizen's words cannot "win" against the good man, like Rhadamanthys, any more than Ixion's violence could succeed against the gods. The poet disassociates himself from such conduct: "I do not share his boldness. May it be mine to love a friend. Toward an enemy as an enemy, like a wolf I shall run below, treading one way, then another on crooked paths." In the next lines, the use of illustration from a political context again moves us away from the particular victory being celebrated to unspecified times and places: "into everything the straight-tongued man bears his right way forth, in a tyranny, and when a hungry army, and when the wise watch a city." Is the tyrant Hieron? is the "hungry army" the Athenians, or the army of which Hieron is "ruler lord" (58)? Who are the wise who watch the city: we cannot say for sure because the statement is general enough to include all these possible identifications, and even more. The statement about the "straight-tongued man" can apply not only to Pindar, but to everyone, and especially to Hieron. Pindar speaks well of his patron and benefactor, and, similarly, Hieron, whenever he yokes his chariot, acknowledges his true debt to the gods: "he calls on the trident-mover god wide in force" (12). Concluding advice gives the message of the myth its widest application: "one must not fight against god." It is not until the next stanza that Pindar returns specifically to the context of victory in games.

        ὃς ἀνέχει τοτὲ μὲν τὰ κείνων, τότ᾽ αὖθ᾽ ἑτέροις
        ἔδωκεν μέγα κῦδος. ἀλλ᾽ οὐδὲ ταῦτα νόον
90   ἰαίνει φθονερῶν· στάθμας δέ τινες ἑλκόμενοι
        περισσᾶς ἐνέπαξαν ἕλ-
        κος ὀδυναρὸν ἑᾷ πρόσθε καρδίᾳ,
        πρὶν ὅσα φροντίδι μητίονται τυχεῖν.
        φέρειν δ᾽ ἐλαφρῶς ἐπαυχένιον λαβόντα ζυγόν
        ἀρήγει· ποτὶ κέντρον δέ τοι
95   λακτιζέμεν τελέθει
        ὀλισθηρὸς οἶμος· ἁδόν-
        τα δ᾽ εἴη με τοῖς ἀγαθοῖς ὁμιλεῖν.

                                     (89-96, epode 4)

The final epode deals particularly with evaluation of one's own achievement. God "holds up first the deeds of some, and then gives others great glory." The wrong conduct of the envious is compared to the right conduct of the man who accepts what he gets: "some drag a standard that is too much and fix a painful wound in their own hearts before they get what they plotted in their minds." Right action is instead to "bear the yoke lightly," like the horses Hieron guides gently to victory (7-8). Wrong action is characterized in terms of Ixion's fall, "kicking against the goads is a slippery road." A final prayer, "may it be that I please and consort with the good," takes us back to the beginning of Ixion's story, when he "seized a sweet existence beside the kind children of Cronus" (25-26). To "please and consort with the good" is not a prayer for success, but for association with those, who like Rhadamanthys, understand right conduct. The stanza has meaning for all who witness another's success. Hieron has won many victories, but he has not won and will not win every contest that he enters. Pindar too sings of Hieron's victory, not his own. Envying the victors will class both Hieron and Pindar (and the audience) with Archilochus, the whisperers, and the deceitful citizens.

    The concentration in this final stanza on acceptance of what god gives may provide some general indication of when the ode was composed. In 476, the triumphant year when Bacchylides and Pindar both wrote odes for Hieron's horse race victory at Olympia, and Aetna was founded, Pindar spoke of his hope to celebrate a chariot victory at the next Olympiad (*Ol.* 1. 108-111). But although Hieron seems to have won the horse race again in 472, we know that he did not win the chariot victory he had hoped for until 468. Was *Pythian* 2 composed sometime after 472, during a period of disappointment?

That we cannot know for sure reveals again the generalizing nature of the victory ode. *Pythian* 2, with its many statements about cooperation and repayment, describes the problems that arise and will continue to arise from success, not just in games, but in war and art, and in every human undertaking. Athletic contests provide a unique means of combining skill and discipline with man's instinctive need for violence and his desire for supremacy. Because *Pythian* 2 grasps and expresses the larger significance of the contest it celebrates, it can instruct all who hear it, both in Syracuse after the victory, and long afterwards, elsewhere.

Conclusions

In the process of answering our first questions about *Pythian* 2, we have at least evolved a method of reading which should help us approach still other odes with more assurance. We would expect that any victory ode would attempt to depict the victory it celebrates as an illustration of human achievement in general, and accordingly to compare it with deeds in the past, both successful and unsuccessful, especially in war or conflict, both by the victor and his family, and by heroes in myth. We would anticipate that the ode would start with some statement of lasting validity, and then go on to talk about the current victory and celebration, moving then to the past in myth, and then again to the present in praise, concluding with practical advice about future conduct. The concentration on the present in the concluding section has a function analogous to the last play in Aeschylus' *Oresteia* trilogy, the *Eumenides*, which directs the mythic action of the first two plays directly to Athens and man's dispensing of justice.[4]

We would also expect that in any ode longer than two or three stanzas reiteration of word and theme would help understand the relationship between the past and present events in the ode. We would look at the proem and the longer narratives to see what themes in particular would be emphasized. The first verse of the ode will be in effect a statement of a theme that will gradually be elaborated: men and horses in *Pythian* 2, "destiny" in *Ode* 5, competition and water in *Olympian* 1, the lyre and music in *Pythian* 1, the importance of god in *Ode* 3, and the reality of death in *Pythian* 3.

The compressed language and unexplained allusions of the opening stanza are expanded and developed fully in the narrative sections of the ode, and reiterated also in the praise and advice of the ode's concluding stanzas. *Pythian* 1 begins with a description of the eagle sleeping on Zeus' staff (6), which gains significance as we learn in more detail of Typhos lying beneath Aetna on a bed that cuts and stabs him (28); the idea of the sleeping eagle comes increasingly to connote peace as we hear of the weariness of Hieron's wars (46) and of both Medes (78) and Hieron's enemies at Himera (80). A long narrative, even where it follows the first praise rather than the proem, will define the language of the other sections of the ode: in *Olympian* 1 the boiling water and feasting in the false story of Tantalus (48-51) shape both Pindar's revision of the myth and the ode's introduction, where water surprisingly comes first in a list of supremacies, and where the first we hear of Hieron is of a gathering round his hearth (11).

Pindar and Bacchylides employ these basic techniques of exposition in recognizably different styles. Bacchylides sets up dramatic contrast between aspirations and achievements, using language that deliberately evokes the epic past or redefines lines from other lyric poetry, to restate for his contemporaries traditional observations about man's life and its limitations and uncertainty. Pindar instead uses new and startling combinations of words and ideas, with more concentration on the powers of art, to express a greater confidence in the enduring capabilities of man's achievement. These observations will be helpful in understanding the many odes we have not discussed, and perhaps in identifying the authorship of epinician poetry yet to be discovered.

These general conclusions can serve only as guides to better understanding; our method of reading is at best an approximation of what an ancient audience heard. Although we can recognize the function of associative repetition in the odes, no theoretical description survives to prove that the ancients were consciously aware of its existence.[5] The poets themselves tell us only that their poetry is meant to praise and instruct concisely and directly, so that their words can be described as arrows; they state explicitly that they can shape inherited narrative as they see fit; their characterization of their song as a journey in the Muses' chariot signifies that they are conscious of the artists' ability to travel backward and forward in time, and to see from a greater perspective than their audience the meaning of the events they have been asked to celebrate.

But the poets seem to have no special terminology for the reiterative vocabulary and syntax that helps connect present with past and praise with positive and negative examples of conduct. "Arrows" or "missiles" only partially characterizes the effect of phrases like "could not digest his great prosperity," and "stewing one's nameless old age" (*Ol.* 1. 55-56, 82-83) and Croesus' "wooden home" (*Ode* 3. 49) without indicating how they are in fact integrated into the overall expository framework of their respective odes. The patterning of associations seems as flexible as the structuring of the basic elements of praise. This unpredictability suggests that even in antiquity the odes were not intended to communicate their meaning instantly to their audience, with the facility that comes from standardized format, as in epigrams and drinking songs. Since victory odes are meant to entertain as well as enlighten, they do not try to reproduce the relentless exhortation of didactic poetry, where the application of metaphors and illustration is made explicit.[6] Their scope is too small to permit the leisurely pace and resulting comprehensibility of epic narrative. Swift changes of subject, postponed conclusions, statements whose meaning becomes apparent only in retrospect—all provide the kind of teasing excitement that comes from deliberate complexity.

It would also be reassuring to gain somehow the precise information about the games and the performance of the odes that has been lost, so we could trace with more certainty the development of each poet's art and more accurately estimate to what degree the poets sought to comment on the historical events that they had witnessed. But even if we cannot discover what has been lost, we can admire and be enlightened by what we can find: the way Pindar transforms the story of Ixion and the centaurs into a statement about the forces that lead men to success, or how Bacchylides uses the story of Meleager both to recall and deny the value of Homeric heroism.

Absence of precise historical data will only become a serious detriment if we allow it to keep us from looking at the odes themselves, or to encourage us to abandon our attempts to understand them. Before the techniques of exposition and structuring in early poetry were rediscovered, there was some justification in reading political allegory into the poet's complex metaphorical statements about his art, or in choosing for comment brief fragments from the odes. But what we know about thematic repetition in epic poetry and the use of polarity and analogy in archaic thought enables us to see (in *Ode* 3) connections between the gold that signifies both Hieron's piety and Croesus', and (in *Pythian* 3) between the far and the near in Coronis' and Asclepius' lives and in ours. Observing the process of association may be sufficient reward for our attention. The juxtaposition of water, gold, fire, and the sun in the opening of *Olympian* 1 intrigues us not just by its obscurity, but by its beauty, which leads us instinctively to feel that it has some deeper meaning both within the poem and for our own perception of reality.[7]

Even aside from aesthetics, or the undeniable pleasure of seeing (even mistakenly) in the past some likeness to ourselves, the odes repay our study because of what they can tell us about intellectual developments in Greece in the fifth century. They help illustrate for us the fact that the sophistic movement in the second half of the fifth century B.C. was not an isolated phenomenon, but a natural outgrowth of the thought of the preceding generation. The sophists were primarily teachers of the art of speaking, of the power to persuade and guide political action. Among their more potent tools was the ability to adapt and reshape myth to suit their special purposes. Gorgias used his rhetorical skill to demonstrate that Helen could not be blamed for the war at Troy (B11A DK).

Conclusions

We have now seen a similarly conscious process of revision in action a generation earlier, in Pindar's exoneration of Pelops in *Olympian* 1, and in the story of Typhos' suppression under Cumae and Aetna.[8] The attempt to express abstractly the enduring meaning of events which we see in the proems to *Olympian* 1 and *Pythian* 1 was to be developed more fully by Thucydides in the composition of his speeches, and in the invention by sophists like Gorgias and Thrasymachus of types of speeches that could be used for standard types of occasions.[9] *Pythian* 3, which seems itself so cut off from any specific event, is one of the first recognizable examples of a process of abstraction that was to result in Thucydides' writing of history as a "possession forever."

Perhaps then it is not essential that we cannot reconstruct the historical settings of all of the odes or trace either Pindar's or Bacchylides' artistic development with the kind of certainty with which we can trace Wordsworth's or Hopkins'. The odes' development of abstractions from myth, and their self-conscious concern with the artists' powers, deserve more of our attention than questions of their performance and provenance, if we are to come to a better understanding of what happens in literature later in the century.

Not long after Pindar's death, Sophocles in the *Antigone* was to write choral odes that seem as remote from the action as the proem to *Olympian* 1 seems from the myth of Tantalus, and that at the same time are in fact as closely relevant to what Antigone and Creon do as "best is water" is to the water in the caldron where Pelops was either washed or cooked (48).

Almost a century after the odes, Plato was to use myth to give emotional force to abstract arguments, basing the dramatic structure of the *Republic* on the "likeness" of the cave, with its traditional narrative of descent to death and darkness and return to life and light. Even Plato's most scientific theory of knowledge is expressed in an analogy to vision, which itself derives ultimately from the value given to light in ancient heroic myth.[10] Because victory odes provide the first real indication of the process of the transformation of myth into abstraction, they can demonstrate perhaps even better than the fragmentary texts of the pre-Socratic philosophers how and why Plato wrote stories rather than treatises. The same process, as we have seen, gives the odes their distinctive form and linguistic character. Aside from all their other merits, the odes can provide extensive documentation of significant trends in the later development of Greek thought.

I hope also that the discussion of these six odes for Hieron has shown, at least indirectly, why Pindarists like to read Pindar (and Bacchylides). To some degree we are drawn by the challenge of deciphering, since as classicists we share the archaeologists' passion to reconstruct from partial evidence a sense of the original whole. But also like the archaeologist we begin with the assumption that the lost past is in some way worth recovering because it has continuing meaning for ourselves.

The odes celebrate the tension and struggle that characterize excellence because they express (especially Bacchylides') the fears of failure and (especially Pindar's) the insistent envy that seem always to accompany success, both in Greek society and in our own.[11] The complexity of association compressed into the language and structure of the odes can still appeal to us because, like all great art, it says more than ordinary discourse can convey. The odes, because they do not say explicitly that *a* is like *b*, or *c* like some *d* in the past, replicate the inexplicable processes by which we relate ideas and impressions to each other in our own minds. The juxtaposition of so much at once—harmony, Typhos, wars, victory in the games, the conduct of government—can be shattering in its intensity. But their elaborate confirmation that man's achievements and perceptions are memorable, even when unsuccessful, is compellingly reassuring.

NOTES

1. References to the games designated in the ode's title occur in the first praise of all Pindar's victory odes except for *Nemean* 9 and *Nemean* 11 (on which see below), and in all of Bacchylides'.

2. The scholia on *Olympian* 13. 156 abc I 386, explaining a reference to Xenophon of Corinth's victory at "games below high crested Aetna," say that there were Isthmian games at Syracuse and Nemean games at Aetna. Unfortunately no external evidence, such as inscriptions, can be produced to verify these statements. But reference to Pythian games at Megara, which also had Nemean (schol. *Ol*. 7, 157 I 232, *Ol*. 13. 156a I 386) is verified in a second century inscription, *IG* IV. 1136; see L. Moretti, *Iscrizioni Agonistische Greche* (Rome 1953) no. 53; cf. also reference to Pythia in Sicyon (schol. *Ol*. 13 155 I 386, *Nem*. 9 inscr. III 149; 20, 25b III 152; 121 III 163 and Moretti, nos. 35 [fourth century] 45, 63); Olympia in Athens (*Pyth*. 9. 101 and schol. 177 II 237 and Moretti, nos. 69, 70, 75, 76, 84). Nemean games were also celebrated in Laodicea in Syria in the third century A.D. Syracusan coins from the mid-sixth century onwards have on their reverse side a picture of a charioteer with a four horse chariot with a Victory flying overhead (e.g., the famous ten drachma coin commemorating the victory of Himera in 479). Since the drivers on the coins do not wear armor the coin could depict victory in games along with victory in war. In view of the statement in the scholia that Nemean games were celebrated at Aetna, one wonders if *Nemean* 1, which celebrates a Syracusan's chariot victory, and refers only to Aetnaean Zeus, does not in fact commemorate the Sicilian Nemea rather than their prototype on the mainland. On the minor games, see Gardiner, *Greek Ath-*

letic Sports (ch. III n. 13) pp. 72-73, and the article "Nemea" in Pauly-Wissowa, *Real-Encyclopädie* 32, p. 2327. A convenient list of minor games may be found in Gildersleeve (ch. I n. 25) p. 236. Young, "Poetical Epistles" (ch. I n. 33) suggests that *Pythian* 2 is Pindar's missing *Olympian Ode* for Hieron's chariot victory of 468; cf. Lloyd-Jones (Intr. n. 3) p. 119 n. 55a.

3. It is important to remember that the present classification of Pindar's odes into books and the order of odes within the books is both late and arbitrary. The practice of dividing works into books began only in the fourth century; see Stephanie R. West, *The Ptolemaic Papyri of Homer* (Papyrologica Coloniensia III; Cologne 1967) pp. 18-20. The first classifiers arranged the odes into books by festivals, in order of the festival's importance: *Olympian, Pythian, Isthmian,* and *Nemean,* with the three anomalous odes now called *Nemeans* 9, 10 and 11 at the end. Within books the odes were arranged in order of the importance of the contest won, with chariot races first. Further reclassification put the *Isthmians,* the shortest book, at the end of the series. Aristophanes of Byzantium (in the third century) put *Olympian* 1 ahead of the *Olympian* odes for chariot victories because it celebrated the founding of the Olympian games. An established practice of grouping odes for the same victor together (e.g., *Olympian* 2 and 3 for Theron, *Olympian* 10 and 11 for Hagesidamus, *Pythians* 4 and 5 for Arcesilaus, and *Isthmians* 5 and 6 for Phylacides) may have accounted for the insertion of *Pythian* 3 (which refers to Pherenicus' horse race victories) after *Pythian* 1 among the chariot victories of *Pythian* 4, 5 and 6. A similar logic may have brought *Pythian* 2 for Hieron once classified by Callimachus as "Nemean" (i.e., anomalous, like *Nemeans* 9, 10 and 11) next to the chariot victory of *Pythian* 1. See Jean Irigoin, *Histoire du Texte de Pindare* (Paris, 1952) pp. 42-44; H.T. Deas, "The Scholia Vetera to Pindar," *Harvard Stud. in Class. Philol.* 42 (1932):48-49; and Rudolf Pfeiffer, *History of Classical Scholarship* (Oxford, 1968) p. 130.

4. If the *Women of Aetna* were the last play of the *Prometheus* trilogy presented in Sicily, as Lloyd-Jones suggests in *The Justice of Zeus* (ch. III, n. 5), it would have had a function similar to the *Eumenides* in Athens of relating past myth to present reality.

5. On the importance of repetition in Pindar's odes, and the difficulties involved in describing its usage: see David Young, "Pindaric Criticism" (Intr. n. 4) pp. 27-28, 30-31, 35.

6. For example, Semonides of Amorgos explains clearly how women resemble certain animals (7W), but the similarities between the eagle in Bacchylides' *Ode* 5 and Pherenicus (and Hieron, and Bacchylides) are never directly stated. Solon's comparison of Zeus' justice to a sudden rain storm is introduced ("just as") and concluded ("such is the vengeance of Zeus") formally (13. 17-25), but the lyre's rain in *Pythian* 1 evolves suddenly from a description of musical signs and then changes into arrows without warning.

7. The odes have appeal for reasons other than their difficulty. The English poet Cowley, like Thoreau, complains of Pindar's obscurity, but at the same time, without saying so explicitly, admires him for his seriousness. Cowley evolved a style he described as "truly Pindarical, falling from one thing to another, after his Enthusiastical manner" for his *Ode on the Resurrection;* (Intr. n. 5) p. 183.

Thomas Gray also turned to the triadic form and a deliberately allusive style to discuss the poet's role in *The Bard* and *The Progress of Poesy*. Ben Jonson similarly used triadic form in his "Ode Pindarick" for Sir Lucius Cary and Sir Henry Morison to describe their "victory" in death. On other Pindaric imitations, see Swanson (Intr. n. 5) pp.215-259.

8. Cf. also Protagoras' revision of the Prometheus myth in Plato's dialogue 320c-323a and Socrates' own adaptation of Hesiod's story of the generations of gold, silver, and bronze, in the *Republic* 413-415c. On the occurrence in later rhetoric of techniques of praise used in the victory odes, see Bundy (Intr. n. 3) I n. 38, II, n. 14, pp. 32, 124, 125.

9. See, e.g., Gorgias' eulogy for Athenian war dead (B 6 DK), Antiphon's model courtroom speeches (*Tetralogies*), and Gorgias' defence of Palamedes, which influenced Plato's *Apology of Socrates;* see James A. Coulter, "The Relation of the *Apology of Socrates* to Gorgias' *Defense of Palamedes* and Plato's Critique of Gorgianic Rhetoric," *Harvard Stud. in Class. Philol.* 68 (1964): 269-303.

10. On the dramatic structure of Plato's *Republic,* see Corinne P. Sze, "Plato's *Republic* I: Its Function in the Dialogue as a Whole," (unpubl. diss. Yale Univ., 1971).

11. On melancholy as a consequence of success, see, e.g., William James, *The Varieties of Religious Experience* (New York, 1902) pp. 133-134. On Pindar's more intense concern with envy, see "Pindar's Lives" (Intr. n. 2) pp. 90-93; and on similarities between the Greek value system and our own, see P. Slater (ch. I n. 43) pp. 440-466.

INDEXES

All numerical references to ancient texts are in italics.

I. The Poems

Principal discussions of poems and stanzas are listed first. Subsequent interpretative citations are also noted, since the full significance of many lines becomes clear only in retrospect.

Bacchylides
Ode 3: 104-105, 125-142; date, 104, occasion, 125; tone, 135, 140; abstraction in, 137
—special emphasis on building, 129, 130, 131, 132, 133; daughters and mother, 132; god and man, 135, 137, 138; height, 128, 130; initiative, 129, 130, 132; light (fire), 136; speech 131, 132, 134, 136-137, 139, 140; superlatives, 129, 132, 134; wealth, 126, 128, 133, 136, 156, 172
—*1-4*, 126, 170; *1-2*, 44, 151; *1-3*, 132; *2*, 127, 128; *3-4*, 135; *4*, 128
—*5-8*, 126; *5*, 130, 136; *5-6*, 127, 128; *5-7*, 164; *6*, 131, 133; *6-7*, 138, 140, 164
—*9-14*, 127; *9-10*, 131, 136; *9-14*, 139; *11-12*, 127, 134; *12*, 128, 132, 134; *13*, 129, 136, 138, 139, 141; *14*, 133
—*15-18*, 127-128; *15*, 134; *15-16*, 138, 160n.20; *15-17*, 140; *17*, 133, 134, 136, 138, 141, 156; *18*, 130, 132, 133, 136; *18-21*, 136
—*19-21*, 128; *19*, 130, 133; *20-22*, 160n.21; *21-22*, 133, 136; *21*, 140
—*22-28*, 128-129; *22*, 129, 132, 138; *25*, 129
—*29-32*, 129-130; *31-32*, 156; *31-33*, 131; *32*, 132, 133
—*33-36*, 130; *33*, 133; *35-36*, 132; *36*, 138
—*37-42*, 130-131; *37-47*, 136; *38-39*, 140; *40*, 132
—*43-46*, 131; *44*, 133; *44-45*, 138; *44-47*, 140; *46*, 132
—*47-50*, 131-132; *47*, 133, 134, 135, 138, 139; *49*, 140, 147; *50-55*, 128-129
—*51-56*, 132-133; *51*, 139; *51-52*, 134, 135; *53-56*, 140-141; *54*, 156
—*57-60*, 133

—*61-64*, 134; *61-62*, 134; *63-65*, 136; *63-66*, 139
—*65-70*, 134
—*71-74*, 135
—*75-78*, 135; *76-84*, 136; *78*, 139
—*79-84*, 135-136, 138
—*85-88*, 136-137
—*89-92*, 138-139; *90-91*, 141; *92-94*, 105
—*93-98*, 139; *96-98*, 166; *98*, 142
Ode 5: 41-76; date (476 B.C.), 42
—special emphasis on colors, 60, 63, 69, 70; destiny, 45, 59, 61, 62-63, 65, 67, 72; female forces, 55, 60, 63, 65, 69, 74; parentage, 60, 62 65; plants, 58, 65, 68, 74; singularity, 47-48; violence, 45, 52, 60, 63, 74; vision, 30, 48, 49, 50, 55, 64, 67, 69
—*1-15*, 44-46, 170; *1*, 52, 65, 70; *1-2*, 49; *1-6*, 152; *1-8*, 126; *1-11*, 79; *2*, 60, 71; *3*, 60, 106; *3-4*, 52, 66; *2-5*, 94; *3-6*, 47-80; *4-5*, 48; *4-6*, 59; *5*, 52; *6*, 73; *6-7*, 46, 47; *6-8*, 62; *6-16*, 156; *7*, 94, 108; *8-12*, 48; *9*, 58, 108; *9-10*, 49, 73; *9-12*, 150; *10-11*, 49, 74, 142, 150; *10-15*, 73; *11*, 52, 80; *12*, 62, 72; *12-14*, 47; *13-14*, 106; *14*, 73; *14-15*, 74
—*16-30*, 46-48, 39n.30, 43, 79, 139, 155n.6; *16*, 72; *17*, 52; *18-19*, 52, 63, 106; *19-23*, 42; *20-23*, 62; *22-23*, 55, 70, 137; *25*, 72; *25-26*, 49, 52, 60; *26-27*, 52; *28-29*, 44, 49, 52, 125; *29*, 60; *29-30*, 49, 56; *30*, 52
—*31-40*, 48-49; *31-33*, 71; *34*, 55, 64; *37*, 49, 58, 70; *37-40*, 72, 164; *38*, 71, 164; *38-39*, 54, *39*, 63, 72, 126, 159n.17; *39-40*, 62
—*41-55*, 51-53; *41*, 76; *42*, 56, 140; *43-44*, 121; *43-49*, 80; *44*, 60, 70; *45*, 65; *46-47*, 60; *47*, 54; *48-49*, 64; *49*, 60; *50-53*, 63, 65, 72; *53-55*, 58-59, 127; *55*, 64

—56-70, 53-54; *57*, 66; *58*, 57; *60*, 61, 158n.6; *62*, 55; *61*, 63; *64*, 62; *65*, 61; *65-67*, 61, 65, 99-100n9; *69*, 68; *71*, 67; *71-72*, 68; *76-77*, 61; *80*, 57, 58; *80-82*, 71

—81-95, 56-59; *81-83*, 64; *84*, 65, 68; *86-88*, 68; *87*, 61, 65; *87-88*, 61; *89*, 60; *90*, 65; *92*, 70; *93-94*, 69; *94*, 65, 66

—96-110, 59-61; *98*, 69; *98-99*, 63; *99*, 71; *101-102*, 61; *104-105*, 62; *108*, 65; *110*, 63

—111-120, 61-62; *111-113*, 63; *113-114*, 64, *117-118*, 63; *120*, 68

—121-135, 62-64; *121*, *122*, 65; *124*, 65, 68, 69; *126*, 69; *129-131*, 68

—130-131, 65, *132*, 72; *132-133*, 67; *134*, 72

—136-150, 64-66; *137*, 65, 68, 69; *142*, 68; *145*, 69; *148*, 72

—151-160, 66-67; *154*, 68, 69

—161-175, 67-71; *169*, 69, 70; *172*, 100n.10

—176-190, 71-72; *184-186*, 105; *186*, 74, 138, 139; *187-190*, 165

—191-200, 73-74; *191*, 76; *191-193*, 140; *199-200*, 96

Dithyramb 16.23-25, 100n.11

Pindar

Olympian 1, 41-43, 76-98; date (476 B.C.), 42; tone, 93, 135, 140

—special emphasis on cooking/eating, 84, 85, 86, 91, 92, 101n.15; god and man, 85-88, 94; fixity/movement, 88, 90, 91; height, 87, 91, 95, 96; light, 78, 82, 85, 89, 93, 96, 102n.21; singularity, 84, 89, 96; water, 78, 171

—1-11, 77-79, 170-172; *1*, 4-5, 44, 83, 125; *1-2*, 90; *1-7*, 137; *3*, 93; *3-4*, 80, 91; *3-5*, 84; *4*, 80, 89, 94; *5*, 93; *5-6*, 95; *6*, 83, 93, 138, 151; *8*, 3-4, 100n.12; *8-9*, 80, 83, 87, 91, 94; *9-10*, 95; *11*, 86, 171

—12-22, 79-80; *12*, 101n.13; *12-13*, 126; *13*, 91, 92, 95; *14*, 72, 84; *14-15*, 91; *15*, 96, 100n.12, 101n.14; *16-17*, 84, 89; *17*, 94; *17-18*, 84; *18*, 90; *18-19*, 83, 85, 87, 88, 91; *19*, 94; *20*, 92; *20-21*, 164; *21*, 93; *22*, 83, 90, 92

—23-29, 81-83; *23*, 94; *23-24*, 91, 92, 138; *24-25*, 129; *26*, 90, 92; *28-29*, 76; *28b*, 84, 119; *28b-29*, 94; *29*, 83

—30-40, 83-84; *30*, 89; *31*, 94, 133; *31-34*, 86; *33-34*, 76, 93; *35*, 76, 85; *35-36*, 86; *36*, 86, 92; *37*, 86, 87; *40*, 89

—41-51, 84-85; *41*, 89, 90, 91; *42*, 88, 89, 93, 95; *46*, 96; *47-51*, 167; *48*, 93, 96; *48-51*, 171

—52-58, 85-88; *52*, 88, 145; *56*, 90, 92, 94; *57*, 145; *57-57b*, 96; *58*, 4, 88, 92; *58-60*, 90

—59-69, 87-88; *59*, 103n.26; *59-60*, 93, 101n.18; *66*, 94; *69*, 90

—70-80, 88-90; *71*, 138; *73-74*, 94; *74*, 96; *75*, 91; *76-77*, 76; *80*, 4

—81-87, 90-91; *81*, 95; *84*, 93, 94, 87, 47, 95, 102n.22

—88-98, 92-93; *88*, 103n.26; *92*, 164; *93*, 103n.26; *93-94*, 138; *94*, 92, 164

—99-109, 93-95; *99-102*, 115; *103-104*, 102-103n.23, 135; *104*, 103n.26; *105*, 96, 100n.12; *107*, 103n.25, 105; *108-111*, 169; *109*, 100n.12; *109-111*, 125, 165

—110-117, 95-96; *111*, 164; *111-112*, 137, 141; *113-114*, 124, 135; *115-116*, 139, 165; *115b-116*, 155

Olympian 2.83-88, 136-137; 3.13, 100n.12

Pythian 1: 104-125; date, 104; occasion, 175n.3; tone, 125

—special emphasis on beginnings, 113, 114, 116-117, 122; building, 112, 119, 120; disorder/order, 105, 110, 112, 114, 118, 119; sound, 107, 110, 119, 121, 123-124, 156; storms/fire, 109, 110, 122; struggle/repose, 108, 116, 122, 123, 171; voyages, 114, 116-117, 122; weapons, 107, 111, 121, 122

—1-6, 105-106, 170; *1*, 44; *2*, 113, 115, 116, 117, 120, 122; *2-4*, 141; *3*, 117; *4*, 110, 112; *5*, 101, 119, 141; *5-6*, 115; *5-10*, 175n.6; *6*, 107, 121, 124, 134, 141, 170

—7-12, 107-108; *7*, 120, 141; *7-8*, 113, 8, 108, 109, 111, 112, 119, 120; *9*, 111, 117; *9-10*, 109; *10*, 113, 115, 118, 124, 141; *10-12*, 115, 117; *11-12*, 108, 122; *12*, 39n.30, 137

—13-20, 108; *13*, 111, 112, 119; *13-14*, 113, 115, 121; *14*, 117; *15-16*, 111; *16*, 112; *17*, 125; *18-19*, 119, 120; *19*, 112, 115, 117, 121, 124; *20*, 141

—21-26, 110-111; *21*, 119; *22*, 121, 141;

Index   179

23-24, 115, 122; 24, 113, 117, 119,
   120, 124; 25, 113, 120; 26, 111, 121,
   123, 141
—27-32, 111-112; 27-28, 118; 28, 117,
   120, 121, 122, 141, 158n.6, 170; 30,
   113, 116, 119, 124; 30-32, 118, 32-36,
   117
—33-40, 112-114; 33-34, 123; 33-35,
   116, 122; 34-35, 117; 36, 119; 37, 116,
   118, 118-119, 124; 38, 119; 39, 164
—41-46, 114-115; 42, 39n.30; 43-44,
   121, 122, 141; 44, 116; 44-45, 141; 46,
   116, 117, 118, 120, 141, 171
—47-52, 115-116; 48, 118, 123; 48-49,
   117; 49-50, 119, 124; 51, 172; 52, 120;
   52-55, 122
—53-60, 116-117; 53, 120, 141; 54, 120;
   57, 129; 59, 118, 122; 60, 124
—61-66, 117-118; 62, 122; 66, 123, 124
—67-72, 119; 67, 120; 69, 124; 70, 120
—73-80, 119-120; 73, 124; 78, 171; 80,
   123, 141, 171
—81-86, 120-122, 165-166; 81, 123; 81-
   82, 40n.41, 125; 81-86, 168; 82-83,
   141; 84, 123; 86, 105, 123, 124, 125,
   141
—87-92, 122-123, 165-166; 88, 89, 90,
   91, 92, 124
—93-100, 123-125, 155-156, 165-166; 94,
   140; 94-96, 112; 96, 125
Pythian 2: date, 170; occasion, 8-9;
   problems of interpreting, 4; anti-
   thesis in, 24-25, 57; subsequent in-
   fluence of, 34
—special emphasis on animals (civi-
   lized vs. feral behavior), 21, 26, 29,
   30, 34; envy, 34; god and man, 21,
   30-31; reciprocity, 15, 16, 17, 20-22,
   24-25, 28, 29, 40n.38, 78, 85; self-
   knowledge, 26, 31; taming/control,
   15, 17, 21, 31; vision, 16, 26, 48; war,
   13, 16, 24-25
—1-8, 13-14, 24, 79, 170; 1, 44, 164; 1-
   2, 16, 23, 33, 49, 78; 1-4, 11-12; 2, 15,
   20, 21; 3, 18, 20, 31, 149, 164; 3-4,
   15, 25, 30, 45, 47, 150; 3-8, 78; 4, 14;
   5, 29; 5-8, 23; 6, 15, 16, 17, 165; 67,
   14, 164; 7, 18; 7-8, 49, 70, 169; 8, 14,
   16, 17, 19, 31, 32, 57
—9-16, 14-15, 24, 79; 9, 16; 9-10, 19;
   10, 15; 10-11, 17; 11, 22, 32, 33; 11-
   12, 31, 165; 12, 16, 17, 69; 13, 15, 18,
   22, 23; 13-14, 18, 19, 22; 14, 25; 15,

37n.19; 15-16, 16, 22
—17-24, 15; 17, 17, 20, 22, 25, 31, 32,
   37n.20, 48; 18-19, 37n.21; 18-22, 81;
   19, 22, 24, 27, 38n.23; 19-20, 21, 25;
   20, 19, 25, 29, 48; 21, 11, 22; 21-24,
   53, 81; 22-23, 70; 22-24, 82; 24, 17,
   22, 25, 38n.24
—25-32, 17-18; 25, 23, 26; 25-26, 30,
   169; 26, 19, 23, 24, 29, 70; 27, 19; 28,
   20, 22, 27, 29; 28-29, 19; 29, 19, 22;
   31, 19, 20, 21, 27, 28, 30, 31; 31-33,
   21, 33; 32, 19, 21, 70
—33-40, 18-20; 34, 11, 12, 22, 26, 30,
   38n.25, 48; 35, 22; 36, 25, 29, 38n.26;
   37, 22, 23, 24, 27, 30; 39, 29; 39-40,
   26, 57; 40, 11, 24, 27, 29, 31, 167; 40-
   41, 21; 41, 22, 27, 31; 43, 30, 38n.28;
   44, 38-39n.29; 44-48, 32; 45, 32, 70;
   46, 23; 46-47, 30; 46-48, 33, 70; 48, 33
—49-56, 21-23; 49, 31, 72; 49-50, 27,
   160n.22; 49-50, 24, 30; 49-52, 93; 51-
   52, 31; 52, 23, 24, 167; 52-53, 11, 31,
   72; 53, 23, 27, 29, 32; 54, 27, 28; 54-
   55, 48; 54-56, 86; 55, 24, 25; 55-56,
   27, 134; 56, 30, 39n.30, 72; 58, 30
—57-64, 23-24; 59-60, 25; 60, 26; 61, 78;
   62, 25; 62-63, 28, 39n.32, 164-165,
   167; 63, 25, 33; 63-64, 29, 31
—65-72, 24-26; 65, 26, 33; 66, 29; 67-68,
   28, 167; 69, 39n.33; 71, 40n.36; 72,
   11, 12, 27, 39n.34; 72-73, 33,
   160n.22, 166, 167; 72-75, 32
—73-80, 26-28, 166-168; 74, 29; 75, 11,
   29; 75-76, 29, 32; 76-78, 86; 78, 31-32
—81-88, 28-30, 168-169; 81, 32; 81-82,
   40n.37; 83, 32; 84, 32, 40n.39; 85, 31;
   86, 31, 40n.40; 86-88, 32
—89-96, 31-33, 156, 169-170; 89, 33; 90-
   91, 40n.41, 78; 93, 32; 93-94, 9, 53;
   95, 33; 96, 96
Pythian 3: 104-105, 142-157; date, occa-
   sion, 157, 163; tone, 156; abstraction
   in, 173; traditional diction in, 155
—special emphasis on death, 143;
   disease/fire, 146, 147, 148; god and
   man, 148, 153; healing, 143, 147,
   149, 150, 155; geography, 143;
   knowledge, 145, 147, 149; near/far,
   144, 147, 149, 151, 155, 156, 163n.39,
   172; parentage, 143, 149; sea voyage,
   154; turning 153
—1-7, 142-143, 170; 1-3, 144, 149; 2, 5,
   145; 5-7, 147; 6, 155; 7, 147
—8-14, 143; 10, 154; 13, 144, 145

180 Index

—15-23, 144; 15, 146; 17, 152; 18, 164;
  18-19, 151; 21, 152, 156, 21-22, 143;
  22, 149; 22-23, 147, 155; 23, 149, 154;
  23-25, 145
—24-30, 144-145; 25, 150; 27, 164; 27-
  29, 147; 28, 148, 155; 29, 146; 30, 150
—31-36, 145-146; 31, 155; 34, 144; 34-
  35, 148, 152, 36-37, 148
—38-46, 146-147; 39, 151; 42, 153; 44,
  148, 154; 46, 149, 152
—47-53, 147-148; 50, 149; 51-53, 152;
  52, 149; 52-53, 149; 53, 153
—54-60, 148-149; 58, 154; 59, 60, 155
—61-69, 149-150; 61-62, 154, 166; 62,
  65, 155
—70-76, 150-151; 72-76, 163n.42; 73-74,
  164; 74, 163n.42
—77-83, 151-152; 78, 153
—84-92, 152-153; 91, 153; 92, 164
—93-99, 153; 96, 153, 155; 98, 149; 99-
  100, 155
—100-106, 153-154; 105-106, 155; 106,
  105; 107-109, 166
—107-115, 154-155

Pythian 5.31, 100n.12; 72-73, 158n.10;
  8.57, 100n.12; 10.41-42, 161n.30
Nemean 1 (occasion), 162n.33, 174n.2;
  3.65, 100n.12; 9, 10, 11 (occasions),
  165
Isthmian 8.9-11, 101n.17
fr. 270, 161n.30

II: Author and Subject

Abstraction: increasing in later odes,
  137, 173; as indication of artistic ma-
  turity, 105.
Adaptation, creative, see Epic diction,
  Hesiod, Homer, Imitation
Admetus, "Sayings for," 136, 162n.32
Aegidae (Dorian tribe), 118, 158n.10
Aeschylus: diction, 33-34, 41n.44, 105;
  development of themes, 10-11, 13,
  36n.9; interest in motivations, 34;
  Aetnaean Women, 158n.5, 175n.4;
  Agamemnon, 40n.41, 105; *Eumenides*,
  175n.4; *Persians*, 140, 158n.6; *Pro-
  metheus*, 175n.4; 250, 135; 365,
  158n.5, 366-369, 159n.14
Aesop: fable 345, 39nn.35-36; 568,
  39n.35
Alcaeus, 307, 161n.30
Alliteration, 52, 57, 62, 107, 110, 111,
  117, 127
Ambiguity: deliberate, 19, 33, 39nn.30
  &32, 40n.41, 46, 48, 54, 63, 68-69,
  121, 137, 148, 149, 150-151, 152, 154,
  175n.6; in first personal statement,
  155; generalizing, 168; associating
  negative with positive examples 125
Anaxagoras, *B 12 DK*, 162n.36
Animals, special emphasis on, see
  Pindar, *Pyth.* 2
Antiphon (sophist), 176n.9
Antithesis: negative and positive
  examples juxtaposed, 43-44, 166,
  168; without exact parallelism, 124;
  increasing in later odes, 105; rhetori-
  cal function of, 162n.36; dramatic, in
  Bacchylides, 140
Archaic style: description of, 10-11;
  analogy in, 11; antithesis, 11, 24-25,
  29, 32; circular time, 70; conclusion
  as introduction, 38n.24, 143; digres-
  sion as statement of theme, 129;
  generalization by accumulated spe-
  cifics, 11-12; myth as illustration, 10;
  narrative, sequence of, 36n.13, end-
  ing of, 70; metaphor as illustration,
  10; transitions, 10
Arion (poet), 939.8, 160n.17
Archilochus: in Pindar, *Pyth*.2, 22, 23,
  26, 27, 28, 30; fr. 23. 14-16, 40n.38;
  55, 101n.17; 81, 39n.35; 82, 40n.36;
  185-187, 39n.35; 80.5 (Diehl), 160n.18
Athletics: ethical function of, 170; in-
  scriptions about, 103n.34, 159n.15;
  javelin contest, 158n.8; javelins as
  measurements, 159n.13; metaphors
  from, 98; professionalism in, 35n.3
Attic drinking songs (*scolia*), 162n.32
Bacchylides: artistry, compared to
  Pindar, 43, 50-51, 76-77, 79, 80, 97,
  133, 135, 137, 138, 139, 140-142, 150,
  171-172, 174
—style, general description of, 2, 75-
  76, 142, 171-172; dramatic tech-
  niques, 55, 66, 68, 74, 133, 140,
  162n.36; innovations, 45, 49, 53, 60,

66, 126, 127, 133, 134, 160n.19; reiteration, 141; traditionalism, 171; use of familiar analogies, 141
—critical interpretation of, 2, 42-43, 76; emphasis on human limitations, 62, 76, 140, 171; evocation of past, 172; reasons for popularity in antiquity, 40; "rivalry" with Pindar, 9, 42; traditional bardic detachment, 141; influence on later philosophy, 162n.36; "imitation" of Pindar, 136-137, 140-141; text (papyrus), 42

Beginnings, special emphasis on, see Pindar, *Pyth.* 1
Bergren, A., 101n.14, 159n.13
Biographical criticism, see Interpretation
Boas, F., 36n.8
Boges (Persian governor), 131
Bowra, C. M., 6n.6, 39n.33
Brannan, P. T.: "Bacchylides' *Ode 3*," 160n.21, 161nn.23, 28-29; "*Ode 5*," 99nn.6-7
Brower, R., 35n.1
Budge, E. A. W., 99nn.2,5
Building, special emphasis on, see Bacchylides, *Ode 3*, Pindar, *Pyth.* 1
Bundy, E., 2, 6n.3, 36 n.31, 176n.8
Burnett, A., 5n.2, 6n.7, 40n.42
Burton, R., 157n.3, 159n.15
Butterworth, E. A., 160n.19
Calder, W., 6n.4, 101n.13, 160n.23
Campbell, D., 40n.28, 98n.1
Carthaginians, 25, 131
Cherniss, H., 35n.5
Coinage, process of, 158n.6
Coins, Syracusan, 106, 134, 157n.3, 174n.2
Colors, special emphasis on, see Bacchylides, *Ode 5*
Conclusion, of victory ode: diction in, influenced by language of proem, 31-32, 71, 74, 75, 96, 104, 117, 123-124, 125, 155; prayers in, 96; addressed to victor and poet, 165-166; focus on present in, 170; concentration on motivations in, 170
Conway, G., 4, 6n.6
Cooking, special emphasis on, see Pindar, *Ol.* 1
Cornford, F. M., 101n.15
Coronis, traditional myth of, 145

Cowley, A., 3, 6n.5, 175n.7
Croesus, life of, 131
Deas, H. T., 175n.3
Death, special emphasis on, see Pindar, *Pyth.* 3
Deinomenes (Hieron's son), 117-118, 159n.15
Delphi, Hieron's gifts to, 127-128
Denniston, J. D., 162n.36
Detail, relevance of, in victory ode, 114, 131, 145, 153
Diagoras (poet) 735.1, 160n.22
Diction: character of, in victory ode, 3, 11, 50, 74-75; deliberate complexity of, 172; deliberate generality of, 33, 154, see also Ambiguity; dramatic, 127; unifying function of, 92, 134; aesthetic function of, 174
—complexity in introductory lines, see Proem; straightforward in myth, see Narrative; selection of language in final section, see Conclusion. Also see Aeschylus, Bacchylides, Pindar
Dike, 29-30, 38n.28, 40n.39, 106
Disease, special emphasis on, see Pindar, *Pyth.* 3
Dorians, 118
Drachmann, A. B., 35n.5
Drama: influence of on victory ode, see Aeschylus, Bacchylides, Euripides, Sophocles; effect of victory ode on, 173
Dramatic technique, see Bacchylides
Dumortier, J., 160n.23, 161n.16, 162n.34
Ebert, J., 103n.24, 160n.17
Eliade, M., 101n.15
Eliot, T. S.: on interpreting poetry, 5, 7n.10; use of repetition, 162n.33
Empedocles, *B130.1 DK*, 37n.20
Envy: emphasis on, in victory ode, 3, 9, 24, 32-33, 43, 72, 85, 86, 119, 121, 134, 167, 169, 176n.11; positive function of, acc. Hesiod, 121; special terminology for, 40n.41
Epic diction: in Bacchylides, 50, 54, 74-75, 76-77, 126; see also Hesiod, Homer
Epigram, describing whirling leaves (1943-44 GP), 100n.9
Etruscans, 109
Euripides: innovations in traditional

format, 125; *Alcestis 252-257, 259-262*, 132; *Hippolytus*, 97; *Trojan Women 1190*, 163n.42
Exposition: pattern of, 16-17; subordination in, 114, 118, 150; in narrative, 104, 129; absence of symmetry in, 43, 124
Fables: generalizing function of, 67. Also see Archilochus
Failure: emphasis on, in victory ode, 33, 41n.43, 44, 77. See also Envy
Farnell, L., 35n.6
Females, special emphasis on, see Bacchylides, *Odes 3, 5*
Fire, special emphasis on, see Bacchylides, *Ode 3*, Pindar, *Pyth. 3*
First personal statement: as transition, 10; representing public persona of poet, 11; generalizing function of, 155
First praise of victor: 150, 164-165, 174n.1; expressed in language of proem, 148
Fixity/movement, special emphasis on, see Pindar, *Ol. 1*
Floyd, E., 103.n25
Fontenrose, J., 158n.5
Galinsky, G. K., 99n.6, 100n.11
Games, references to in odes, 164-165
Gardiner, E. N.: *Athletics of Anc. World*, 35n.3, 37n.15, 100n.12; *Greek Athletic Sports*, 159n.13, 174n.2
Generalization, see Victory Ode
Geography, special emphasis on, see Pindar, *Pyth. 3*
Gerber, D., 5, 40n.38
Gildersleeve, B., 38n.5, 175n.2
God, cf. to man: see Bacchylides, *Odes 3, 5*; Pindar, *Ol. 1, Pyth. 2, Pyth. 3*
Gorgias: *B 6 DK*, 176n.9; *B 11A DK*, 172-173
Gouldner, A., 41n.43
Grant, M., 162n.30
Gray, T., imitation of Pindar, 1, 176n.7
Greengard, C., 2, 3, 6n.3, 37nn. 16-17, 159nn. 12 & 16
Hamilcar (Carthaginian general), 131
Hamilton, R., 5n.2, 35n.2, 37n.14
Harris, H. A.: *Greek Athletes*, 37n.15; *Sport in Greece*, 158n.8
Headlam, W., 162n.35
Healing, special emphasis on, see Pindar, *Pyth. 3*

Height, special emphasis on, see Bacchylides, *Ode 3*, Pindar, *Ol.1*
Heracles, and Meleager, myth of, 100n.9
Heraclitus: adaptation of epic, 140-141; *B 51 DK*, 107; *60, 62*, 162n.36; *67*, 11, 162n.36; *82-83*, 26, 166; *114*, 162n.36
Herodotus: *4.36.1*, 162n.30; *7.197, 167*, 161n.25
Hesiod: *Theogony, 770-773*, 40n.37; *Works and Days*, 10; fr. *286 MW*, 27, 30, 39n.36, 167; *323*, 37n.20
—adaptations by Bacchylides, *Theog. 81-93*, 73; *99-103*, 45; *100*, 73; *364*, 133; *Works and Days 167-171*, 133
—adaptations by Pindar, *Theog. 88-93*, 122; *99-103*, 156; *869-880*, 109, 111; fr. *60.4 MW*, 163n.39
Hieron: importance of, 4; selection of poets by, 140; life, 4, 104, 127-128, 157, 158n.9, 160n.21
History, general reflection of, in victory ode: 104, 114, 131, 134, 139-40, 151, 161n.25, 169; difficulties in determining, 170, 172, 173; focus on current events in ode's conclusion, 170
Holland, N., 35n.2, 37n.14
Homer: *Il. 6. 149*, 10; *Od. 4. 465*, 19;
—adaptations by Bacchylides, 127, 136; of epithets, 45, 47, 53; of pattern of inquiry, 58; of simile style, 49; of *Il. 1.515*, 57; *4.116-126*, 55; *4.461*, 160n.19; *6.146-149*, 53-54; *9.497*, 59, 60; *9.540-542*, 60-61; *9.543-545*, 61; *9.591-594*, 131; *15.170-172*, 52; *16.856-857*, 66; *17.53-58*, 100n.9; *17.565*, 133; *18.56-60*, 58; *20.46*, 55; *22.134-135*, 55; *22.362-363*, 66; *24.480-484*, 57, 58; *24.524-526*, 52, 68; *24.629-631*, 55; *24.781*, 129; *24.792*, 133; of *Od. 2.97*, 160n.19; *3.316*, 57; *5.221-222*, 67; *7.86*, 129; *8.459*, 55; *9.485-486*, 60; *10.3-4*, 161n.24; *11.90-91*, 54, 55; *11.93-94*, 56; *11.617-619*, 67; *11.620-624*, 53; *14.1*, 57; *14.174*, 130; *15.13*, 57; *16.109*, 131; *19.518-523*, 139; *21.420-421*, 52; *23.204*, 74
—adaptations by Pindar, of *Il. 1.348-351, 359-362*, 89; *2.783*, 109; *9.98-99*, 80; *10.159*, 101n.14; *24. 534-548*, 152; of *Od. 8.105*, 80; *9.121*, 112; *10.548*,

101n.14; *11.128*, 82; *11.582-592*, 87; *19.565*, 91
Homeric Hymns: adaptations by Bacchylides, of *2.379*, 47; *2.380-383*, 46-47; of *19.18*, 46
Hymn form, in victory ode, 44, 78, 106
Image, see Metaphor
Imitation: by Bacchylides of Pindar, 136-137, 140-141; as creative adaptation, 162n.33
Initiative, special emphasis on, see Bacchylides, *Ode 3*
Innovation, as cause of obsolescence, 125, 157. See also Bacchylides, Pindar
Inscriptions: describing games, 160n.17; describing victors, 160n.21, 163n.42
Interpretation: biographical criticism, 2, 9, 35n.5, 42-43, 158n.9; emphasis on conventional elements, 5n.2, 35n.2; by hypothesis, 8-9, 35n.4; methodology in this book, 12; misclassification of odes, 39n.33, 104; problems involved, 1-2, 5, 7n.10, 34, 98, 102n.22, 103n.25, 157n.4
Irigoin, J., 175n.3
Irwin, E., 100n.10
James, W., on success, 176n.11
Jebb, R., 99n.5, 160n.18, 161n.26
Jonson, B., imitation of Pindar, 1, 176n.7
Julian (emperor), reads Bacchylides, 99n.5
Katz, P., 37n.19, 40n.38
Keats, J., ode form, 10
Köhnken, A., *Funktion des Mythos*, 6n.3, 35n.5; "Hieron und Deinomenes," 159nn.15, 16; "Pindar as Innovator," 101n.16
Knowledge, special emphasis on, see Pindar, *Pyth. 2, 3*
Lamprocles (poet), *735.2*, 161n.23
Language, see Diction
Lattimore, R., 6n.6
Lebeck, A., 33, 36n.9, 40n.41, 41n.44
Lefkowitz, M.: "Bacchylides' *Ode 5*," 7n.9, 99nn.5 & 6, 162n.33; "Cultural Conventions," 35n.6, 38n.28, 40n.40, 99nn. 5, 9; "First Person in Pindar," 6n.9, 158n.10, 163nn.40 & 41; "Influential Fictions in Scholia," 7n.9, 35n.4, 99n.4; "Pindar's Lives,"

5n.2, 35n.5, 176n.11; review of Hamilton, 5n.2
Lessing, G., on translating Pindar, 6n.5
Lévi-Strauss, C., on myth, 101n.16
Libanius, on memory, 36n.8
Light, special emphasis on, see Bacchylides, *Ode 3*, Pindar, *Ol. 1*
Lloyd, G. E. R., 36n.12, 38n.24
Lloyd-Jones, H.: *Justice of Zeus*, 158n.5, 175n.4; "Modern Interpretation of Pindar," 2, 6n.3, 34, 35n.5, 37nn.20 & 21, 39nn. 30 & 33, 40n.42, 41n.43, 175n.2
Locri, Epizephyrian (in war) 21, 37-38
Lycambes, 26, 40n.38. See also Archilochus
Maehler, H., 5
Matheson, W., see Ruck
Memorization and Memory: function of, 36n.8, 96; in archaic poetry, 74; in pre-literate society, 36n.8
Metaphor: as a form of abstraction, 173; complexity of, 3, 30, 122, 141; determined by myth, 156; general function in ode, 32-33; in Homer, 10; imprecision of, in victory ode, 110n.12; increasing abstraction of, in later odes, 105; in initial lines, 18, 170; lack of ancient terminology for, 171; of light, influencing later thought, 97; in Pindar and Bacchylides, contrasted, 141; poet's choosing of, 36n.10, 156; simple, 156; variation in association, 80, 133, 136, 171-172. See also Diction, Proem
Metrical structure, in victory odes: function of, 12; suspense in, 15, 18, 20, 24, 39n.30, 45, 46, 58, 62, 66, 67, 76, 82, 95, 109, 134, 135, 136, 138
Miller, H., on water in Greece, 6n.8
Milobenski, E., 40n.41
Moralizing statements, in victory ode, 11
Moretti, L., 174n.2
Morpurgo, A. 37n20
Mothers, special emphasis on, see Bacchylides, *Ode 3*, Pindar *Pyth. 3*
Motivations, emphasis on, see Pindar
von der Mühll, P., 38-39n.29
Murray, G., 99n.5
Myth: determines choice of metaphors,

156; general function of, 1, 101n.16; in Homer, 10; as illustration, 15; as negative illustration, 85; Pindar's revisions of, see Pindar. See also Archaic poetry

Nagy, G., "Iambos," 40n.38; "Perkunas," 159n.14

Narrative: exposition of, 104; selection of detail in, 153; first sentence as introduction in, 17, 129. See also Diction, Exposition

Near vs. far, special emphasis on, see Pindar, *Pyth. 3*

Negative examples, function of, 12. See also Archaic poetry, Myth

Nisetich, F., 37n.15, 100n.12

Newman, F. S., 103n.26

Nilsson, M. P., 161n.25

Nomos, 11, 29, 38n.28, 40n.40

Notopoulos, J., 36n.8

Oates, J., 39n.33

Occasion of victory, difficulties in determining, 157

Ode, post-classical versions of, 1, 10, 175-176n.7. See also Cowley, Gray Jonson Keats

Olney, J., 36n.10

Onomatopoeia, 110

Opposites, see Antithesis, Archaic style

Ostwald, M., 38n.28, 40n.40

Palmer, L. R., 40n.39

Parentage, special emphasis on, see Bacchylides, *Ode 5*, Pindar, *Pyth. 3*

Pedley, J., 161nn.24, 25

Pelops, traditional myth of, 86, 101n.14

Pfeiffer, R., 175n.3

Pherenicus (Hieron's horse), 51, 80, 128, 151, 175n.3

Philosophy, influence of victory odes on, 173

Pindar: name, 158-159n.10; in Sicily, 158n.5; criticism of, 13, and see also Interpretation; comparison with Bacchylides, see Bacchylides

—emphasis on motivations for success, 97, 156, 168-169, 171-172; esp. in last stanza of ode, 169

—innovations in vocabulary, 113, 122; in format, 117, 125; revisions of convention, 142, 150; of myth, 81, 82, 86, 87, 89, 97, 101n.16, 109, 110, 111, 173

—style, 1, 83; animation of inanimates, 76, 106; antithesis, 85; apposition, 102n.18; metaphors, 76-77, 97, 156, complex, 141, 171, simple, 156, reasons for choice of, 156, generalizing function of, 76; postponed conclusions, 97, 115

—poetry imparts impression of personal commitment, 141, of combative poet, 142; influences drama, ethics, 97

Plants, special emphasis on, see Bacchylides, *Ode 5*

Plato: *Apology*, 176n.9; *Republic*, 97-98, 173, 176n.19

Poet: persona of, 11; signature, 45; traditional role, 28, 34, 37n.14, 45, 47, 94, 107, 141-142; reference to as transition, 10, 15; as appraiser, 10, 21; as competitor, 31, 78, 89, 115, 121, 137; as exemplar, 165-166; as victor, 155, 165

Poetry, ancient terminology for, 23, 171

Polarities, 70-71, 124, 133. See also Antithesis, Archaic style

Politics, reflection of, in victory ode, 32-33. See also History

Porter, H., 38n.27

Praxilla (poet), 749, 162n.32

Preoccupation, impressions of, 33. See also Repetition

Proem, of victory ode: 3, 4; style of, 79, 104, 143, 170-171; initial complexity of, 48, 108, 113; as introduction to themes in ode, 79, 104, 106, 142, 147-148; extraordinary length of in some odes; 105; statements about poet in, 79

Puns, 21. See also Repetition

Recollection, see Repetition

Reminiscence, deliberate 140-141. See also Bacchylides, Epic Diction, Hesiod, Homer

Renehan, R., 100n12

Repetition: function of, 6n.4, 33, 36n.10, 64, 157n.1, 160n.22, 162n.33; importance of, 175n.5; ancient terminology for, 171; poets' usuage of, contrasted, 51

—verbal, direct, 16-17, 18, 19, 22, 27,

29, 30, 43, 45, 49, 52, 64, 93, 95, 103n.26, 113, 115, 120, 140, 160-161n.13; in puns, 31, 45, 63, 69, 100n.11; as conclusion, 22, 25, 147; at end of ode, 71; absence of fixed patterns in, 124; increasing abstraction of, in later odes, 105
—syntactic, 89-90, 112, 114, 118, 149, 150; thematic, 3, 29, 31, 43, 47, 54-55, 56, 59, 70, 111; in Aeschylus, 10-11; in Homer, 10; as conclusion, 52, 62, 73, 91, 92, 94, 108, 111, 139, 160n.21
Riddles, 27. See also Metaphors, Proem
Roberston, D., 37n.18
Rose, P., 6n.2, 163n.43
Ruck, C.: translation of Pindar, 6n.6, 39n.33; "Marginalia Pindarica," 99n.7
Sandys, J., 6n.6
Scholia (ancient commentaries on Pindar): evaluation of Bacchylides in, 42; classification of odes in, 165, 175n.3; on games, 160n.21, 165, 174n.2; interpretation of poetry, 8-9, 39n.33, 157n.4, 158n.9, 163n.41; research methods, 35n.4
Segal, C., "Croesus," 161n.25; "Ol.1," 102nn.19, 20, 21
Semonides, 7, 175n.6
Shamanism, 101n.15
Silk, M., 99n.8
Simonides: *519 fr. 35b7*, 106n.17; *586.2*, 69; epithets, 98n.1, 159-160n.17; victory odes by, 42
Simpson, M., 157n.3
Singularity, special emphasis on, see Bacchylides, *Ode 5*, Pindar, *Ol. 1*
Skulsky, S., 2, 3, 6nn.3 & 4, 157nn.1-2, 158n.7, 162n.33
Slater, P., 41n.43, 176n.11
Slater, W., 6n.6
Smethurst, M., 36n.9
Smith, A. H. 161n.25
Snell, B., 5, 37n.22
Socrates, 97
Solon: *13.9-10*, 160n.19; *13.17-25*, 175n.6
Sophia, 148
Sophists, 97, 172, 176n.9. See also Anaxagoras, Gorgias, Plato, Thucydides

Sophocles: *Ajax 394-397*, 162n.36; *Antigone*, 173; *Oedipus Tyrannus*, 97, *1182*, 66; *Trachinian Women*, 100n.11
Sound, special emphasis on, see Pindar, *Pyth. 1*
Sourvinou-Inwood, C., 38n.21
Speech, special emphasis on, see Bacchylides, *Ode 3*
Stanza end, predictions in, 58-59. See also Metrical structure
Stein, G., on genius, 103n.27
Stern, J., "Metrical and Verbal Patterns," 161nn.26, 27; *Pindar and Bacchylides*, see Calder
Stockert, W., 36n.8, 38n.27, 39n.31, 103n.26
Subject, abrupt changes in, 33. See also Proem
Superlatives, special emphasis on, see Bacchylides, *Ode 3*
Swanson, R. A., 6nn.5 & 6, 40n.40, 41n.43, 176n.7
Symbol, see Metaphor

Taming, special emphasis on, see Pindar, *Pyth. 2*
Tantalus, traditional myth of, 87
Taylour, W., 161n.24
Theognis: 162n.32; *101*, 160n.18
Thoreau, H. D., translation of Pindar, 1, 5n.2, 8, 35n.1
Thornton, H. and A., 36n.13
Thrasymachus (sophist), 173
Thummer, E., 5n.2, 39n.34, 40n.42
Thucydides, 157, 173
Time, archaic concept of, 11-12
Transitions: by reference to first person, 10, 11; to poet, 10, 15; by brief reiteration of first praise, 81; also see Conclusion
Translation: difficulties involved, 3-4, 6n.6, 35n.6; used in this book, 3-4, 39n.30
Townsend, E. (Vermeule), 160n.23
Turning (change), special emphasis on, see Pindar, *Pyth. 3*
Type of victory, definition of in first praise, 164
Typhos (Typhoeus), traditional myth of, 109, 158n.5

Value System, in victory ode, 33, 41n.43
Van Groningen, B. A.: *Composition*

littéraire, 36n.8; *Grip of Past*, 36nn.11, 24
Vergil, *Aen*. 6.309-312, 99n.9
Victory: description of, in ode, 51, 80, 114, 126; celebrated by two poets, 99n.1
Victory ode: 170-174; basic contents of, 34, 49-50, 104, 170; basic format of, 43, 49, 75; variations in, 75, 117, 125; structure of, 10. See also Antithesis, Conclusion, Exposition, Myth, Proem
—diction in, see Ambiguity, Diction, Exposition, Metaphor, Repetition
—function of, general, 33; aesthetic, 172; ethical, 32, 44, 81, 97, 159n.15, 166, 169, 171, and see also Pindar, revision of myth; paideutic, 170; social, 163n.43; universalizing, 70, 156-157, 167, 169, 170
—influence on contemporary literature, 1; on trends in Greek thought, 172-173. See also Bacchylides, Pindar
—present-day appraisals of, 1-2, 8; present study, function of, 2-5. See also Interpretation
Violence, special emphasis on, see Bacchylides, *Ode 5*, Pindar, *Pyth. 1* (disorder, storms, struggle)
Vision, special emphasis on, see Bacchylides, *Ode 5*, Pindar, *Pyth. 2*
Voyages, special emphasis on, see Pindar, *Pyth. 1, 3*
Water, special emphasis on, see Pindar, *Ol. 1*
Wealth, special emphasis on, see Bacchylides, *Ode 3*
Weapons, special emphasis on, see Pindar, *Pyth. 1*
West, S., 175n.3
Whitman, C., 159n.14
Wilson, J. A. 99n.2
Wind, R., 162n.33
Woodbury, L., "Bacchylides," 162nn.33, 34; "Isthmian 2," 162n.33; "Pythian 2," 39n.34
Woolf, V., on choosing metaphors, 36n.10
Word order: emphatic, 19, 83, 93, 109, 110-111, 112-113, 132, 143-144, 147; metrical echo, 107; suspense in, 18
Young, David, *Isthmian 7*, 5n.2; "Pindaric Criticism," 6n.4, 35n.5, 175n.5; "Poetical Epistles," 39n.33, 163n.42, 175n.2; *Three Odes*, 2, 3, 6n.3, 103n.26; 162n.37, 162-163nn.38, 39, 40
Young, Douglas, 102n.22, 103n.23
Xenophanes: 162n.36; *1 DK*, 162n.32
Zeitlin, F., 36n.9

OHIO UNIVER